P9-EEE-164

Christmas 1981

To Richie

With much love
from
Jim and Marian

YOSEMITE

YOSEMITE

ITS DISCOVERY, ITS WONDERS,
AND ITS PEOPLE

Margaret Sanborn

RANDOM HOUSE NEW YORK

Grateful acknowledgment is made to the following for permission to reprint previously published material:

Houghton Mifflin Company: Excerpts from *The Life and Letters of John Muir*, 2 volumes, by William Frederick Badè. Copyright 1923, 1924 by Houghton Mifflin Company. Copyright renewed 1951, 1952 by John Muir Hanna. Excerpts from *The Life and Letters of John Burroughs* by Clara Barrus. Copyright 1925 by Clara Barrus. Excerpts from *My First Summer in the Sierras* by John Muir. Copyright 1911 by John Muir. Copyright 1916 by Houghton Mifflin Company. Copyright renewed 1939 by Wanda Muir Hanna. All are reprinted by permission of Houghton Mifflin Company.

Sierra Club Books: Short excerpts from *The Bulletin* are reprinted by permission of Sierra Club Books.

Library of Congress Cataloging in Publication Data
Sanborn, Margaret.
    Yosemite : its discovery, its wonders and its
people.

    Includes index.
    1. Yosemite Valley (Calif.)—History. 2. Muir,
John, 1838–1914. I. Title.
F868.Y6S197   979.4′47   81–40237
ISBN 0–394–51794–6   AACR2

For Karla and Lillian,
and for Mary

CONTENTS

YOSEMITE

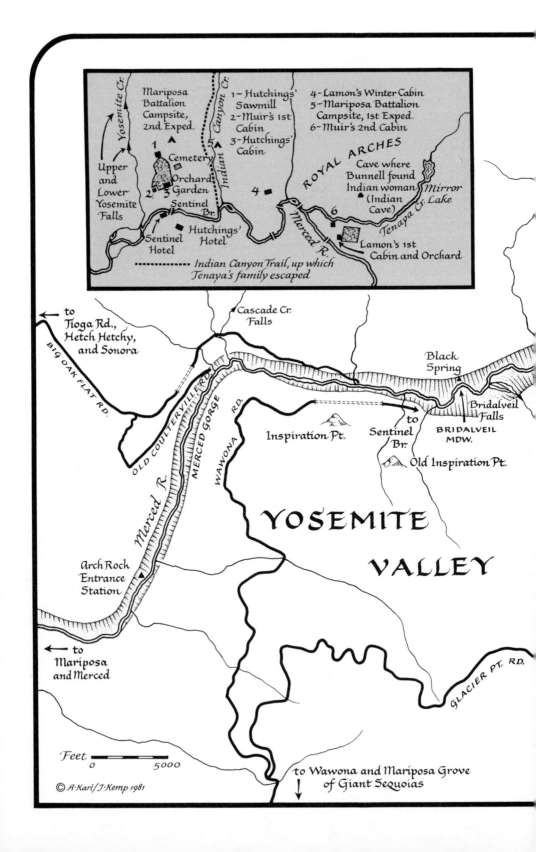

Mariposa
Battalion
Campsite,
2nd Exped.

1~ Hutchings'
   Sawmill
2~ Muir's 1st
   Cabin
3~ Hutchings'
   Cabin

4~ Lamon's Winter Cabin
5~ Mariposa Battalion
   Campsite, 1st Exped.
6~ Muir's 2nd Cabin

Yosemite Cr.

Indian Canyon Cr.

ROYAL ARCHES

Upper
and
Lower
Yosemite
Falls

1

Cemetery

Orchard
Garden

Sentinel
Br.

4

Cave where
Bunnell found
Indian woman
(Indian
Cave)

Mirror
Lake

Tenaya Cr.

2
3

6

Merced R.

Sentinel
Hotel

Hutchings'
Hotel

Lamon's 1st
Cabin and Orchard

---------- Indian Canyon Trail, up which
           Tenaya's family escaped

to
Tioga Rd.,
Hetch Hetchy,
and Sonora

Cascade Cr.
Falls

Black
Spring

BIG OAK FLAT RD.

OLD COULTERVILLE RD.

MERCED GORGE

WAWONA RD.

Merced R.

Inspiration Pt.

to
Sentinel
Br.

Bridalveil
Falls

BRIDALVEIL
MDW.

Old Inspiration Pt.

YOSEMITE

VALLEY

Arch Rock
Entrance
Station

to
Mariposa
and Merced

GLACIER PT. RD.

Feet
0   5000

© A. Karl / J. Kemp 1981

to Wawona and Mariposa Grove
of Giant Sequoias

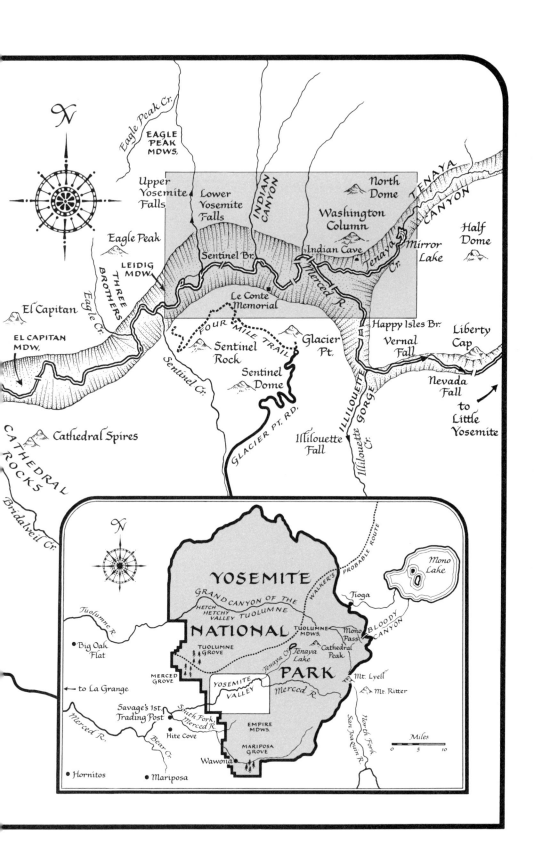

1

DISCOVERY

*I*N THE FALL of 1833 a party of fifty-eight fur trappers and
hunters—French Creoles from Canada and Louisiana (many of
them former voyageurs), Indian half-breeds, and Western fron-
tiersmen—pushed slowly along the high rugged divide between
the Merced and Tuolumne rivers in California's Sierra Nevada
Range. Their leader was thirty-four-year-old Joseph Reddeford
Walker of Tennessee, six feet in height, "strong built . . . brave in
spirit though mild in manners," who had been by turn mountain
trapper, Santa Fe trader, Indian fighter, and border sheriff. His
dark eyes were keen, his bearded face slender, the features even;
his curling brown hair fell free to his shoulders. Like his comrades
he had adopted practical Indian dress, and wore the buckskin
hunting shirt which hung below the knees; long leather leggings,
the outer seams sewn with strips of scarlet cloth, fringe, and
hawk's bells; and moccasins embroidered with colored porcupine
quills and glass beads. His hat of stiff wool was wide-brimmed and
high-crowned; about it he had tied a scarlet band, and fitted into it
a tuft of wild bird feathers.

Walker and his men were making the first east-to-west crossing
of the Sierra through country no white man had ever seen. They
were on their way to hunt beaver in California, that fabled land
where three centuries earlier Spanish adventurers had searched

for griffins, and for the mythical Queen Califia's hoard of pearls and gold.

Weak from hunger, their feet bruised and frostbitten, Walker's men stumbled over masses of shifting talus, up steep granite cliffs slick with glacial polish, through forests cluttered with fallen trees, and across vast banks of deep snow, covering but a few miles each day.

Nearly two weeks before they had eaten the last of their dried buffalo meat, and every night since then their hunters had come in empty-handed. The party kept alive by eating the lean, tough meat of those horses that dropped from starvation and exhaustion (twenty-four horses were to give out on this passage over the Sierra), for the time was well past mid-October at an elevation of over eight thousand feet above sea level. Winter had come early that year and snow had buried the herbage that would have sustained their animals, now too weak to carry either packs or men. Every night brought hoarfrost, and during the day winds of numbing coldness swept down from icy pinnacles and hissed shrilly through the branches of contorted junipers and pines.

"Our situation was growing more distressing every hour," wrote Zenas Leonard, the party's clerk and chronicler, "and all we now thought of was to extricate ourselves from this inhospitable region."

Their plight was the result of a frontier army officer's decision to explore the country lying between the Rocky Mountains and the Pacific Coast. In his application for a two-year leave, Captain Benjamin Louis Eulalie de Bonneville, a French-born graduate of West Point, stated that he intended to collect geographical information; map the area; gather material on the Indians; observe the British Hudson's Bay Company installations in Oregon Territory, for England and the United States traded there jointly; and report on ways in which American citizens could make the best use of that vast and little-known region, thus challenging British monopoly. It was a plan that appealed to the War Department, and the leave was granted.

To finance the expedition Bonneville entered the Western fur trade. Backed by several New York capitalists, he assembled and outfitted a party of one hundred and ten trappers and hunters at Liberty, Missouri, and hired two able and experienced assistants. One of them was Joseph Walker. When the captain later detached a company to trap beaver in California and report on the fur-trade potential there, he chose as its leader Joe Walker, whose "chief delight," a comrade wrote, was "to explore unknown regions." With instructions to meet Bonneville at the end of the year in Utah's Bear River Valley, Walker set off late in July 1833.

About one hundred miles west of the Salt Lake, Walker and his men came upon the Humboldt River, and followed it across the Great Basin of Nevada to its terminus in Humboldt Lake. Riding south from there they saw on their right the distant line of the snow-clad Sierra, running lengthwise 430 miles along the eastern border of California, rising almost sheer from the plain and forming a towering crenelated wall that seemed to defy entry. They observed its changing outline carefully as they moved parallel to it, watching for some suggestion of gap or passage that might lead them west. Reaching at length a large lake formed by a river rising in those mountains (both lake and river were later named for Joe Walker), the company pushed up the stream's east branch, and passed over the crest near its headwaters. They soon found themselves confronted with a maze of rugged canyons and ridges, of lakes and rushing streams, and a confusing possibility of routes. A few were Indian trails leading straight up one canyon wall and down another, for the Miwoks of the region were almost airline in their directness. With their horses growing daily weaker, the men would have chosen to follow one of the less tortuous and craggy tributaries to the Tuolumne. Upon reaching that river they forded it and worked their way over to the divide, coming to it perhaps near Tenaya Lake. From there they turned west, to parallel in part the ancient Indian trade route and the present Tioga Road.

Streams flowing from north to south now darted across their trail. Following the course of the largest of these in the hope it would lead out of the mountains, the men found themselves unexpectedly at the brink of a deep gorge. There they saw that these streams did not wind gently down as they had expected, but plunged over the verge with a thunder and crash, hurling themselves from "one lofty precipice to another" until they were "exhausted in rain below. Some of these precipices appeared to us to be more than a mile high." What Zenas Leonard and his companions were seeing were the waterfalls and tall granite cliffs of Yosemite Valley.

With his spyglass Joe Walker scanned the meadows far below,

deep in grass now golden and dotted with stands of oaks turning red and yellow; the cliff bases edged with pine forests; and the sinuous river, silvery from that distance—the Merced, or river of mercy, named long before by a Spanish explorer in gratitude after a forty-mile march in the midsummer sun across an arid plain. In that snowmelt river Walker knew there would be fine fish, and in those woods fat bear and deer. The rich herbage of the meadows, and the thick coppices lining the stream would restore his horses.

He let his spyglass rest on each straight wall, searching closely for some suggestion of trail or passage. Although there was none, he still sent scouts to investigate; but they "found it utterly impossible for a man to descend, to say nothing of horses." Resignedly the party turned back to the divide, continuing to break paths for their animals, to scramble over ledges of rough granite and flounder through snowdrifts—hungry, ever hungry, as mountain man Joe Meek never forgot.

By October 25, Walker found his men more discouraged than he had ever seen them. A few had even given up hope. That morning he sent several scouts with the hunters to search for some direct route to the lowlands. But that evening both parties reported failure. In silence the men turned to the carcass of a horse, carved off slices, skewered them on twigs, and set them to broil over the fire. One hunter had not yet come in, and some of the men held slender hopes that he would not return empty-handed. When he at length strode into the firelight and they saw that he carried a large burden basket filled with acorns, he was given a hero's welcome, Leonard wrote. Quickly the acorns were buried under the hot coals to roast. Cooked, they proved mealy and sweet, and to some tasted better than the finest chestnuts they had ever eaten.

The Indian who had dropped his load and fled at the sight of their hunter was a good omen: the end of these hostile and seemingly interminable mountains was in sight. Rivers and fertile plains abounding in elk, antelope, deer, and bear could not be too many days away. With renewed spirit the party set off in the morning. Even the way seemed easier. Although snowbanks were still numerous, these were not as deep, and there were fewer fields of rough granite to pick their way over and not as many massive boulders to avoid.

Three more days of travel in the mountains north of Yosemite Valley brought them to a point from which they could see the plains of central California. Through the spyglass these seemed to merge with the Pacific and to be bounded only by the pale blue horizon. Still there was no way down. The eminence on which they stood dropped "almost perpendicular; a person cannot look down without feeling as if he was wafted to and fro in the air, from the giddy height." There, within view of the party's destination, they made camp, and not long afterward their scouts came in to report finding an Indian trail, and fresh signs of deer and bear.

The trail proved steep and tortuous and ended abruptly at the edge of a cliff of "great height, extending eight or ten miles along the mountain." There they halted, and again sent out men to reconnoiter. Several hours later these scouts returned without having found any passage. One of them, however, brought in a small deer he had killed. "This was dressed, cooked and eat in less time than a hungry wolf could devour a lamb," Leonard wrote. For men accustomed to consuming five to ten pounds of rich buffalo meat at a meal, the venison was a mere appetizer. Still, with some of the hunger pangs eased, the problem of that rock wall was readily solved by lowering the horses in rope slings. Although it was nearly nightfall before all animals, baggage, and men were safely down, their hunters started off in search of game. The main party pitched camp in a little oak glade and built a blazing fire. Soon after dark the hunting party brought in the makings of a feast: two large deer and a black bear, "all very fat and in good eating order. This night we passed more cheerful and in better heart than any we had spent in a long time."

The worst was now over. Game became plentiful in the lower elevations; the only regret for these mountain men was that there were no buffalo. There was a thick undergrowth of wild plum and buckbrush, and the open ground was dotted with clumps of dry grass and bracken, all life-giving to their failing animals.

One day during their march the company came to a stand of trees "of the red-wood species, incredibly large—some of which would measure from sixteen to eighteen fathom round the trunk . . . at the height of a man's head from the ground." Walker and his men had made another discovery: the Giant Sequoia or Big Tree (*Sequoiadendron giganteum*), of which there are two groves, the Tuolumne and the Merced, northwest of Yosemite Valley.

They traveled south from the sequoia, following one of several streams flowing into the Merced River. Once in the Merced Canyon, by turning east, they could have entered that steep-walled valley of dashing waterfalls they had seen from above. But it was by then the first of November, the year was fast waning, and Walker was anxious to reach those lowland rivers where he hoped to reap a rich harvest of beaver fur.

Most mountain men were notably indifferent to scenery. However, the Sierra's "natural curiosities," as Leonard termed them— particularly Yosemite Valley and the Big Trees—impressed the Walker party as extraordinary, and "every man expressed himself fully compensated" for the hardships. Even the Merced, which they were following into the plains, had "more wonderful curiosities than any other stream we passed"; and they remarked about its boulders "piled perpendicular to such a height that a man on top, viewed from the bed . . . does not look larger than a small child," and spoke of its turbulence, how it tossed and pitched and foamed "to such a degree that no Indian has the courage to attempt to navigate it with his canoe."

One night Joe Walker announced that it was time to stop admiring scenery and start setting traps. Accordingly, "we all the next morning commenced traveling down the river at a slow gate carefully examining for beaver signs." Their hunters likewise got busy, and "laid up a large supply of deer, elk, and bear meat, of the best kind."

The Ahwahneeche Indians, dwellers in Yosemite Valley, whose scouts had been secretly trailing the Walker party, heard with relief the report that the mountaineers had left the foothills and reached the plains. No white man had yet entered their home valley, and so far as is known, sixteen years were to pass before any even saw it again. Then, one October day in 1849, two gold miners who were following the tracks of a grizzly bear in the mountains above the South Fork Merced were lost and had to spend a night in the woods. While hunting for their way back to camp the next morning, they came on an Indian trail. Taking it, they were eventually led "past a valley enclosed by stupendous cliffs rising perhaps 3000 feet from their base which gave us cause for wonder. Not far off was a waterfall dropped from a cliff below three jagged peaks . . . while farther beyond a rounded mountain stood, the valley side of which looked as though it had been sliced with a knife as one would slice a loaf of bread." They were seeing

Yosemite Valley's Bridalveil Fall, Cathedral Rocks, and Half Dome. They made no effort, either, to enter it.

At the time Joe Walker's discovery of Yosemite Valley meant little to him. But after it grew famous, and its discovery was claimed by another, Walker refuted that claim by telling the story of his harrowing crossing of the Sierra in the fall of 1833, and of how he and his men had looked into the valley from its rim and had seen its domes and cliffs and waterfalls.

Although he was to have a river, a lake, a pass, and a trail named after him, for he became a noted guide and opened a number of new routes into and out of California, his greatest pride seemed to lie in his discovery of Yosemite Valley. Anxious that this not be forgotten, he asked in his old age that the fact be recorded on his tombstone. Over his grave in a small town in central California stands a marker on which the most important events in a long and full life are condensed into nine short lines. One of these states that he camped at Yosemite in November 1833.

2

THE SCENE AND THE SPELL

*T*HE VALLEY called Yosemite, a name derived from a Miwok Indian word meaning grizzly bear, lies in the very center of California's Sierra Nevada Range, near its crest on the western slope. Only seven miles long and from one to two miles broad, the valley is actually but a widened portion of the prevailingly narrow canyon of the Merced River, which meanders the length of the valley from east to west and is in part responsible for its creation.

From a distance there is nothing to indicate the valley's existence on the Sierra's predominantly forested west side. Set nearly a mile deep in the range's solid granite flank, it is so well hidden in the rugged wilderness that white men did not find a way into it for nearly twenty years after Joe Walker's discovery. Even the traveler bound there has no hint of its proximity until a clearing in the forest or the unexpected opening of the Merced River canyon reveal it with such startling suddenness as to suggest unreality. What was written in 1863 remains true: "Our dense leafy surroundings hid from us the fact of our approach to the Valley's tremendous battlements, till our trail turned at a sharp angle and we stood on 'Inspiration Point.' " But because of its configuration the entire valley is not revealed in these first views, only an enchanting foretaste of wonders to come.

When the great landscape architect and conservationist Frederick Law Olmsted first saw Yosemite Valley in 1864, he was struck by its parklike character: the nearly level floor spread with broad meadows deep in grass and wildflowers of many kinds and colors; the thickets of azalea; the stands of towering pines and groves of great oaks in whose dappled shade carpets of tall bracken grew; the sinuous riverbank lined thickly with maple, cottonwood, willow, dogwood, spice-bush, and sweet-scented alder; the mossy ledges crowded with ferns; the open rocky steeps dotted with clumps of rosy buckwheat and orange and yellow wallflower; the quiet pools that mirrored tiger lilies and scarlet columbine. He heard robin, yellow warbler, thrush, and grosbeak sing in meadow and grove. It was a kind of park he had never imagined before, a "wild park" created over the ages without man's intervention, and which man had no right to alter. He was among the first to work for its preservation.

Olmsted saw it in late spring. In summer and fall other flowers bloom on the grasslands and dry slopes; the songs of other birds, resident and migrant, are heard throughout the valley. Seared by the frosts of autumn the meadows turn tawny, but oak groves, stands of cliffside aspen, and riverbank maple, willow, and dogwood glow contrastingly in shades of scarlet and crimson, bright yellow, gold, and amber.

Walling the valley are cliffs of gray granite, mountains in height and size, infinitely varied in form and character and differing wholly one from another—some smooth and sheer, some intricately carved, some crowned with domes or spires; all are separated by wooded ravines or deep shadowy canyons threaded by streams and cascades. Many of these landmarks—El Capitan, Half Dome, the Three Brothers, and Sentinel Rock—are known the world over. El Capitan, standing 7,569 feet above the sea, is one of the largest exposed granite blocks in existence, while Half Dome, which at 8,842 feet dominates the upper end of the valley, is one of the strangest mountain forms, appearing to have been cut in two with some giant axe.

Sharing their fame are the waterfalls, which like the cliffs are of various forms. Outstanding are those making free leaps of such immense height as to set them apart from all others. Yosemite Falls, which even more than El Capitan and Half Dome have given this valley its renown, is composed of a large upper fall, a smaller lower fall, and a connecting chain of cascades, having a combined height of nearly half a mile. The Upper Fall, 1,430 feet, is the highest known free-leaping waterfall in the world. Comparatively, the Lower Fall seems unimpressive until it is realized that its 320-foot drop is twice the height of Niagara. Ranked next to Yosemite Falls in beauty and grandeur is Nevada Fall, which occupies a side canyon and must be sought. At that point in its gorge the entire Merced River, one of ten master streams that rise in the High Sierra and furrow deeply the range's western slope, leaps 594 feet down a craggy precipice. It is the whitest of the valley's falls, since before coming to its brink, it races through a rough, rocky channel where it is beaten and swirled into snowy foam.

Yosemite Valley's 4,000-foot elevation places it within the Transition Zone. However, because each clear day its towering north walls are heated by the sun, while those on the south side remain in shade and are always cool, unusual conditions prevail. These extremes in temperature create additional interest by offering winter residence to creatures that normally would migrate, and by making it a meeting place for flora and fauna from other zones—Lower and Upper Sonoran as well as Canadian—which mingle with indigenous plants and animals. The naturalist John Muir observed that all the birds of the area knew this difference of climate between the two sides of the valley and sought out the warmest nooks on the north to winter. In early January he noted the activity of wrens, bluebirds, jays, and titmice, and found currant and California laurel flowering while just across the valley the south side was still blanketed with snow and deep in silent shadow.

Beyond the valley's cliff tops, to the north and south, and spreading among the crest peaks of the Sierra, lies another world (all within Yosemite National Park) of shimmering alpine lakes set in granite basins; of flower-filled meadows ringed by conifer forests; of streams and waterfalls; of ice-sculptured spires and domes; of little rock gardens blooming with heather and penstemon, fuschia and phlox, and tiny golden violets. Near the park's western boundary, north and south of the valley, are three groves of rare Big Trees, relics of some forty species of sequoia that flourished in the Northern Hemisphere about sixty million years ago. There are birds and mammals in number throughout this high country: tanager, flycatcher, grouse, quail, owl, and kingfisher; deer of three subspecies; coyote, marmot, badger, chipmunk, pika, pine marten, and black bear (the last grizzly bear of record in Yosemite was killed around 1895).

Some twenty miles to the north of the valley is another widened river canyon, the canyon of the Tuolumne, called Hetch Hetchy Valley, a name derived from the Indian word *hetchetci*, a grass growing there whose seeds were ground and eaten as porridge. This valley is said to have been discovered by a gold-seeker while hunting for game in 1850, a year before Yosemite Valley was entered by white men. Although it also contains domes, granite cliffs, and waterfalls, it is approximately half the size of Yosemite Valley and its features are on a less grand and awe-inspiring scale. However, in flagrant disregard of its importance as one of the scenic wonders of the park, its lush meadows and fine stands of oak and pine were drowned by a reservoir in 1923.

But it is Yosemite Valley that has always cast a spell. Incomparable, John Muir called it, for nowhere has there been found another to equal it. It seemed to him "as if into this one mountain mansion Nature had gathered her choicest treasures."

In the beginning it was the Indian who responded to its aesthetic appeal, and once his home was made there, succumbed to its magic. Desperately he struggled to keep it first from the white man's knowledge, then from his grasp. After he was driven out, he came back secretly to live a necessarily furtive existence in its most secluded east end, with readily accessible escape routes to the valley's rim and High Sierra by way of caves, hidden passages, and treetop tunnels. When white men began settling the valley, the Indian did not dare try permanent residence until he had tested their attitude. But once he found that relations were amicable, then he put up his bark huts.

With the first party of white men to enter Yosemite in 1851 was a young physician who responded immediately to its beauty, was awed by it, and was responsible for naming the valley and many of its landmarks. Three years later Grizzly Adams, the famed bear hunter and trainer, found himself held "as if spellbound" by his first view of that "sublime scenery." Among the earliest sightseers the next year were a number who felt Yosemite's call and returned prepared to build log cabins and plant subsistence gardens. When the valley became a state park in 1864 and private holdings were no longer recognized, these pioneer settlers reacted just as the Indian had, stubbornly resisting all attempts to wrest from them the privilege of living at the foot of Yosemite Falls and within the shadow of Half Dome, Sentinel Rock, and the Royal Arches.

The early photographers who packed into Yosemite with their cumbersome equipment soon came under its spell, and finding limitless possibilities, explored the entire region for months at a time and came back year after year to experiment with different approaches. Some won international fame for their Yosemite views. Landscape painters were also caught by the compelling scenery, and for many it became a favorite painting ground to which they returned often and at all seasons. A few were so drawn by it they set up studios in the valley and painted it the year round.

Poets were inspired by it. One British author, completely captivated, spent many months in the valley writing a novel set in Yosemite. Dr. Joseph LeConte, a noted geologist, botanist, and research scientist who went there first to study, became enchanted and returned summer after summer for over thirty years. John Burroughs, the great bird and nature essayist, cherished the memory of his days spent there, and wrote about the valley's spell. President Theodore Roosevelt, who camped in Yosemite one spring, was touched by its magic and never forgot the experience.

John Muir was held in Yosemite's spell for nearly fifty years. He went there in 1869, completely unknown, to work as a sawyer and carpenter. Yosemite developed, matured, and nourished him intellectually, spiritually, and physically. It stimulated him to make profound, dedicated, and exhaustive studies of nature; later when he began to write, Yosemite evoked his most poetic imagery. With the region as his mentor, he grew to be a master of geology and botany. His important discovery that glacial erosion was chiefly responsible for the creation of Yosemite Valley led him to an extensive study of the origin of the Sierra Nevada Range, then to an investigation of all the mountains of California, of Alaska, and finally, of the world.

In his lone rambles through Yosemite, his mysticism evolved; his perception was sharpened, his susceptibility to beauty was expanded, and he became preternaturally sensitive to impressions. Ceaseless exertion in high altitudes restored his health and hardened his body to almost limitless endurance. Because his spirit was "pitched in the right key," he said, he could live in the mountains almost exclusively on dry bread and tea.

He became so attuned to Yosemite, so dependent upon its life force, that he literally withered and sickened when separated from it for any length of time. But once he had returned, his recovery was immediate and total. Later in life when he was trapped by prosaic duties that taxed him spiritually and physically, he would escape periodically to Yosemite and find renewal. The effect of landscape upon man was never more apparent.

3

DWELLERS IN AHWAHNE

*I*NDIANS WERE AWARE of Yosemite Valley at least five thousand years ago. In Mesopotamia men were just then laying the bases of modern culture with the invention of the wheel, and Egyptian scholars were making the first known use of numerals. Europe and much of the rest of the world was still in darkness, but in California, Indians were living essentially as their ancestors already had for thousands of years, and as their descendants would live until the coming of white men. By 1000 B.C. they were already established in Yosemite. The valley's isolated position, easily defended; its abundance of water, game, fish, and plant foods; and its exceptional beauty would have attracted them early in their wanderings about the Sierra. Although Indians selected their village sites primarily for practical reasons, aesthetics also influenced choice.

Within historic times, but doubtless for centuries before, those Indians known as *Ah-wah'-nee-ches*, a subtribe of the Southern or Sierra Miwok, made Yosemite their home. Miwok is not a tribal name, but the native word for people, being the plural of *miwü*, meaning person. The Miwok are members of the Penutian phylum, one of the six linguistic stocks recognized in native North America, five of which are represented in California. Because the Miwok were bordered by the Yokuts, Wintun, Maidu, Washo, and Mono or Paiute tribes, various influences have been recognized in their culture.

Due to the abundance of its natural resources the Yosemite region could support a relatively large population. Thirty-six living sites have been located on the valley floor, and one in Little Yosemite, beyond the head of Nevada Fall. There were doubtless more, overlooked or forgotten by native informants at the time of the count, which was begun in the 1870s. Three types of settlement existed: villages occupied all year; seasonal villages lived in from May through October; and hunting and fishing camps, each site definitely located and regularly occupied at a particular time by adjacent Miwoks and other allied tribes.

These villages and camps were established north and south of the Merced River on sites dictated not by personal preference but by the precepts of totemic moieties: nature was divided into a land half and a water half, and everything in the world belonged to one half or the other. Those villages located north of the river were occupied by people belonging to the land moiety, while those south of it were lived in by members of the water half. When a native spoke of that north side, he might refer to it as the inside, the land side, the grizzly bear side, or the blue jay side; the south he might call the outside, the water side, or the coyote side.

Koom-i-ne, the largest and most important village in the valley, was on the land, grizzly bear or blue jay side, just below Yosemite Falls. It extended southwesterly along the base of the cliffs for three-quarters of a mile to that group of symmetrical summits known as the Three Brothers. In this ruling town lived the celebrated chief Tenaya, and here beside a gigantic oak he had a large round earth-covered ceremonial house, a *hang-e*.

To the east of this settlement was the village of *Ah-wah'-ne*. It was customary to attach the name of the village to the land belonging to it. Since Ahwahne's lands comprised the most extensive tract of open, level ground in the area, outside tribes began calling the entire valley Ahwahne, and those who lived there became the Ahwahneeches.

In these villages there were dwellings of two types: tepee-shaped huts of bark, ranging from eight to fifteen feet in diameter; and round earth-covered semi-subterranean houses built on the plan of the ceremonial room. For the hut, slabs of bark (preferably incense cedar, stripped only from dead trees) were leaned

together over a framework of poles and secured in place by grape-
vine withes. The doorway, merely an opening in the sloping side,
faced east, a traditional direction with North American Indians; it
was closed by setting in place an unattached bark slab of proper
size.

For the partially underground house, a domed roof covered
with thatch and earth to a thickness of several feet and supported
by heavy beams and upright posts was erected over a pit. It was
entered by way of a ladder through a hole in the center of the roof,
strongly suggestive of Pueblo Indian influence from the Southwest. As in the bark hut, there was a shallow depression in the
middle of the earth floor for the fire, which furnished warmth and
light. Next to it was a pit oven, where during the winter acorn
bread, roots, greens, meat, and fish were baked or steamed by
means of heated stones; during the other seasons cooking was done
out-of-doors.

Living arrangements were simple. Although a chief might sleep
between bear hides on a platform of willow poles, the usual bed
was merely a deerskin spread over a thickness of pine needles on
the floor, with more hides or a rabbit-skin blanket for covering.
Occasionally small stumps or blocks of wood served as stools, but
the Ahwahneeches customarily sat on the piles of bedding or on
the ground.

Although life for the Ahwahneeches was easier than for many
other Sierra Miwoks, the quest for food was constant, since they
were neither farmers nor herdsmen. Theirs was not, however, an
uncertain, day-to-day subsistence, for wild crops were harvested—
greens and bulbs in spring, seeds and fruits in summer, acorns and
nuts in fall, and mushrooms in winter—and nearly every family
had large reserves of these, as well as meat and fish, dried and
stored in granaries and baskets. Available supplies of food were
bountiful in variety if not always in quantity: if one source failed,
there were a dozen others to replace it. Movements to different
altitudes prolonged the seasons, and trade enlarged the supply.

Nearly everything edible in the plant world was used for food or
medicine, while most mammals, birds, fishes, reptiles, and several
kinds of insects were eaten. Acorns were the staple of the California Indian's diet. In the Yosemite region, three varieties of oak
—black, canyon live, and scrub—furnished abundant crops most

years. In times of scarcity buckeye nuts were substituted, and woodpeckers' caches were raided for freshly stored acorns.

The shelled, dried acorn kernels were ground into meal by the women, not in portable mortars, for these were revered for their supernatural origin, having been invented by Coyote, one of the creators, but in mortarlike pockets that generations of pounding had worn in flat outcroppings of bedrock found in or near oak groves throughout the Sierran foothills. Here at these communal mills the women chatted or sang in chorus as they worked.

Tannin in the acorns necessitated leaching the meal in a sand basin by pouring water over it slowly. As the water seeped through the fine meal it dissolved the acid and leached it down through the porous sand. Ten baskets of water—the first two or three cold, the next several lukewarm, and the final ones hot— were usually enough to remove the tannin. Then the meal was ready to be made into soup, mush, and biscuits or bread, which were simply variations of one process: boiling a mixture of meal and water. Boiling was effected by placing perhaps a dozen stones (often steatite) at white heat in a tightly woven cooking basket containing a small amount of acorn gruel. As soon as the boiling slowed, the stones were replaced with more hot ones. To keep the basket from burning, the mixture was stirred constantly with a looped stick (of Yokuts origin), which was also used to remove the cooled stones. As cooking progressed, more meal or more water was added, the proportions dependent on the desired results.

Food was being prepared throughout the day, since with the exception of breakfast, which was eaten at sunrise, people ate when they were hungry, and meals were taken at irregular times. Methods of cooking were various. Quail, grouse, trout, rabbit, squirrel, or gopher was either broiled whole over the live coals of an open fire or roasted in hot ashes, the skinning or picking done afterward. Large animals were skinned, the flesh sliced with an obsidian blade, and the pieces broiled over coals. Sometimes this meat was boiled by the hot-stone method or in steatite bowls, which could be put directly on the fire. A favorite way of preparing dried fish was to coat it with acorn mush before broiling it; acorn biscuits were always eaten with this dish. The bulbs and roots of corn lily, anise, mariposa tulip, brodiaea, blue camas, and yampah were baked in hot ashes, boiled, or steamed in the earth oven, which was first lined with preheated stones over which were laid sunflower or wild grape leaves. A thin layer of food was then spread over the leaves, which were covered with more leaves and hot stones, then another layer of leaves and food, and still more heated stones, until the pit was filled. For steaming, water was poured at intervals around the edges of the pit; for baking, a fire was built on top of the oven.

Thirty-seven species of greens were eaten. Some were consumed as soon as picked, but most were either stone-boiled or steamed. The berries of four varieties of manzanita were crushed to make a sweet, unfermented cider used as a refreshing summer drink, as a beverage at feasts, or as a cure for stomach disorders when dipped with a plumed stick from its container and sucked off the feathers. (The curative powers lay not in the manzanita but in the hawk plumes tied to the wand.)

Sierra currant, wild plum, gooseberry, blackberry, grape, and chokecherry—this last favored by singers because it was "good for voice"—were eaten fresh. The fruit of the toyon and elderberry were cooked first. The much-relished nut of the sugar pine was not only eaten in abundance when harvested but was ground, shell included, into a stiff, buttery paste called *lopa*, which was served with acorn soup and manzanita cider at feasts.

First-fruit rites attended the harvesting and eating of wild crops. These were linked with world-renewing ceremonies that took place in April and in September or October. Their purpose was to bring rains to nourish the earth; to regenerate or maintain bountiful crops and an abundance of animal food; and to prevent floods, earthquakes, and other disasters. Before any of the new harvest might be eaten, the shaman had to first blow breath, or tobacco smoke from his ceremonial pipe, upon those present, and to press their bodies with his hands.

Deer hunting was also accompanied by rite. First the hunter sweated and bathed for ceremonial purity, to give strength to his legs and to remove human odor. He entered the sweat-house—a low, conical earth-covered structure—before sunrise, and after adding his oak wood to the fire, kneeled with his face on the floor (to prevent suffocation). After remaining in this position from one to three hours, he ran out and plunged into the nearest stream or pool. This process was repeated once or twice. After bathing for the final time, he rubbed his body with angelica root to ward off rattlesnake bite and confer good luck. Upon killing a deer, he thanked its spirit for having cooperated. Man shared his existence with animals and plants, and felt responsible for them. By respecting other forms of life he did not abuse his relationship with them.

Hunts were of two kinds: individual and communal. A group of men or an entire village might drive deer over a cliff or past hunters concealed in pits beside the trail. Such drives were never undertaken without prayers and magical observances, while strict taboos were observed by the hunters' relatives. Individuals often ran an animal down by foot, for a swift and hardy runner could tire a deer in a day; or they stalked deer in disguise—a tight-fitting cap of long grass that masked the hunter as he crawled through the brush, or a cluster of pine twigs tied to his head, to suggest antlers. The latter disguise was used mainly in the fall, when a buck would attack almost anything and in his rage would come close enough for the hunter to stab him. Bears were also irritated by such a sham buck. One man told of killing four bears in two days: two of the bears had tried to eat him, he said.

But the most highly prized disguise was the entire skin of an antlered buck. Magical properties were attributed to it; it was put on in secret, and when not in use it was kept hidden from the supposed contamination of contact with women and children. This hunter dressed in deerskin would imitate every move of the herd and thus be accepted by it, allowing him to follow closely and kill as many deer as he needed with his silent arrows.

Fish were caught with dip nets, by hand, by hook, with weirs, and communally by poison, when large quantities of crushed soaproot or buckeye nuts were fed into the Merced River and other streams at low water in late summer. The stupefied fish that floated to the surface were picked out by hand or scooped up in baskets. Their flesh proved harmless to those who ate it. Grasshoppers, tasting like shrimp, were highly esteemed as food. In summer a large meadow would be encircled by people from one or several villages. Swinging small boughs back and forth like brooms, men, women, and children would drive the insects into deep, narrow pits dug by each family for the purpose. As soon as the grasshoppers were trapped, smudge fires were lighted among the pits: the wings of those that tried to fly were singed; the rest suffocated. Part of each group's catch was parched with hot coals in an openwork basket to be eaten at once; the rest of the insects were dried for winter use.

The bow used in hunting and for war was about three feet long and some two inches wide at its broadest part. The Ahwah-neeches shaped it from an incense-cedar limb, trimming it first with a sharp-edged stone, then working it down with an obsidian flake. The smoothing was done with sandstone, and the final polishing with scouring rushes still found growing on the banks of the Merced. While yet green the bow was bent into shape by warming it over a fire. After nearly a week of seasoning, dried deer sinew, chewed to workable softness, was pasted on the bow in thin layers as reinforcing, soaproot juice serving as both adhesive and water seal. The bowstring was of sinew or twisted milkweed fiber. Around its center was bound a half-inch strip of otter fur, hair side out, to offer better grip for the arrow nock. To silence the string, another narrow piece of fur was wrapped some six inches from the top. It took about ten days to complete a bow. Nearly every man owned one, but not every man made it himself.

Arrows were always fashioned by a specialist—the bow maker —from select young shoots of western spice-bush, elder, or willow, and paid for with beads. For big game and for war, there was a foreshaft of live oak. The arrowhead was usually obsidian, which works finer and sharper than flint. The arrow base was notched, painted red, and fitted with three or four half feathers of red-tailed hawk, although for deer hunting, roadrunner plumes were preferred because of a magical association between the swiftness of that bird on foot and the lethal properties of the arrow carrying its feathers.

Basketry was the California Indian's most highly developed art. Sierra Miwok basketry shows the influence of neighboring tribes, employing several varieties of the two techniques, coiling and winding, and a wide range of shapes and materials. Yet in their decorative designs the Miwoks developed a distinctive style characterized by lightness of touch.

Twining or winding was the method used for such utensils as seed beaters, winnowers, and sifters; for burden and storage baskets; and for cradles. The Miwoks' fine baskets, coiled with foundation rods, were decorated with abstract geometric designs in maroon (the outer bark of redbud) and black (dyed fern root).

For special uses they were further ornamented with the red feathers of woodpeckers, the yellow feathers of meadowlarks, the green feathers of mallards, and the crests of mountain quail. These tightly woven baskets were multiform and -purpose: the flaring, the straight-sided, the globose, and the elliptical shapes all being used for cooking and serving acorn mush, soup, and bread, as well as for storage. Very small flaring baskets served as dippers to ladle food, or for drinking water and manzanita cider. In a shallow, broad basket the seeds of wild oats, paintbrush, evening primrose, clarkia, tarweed, and buttercup were parched. On a flat woven tray, gamblers cast their dice.

Clothing for the Sierra Miwoks was scant at all seasons. When men wore anything, it was simply a piece of deerskin folded about the hips, or a leather breechclout attached to a narrow girdle, although the clout may not have been aboriginal. Women's dress consisted of a two-piece skirt of buckskin, the rear and longer part put on first, and the smaller front apron wrapped around to overlap. The skirt reached about halfway between the knees and ankles, and the bottom edge was slit into fringes several inches long. Under the skirt was worn a buckskin clout similar to the man's. Children went naked until they were about ten years of age. As protection against the cold, both sexes of all ages wore the dressed skins of deer, bear, mountain lion, and otter, and occasionally buffalo robes obtained in trade from the Monos and Washos, who lived east of the Sierra and had contact with Plains tribes. These skin blankets were thrown about the shoulders like a cape or wrapped snugly around the body or passed over one arm and under the other and tied in front. Another cloak valued highly for its warmth was the rabbit-skin blanket, also obtained through trade.

Around the village and for ordinary excursions, feet were left bare; but for long journeys, for war, and in cold weather, people wore single-piece moccasins lined with shredded cedar bark. These were made by the men, who also cured the hides. For travel over snow in the High Sierra, small oval hoops of wood in which two to four thongs were tied crosswise, and one or two longitudinally, served as snowshoes. The closest parallels to these were discovered in the prehistoric cliff dwellings of ancient Mesa Verde.

Since clothing was minimal, there was little opportunity or incentive to express an innate love of finery by decorating it with paint or with colored quill or bead embroidery. Aside from skirt fringes, for everyday use there is record only of a buckskin sash covered either with shell beads or with the scarlet scalps of woodpeckers, and hung with pendants of olive-shell disks. But this was worn mainly by villagers of wealth and importance, as was the hair net tied with abalone-shell bangles, and the feather plume. Children wore the flowers of rattlesnake grass in their pierced ears, and like their elders decorated their hair, left uncut except for mourning and kept glossy by frequent washing, with feathers and blossoms. Garlands of tiger lilies, common monkey flowers, and Mariposa tulips were worn about the head.

The round of ceremonies, and major and minor dances—at least twenty-six—continued throughout the year, and called for the frequent use of ceremonial paraphernalia. On these occasions participants dressed in capes and skirts of magpie, crow, great horned owl, or red-tailed hawk plumes (never eagle, for these brought bad luck). They tied on long headbands of flicker feathers, the ends left free to hang down the back; and tall crowns of magpie tail plumes, the quills painted red. From these plumes projected single or double rods tipped with the down of owls or hawks and strung with little dangling mats of salmon-pink flicker quills. In their ears were shell bead pendants or plugs of incised bird bone or polished wood tipped with scarlet woodpecker feathers and the showy crests of quail. Nose sticks of shell or polished wood were also worn. Women carried feather ropes; and men, arrows, strings of beads, and plumed sticks. Face and body paint was used in certain dances. For the *Oo-hoo'-ma-te* (from which the name Yosemite derives), or grizzly bear ceremony, performers who imitated the bear attached curved pieces of obsidian to their fingers to simulate claws.

The presence of the Kuksu cult, a men's esoteric religious society adopted from the neighboring Maidus, gave the Miwoks additional ceremonials and dances that included spirit and deity impersonations. Although no true masks were developed, such as are found among many aboriginal secret societies around the world, spirit and god impersonators were disguised with heavy paint and face curtains of feathers, buckskin, or grass. Unlike other tribes who followed the Kuksu ritual organization, Miwoks allowed their women to witness all dances and to take part in every one except the *Kuksuyu,* an especially sacred ceremony in which at least three deities appeared.

The large, semi-subterranean assembly house, around forty feet in diameter, was nearly always a feature of the Kuksu cult. The Ahwahneeches had two in Yosemite Valley. In the round earth-covered dwelling, entrance was made by ladder through a hole in the dome roof. In the ceremonial chamber, after which the living house was patterned, the opening in the apex of the dome was a smoke hole, and entrance was gained through a doorway in the side. No evidence was ever obtained from Miwok informants as to whether this smoke hole was originally an entrance, and the side doorway developed from a former ventilator shaft, as is found in the kivas of the Southwest, for some striking resemblances exist between these Miwok ceremonial rooms and those of the Pueblo Indians.

A large foot-drum, eight to ten feet long, made whenever possible from a naturally hollowed trunk of white oak, was the lodge's most sacred adjunct. Half of the log was placed over a pit dug between the two rear supporting posts, which during construction of the room had been treated ceremonially. Both ends of the log were left open, and the pit acted as a resonance chamber. A possible connection between this foot drum and the kiva's *sipapu,* or spirit entrance from the world below, is suggested.

Depending upon the ceremony, the drum was stamped upon by the drummer either alone or in company with the dancers. During rites, the space around the drum was reserved for the singers, who shook butterfly-cocoon rattles and struck their palms with split-stick clappers that sounded like castanets. Dancers blowing bird- and rabbit-bone whistles accompanied them. The Ahwahneeches had the bull-roarer, which was rare among California Indians. The roaring sound was produced by whirling a pine slat attached to a thong. Its function is not thoroughly understood, but it is believed to have been used to summon villagers to a religious ceremony, and during the rite, as a signal to begin and end.

Although most songs were connected with medicine rites and other religious ceremonies—songs for curing; for adolescence observances; for mourning; for good luck in hunting, gambling, and war—there were also many love songs, lullabies, and play and work songs in daily use. This was also true of musical instruments:

only the flute and resonant bow were used for pleasure. The reedless elderwood flute with six to eight holes, innocent of any definite scale, was played evenings by a young man in love within hearing of his chosen girl, as a part of courtship; or it might be played solely for recreation. The musical bow was the only stringed instrument native to California. It was pressed tightly against the lips, thong uppermost, and the player hummed as he plucked the string with his fingers or tapped it with an arrow. This instrument was also used to communicate with one's guardian spirit.

There was a distinct interweaving of shamanism in the Sierra Miwok celebration of the Kuksu cult, since dances pertaining to the cult were also held to cure and prevent disease, believed due to the presence of some malevolent object in the body, introduced through the wizardry of spiteful shamans. It was the spirit shaman's function to rid the patient of these disease objects, or "pains," by singing and through prolonged sucking of a scarified area. The pains so removed—bits of bone, wood, pebbles, teeth, live insects even—were exhibited to those attending the curing and then buried ceremonially or caused to vanish by rubbing between the palms.

The shaman's power for treating or producing illness rested on his or her (for there were many respected women shamans) possession of guardian spirits and the ability to communicate with them. These supernatural beings sometimes appeared unsought in dreams, but were usually obtained by conscious effort through the vision quest. They were often animals, but among the mountain dwellers were more frequently those spirits known to inhabit high peaks, rocks, springs, lakes, streams, and waterfalls.

The curing shaman employed some eighty-two herbs in conjunction with his rites. Sixty-seven of these plants, used for the relief of colds, coughs, headache, rheumatism, toothache, colic, snakebite, wounds, broken bones, and general debility—the gamut of human ailments—have been identified. The roots, stems, bark, leaves, or flowers were ground and boiled for inhalation of the heated vapor or as a decoction to be taken orally; they were sometimes steeped for washes and baths, mashed for poultices, or dried and pulverized for dusting on wounds and open sores.

Sagebrush was believed to possess extraordinary properties. A decoction of its leaves was drunk to cure rheumatism, and fresh leaves were inserted in the nostrils to relieve headache; but most important, it was thought to have the additional power of protecting against ghosts. A person who wore a necklace of its leaves might walk about at night without fear of encountering them. Those who prepared the bodies of the dead for cremation or burial rubbed themselves thoroughly with sagebrush to keep from being haunted by spirits of the departed.

The shaman himself sometimes ate the raw root of the large-flowered datura or drank a tea made from it to induce hallucinations and so maintain his contact with the supernatural and his ability to see into the future.

Excluding the Yokuts, the so-called tribes of California were in reality nonpolitical ethnic nationalities. Every California Indian belonged to a definite unit. Each of these units, or nations, was autonomous and laid claim to a certain territory for its specific use, a right that was acknowledged and respected by the others. Chieftainship was well-defined and concepts of rank clearly developed among the Miwoks. There were head chiefs, such as Tenaya of the Ahwahneeches, whose authority was acknowledged over districts of considerable size; chiefs in individual villages to represent each moiety, and speakers or subchiefs.

The office of head chief was hereditary, and the title passed to women in the male line. In the event of a chief's death, his wife assumed his powers, which she held until a son became old enough to rule. The chief was solely a civil official. If he led in battle it was only because he also happened to be a distinguished warrior. He acted as adviser to his people and manager of natural resources. It was his responsibility to prevent trespass on the hunting and gathering territory of his people. He decided the best time to begin the acorn harvest; he acted as an arbitrator in disputes, had the final word in settling arguments, and was responsible for the punishment of such criminal offenders as poisoners or witches. His approval was necessary before any public ceremony could be held, and he acted as sponsor for all religious and social affairs, issuing the invitations to other chiefs and providing food for the guests.

Among the Miwoks war was never waged for plunder, oppression, or honor. Revenge for murder and for death related to trespass was the most common cause. (The usual penalty for trespass was death, which in the eyes of the dead person's village became

murder and called for avenging.) Miwok warriors prepared for
battle with prayer, purification, and magic rites, during which
faces were painted black with soot. They did not wear rod or elk-
hide armor or carry leather shields, as did some of their neighbors,
but in open fighting depended on their ability to dodge arrows. As
much as possible a warrior kept the side of his body (being narrower) toward the enemy and danced about continuously to frus-
trate the enemy's aim. The principal weapon was the bow;
obsidian-tipped spears and oaken clubs were used only in hand-to-
hand fighting. Rocks flung from buckskin slings or rolled upon
the enemy from above were used by such mountain dwellers as
the Ahwahneeches.

Attacks were made at dawn. The files of naked fighters, black-
ened features invisible in the half light, chanted as they rushed in
upon a sleeping village. Scalps, deftly severed with a razor-sharp
obsidian blade, were taken home, strung on poles, and celebrated
over in the ceremonial house with a dance of triumphant revenge,
accompanied by stamping on the foot drum.

The dead were thought to travel west to an island across the sea,
which the Miwoks believed—if white interpretation is correct—to
have been their ancestral home. A favorite tale very like the Greek
myth concerning Orpheus and Eurydice describes the journey of a
Miwok to this land of the dead in search of his wife.

The great annual mourning ceremony, known in English as
"burning" or "cry," held in September or October, was the
Miwoks' most important rite connected with the dead, and their
most significant religious observance. The purpose was not only to
mourn the deceased but also to supply their spirits with food,
clothing, and personal property. The ceremony was individual
rather than general, since each family gave only to its own dead. It
was held inside a circular brush enclosure some six feet in height
and ranging from fifty to a hundred feet in diameter, with one
opening facing west toward the island of the dead, and usually a
second one opening east. The ceremony was in the charge of a
director, generally a shaman, whose most important duties were to
deliver the opening and closing orations, to supervise the dispatch-
ing of knotted-string invitations* to neighboring and allied tribes

---

* The number of knots indicated the number of days before the gathering,
one knot being untied by the messenger at the end of each day.

and the setting up of poles on which the offerings for the dead were hung.

Around sunset on the first evening the chief mourners visited the site to cry and wail, and so notify the dead that the rite was to take place. The next afternoon the families gathered inside the shelter to hang the poles (often twenty feet long) from top to bottom with objects to be burned. These were mainly baskets of the finest weave and design, made during the year for this purpose. After the finished poles were set up north and south of the fire pit, baskets and trays of acorn bread and flour, seed meal, pine nuts, acorns, dried fruit, meat, and fish were piled around their bases. Then an old man from the home village came forward and lighted the fire. This was a sign to begin the selling or trading of objects brought for burning. As soon as this bargaining period was over and the din had subsided, the director made his opening address. At its conclusion he began to cry, and the others then began their lamentations, which continued throughout the night.

From time to time, bits of meat, bread, and fish were thrown into the fire. At early dawn the climax of the ceremony came with the stripping of the poles; as the objects were removed, they were thrown singly or by the armful into the flames. Crude secular images made for the dead of rank were also cast into the fire. Old people swayed from side to side and wailed with increased fervor. Mourners beat their heads rapidly with their hands and expelled air forcibly as though to blow away things unseen. In their frenzy, old women had to be restrained from throwing themselves into the flames. Outside the enclosure, dogs barked and howled incessantly.

After it grew light, a period of rest was followed by a ritualistic washing of the mourners-in-chief by members of the opposite totemic moiety. Then the director made his closing oration, in which he invited all to the dance house: "There we will eat, for it is not well to go home hungry. You may gamble there. The fire is burning in the dance house, and the house awaits your coming. Gamble and make merry. Let us go! I will lead the way."

For a day or two more there would be a round of feasting, gambling, and field sports. Both men and women had a game of shinny played on a field much like a football field in size and arrangement. In Yosemite Valley the Ahwahneeches used what is now called Leidig Meadow for their sports. In the women's version of shinny, players used sharp-pointed willow poles to toss a cordage ring some two feet in diameter, or a yard-long braided buckskin, toward the goalposts set up at either end of the field. During the play the ring or braid could not be carried on the poles or touched with the hands. For men's shinny, each player had a wooden club, curved at the end, to strike the ball down the field. It was the object of each team to get the ball between the two goalposts. Another game, played only by women and girls—often land moiety against water moiety—was similar to lacrosse. As with shinny, spectators and participants bet heavily on the outcome. Yet another competitive sport was ring and dart. Among the Sierra Miwoks the contestant ran after a small ring sent rolling along the ground, trying to impale it with a ten-foot lance. There was also spear-throwing by means of a buckskin thong attached to a rod, suggesting the ancient Roman way. The farthest cast won. Archery contests and footraces gave further opportunity for wagering.

But the favorite gambling game, the one subject to the greatest excitement and heaviest betting, was known as "hand." For the men's version of this guessing game, two pairs of flat bones, one of each pair being plain and the other grooved or marked, were used. The object was for one side (two players) to guess in which hand their opponents held an unmarked bone, or in some areas, a marked bone. The two men whose turn it was to hide the bones rolled them about in bunches of grass or heaps of pine needles in time to their gambling songs, which brought them good luck but confused their opponents. When ready, those players who held the bones revolved their clenched fists in front of their chests and swayed in rhythm to the songs until the guess was made. Singing and swaying helped control any expression that might betray them. Skilled players relied on their ability to conceal as well as to read facial and body expressions. Ten counters were used to keep score, two counters being awarded for each two correct guesses. The play continued until one side held all ten counters; then the wagers were collected. It was a game that called for instantaneous decisions and reactions, and demanded tremendous concentration and energy. The women's version differed only in minor details relating to the tokens. Hand was so popular that even children played a simplified form, wagering their prized acorn tops, goose-quill whistles, bows and arrows, and soaproot-leaf dolls.

Evenings after the first rains of winter, the Ahwahneeches gathered around a flickering fire in their ceremonial chambers and listened to the storyteller. The tales they heard, abounding in magic, had been told for generations, nothing lost and nothing added through the countless retellings. Many stories dealt with Miwok religious history, narrating the exploits of Coyote the Creator, a deity of mysterious origin and paradoxical character; of Falcon, his grandson and companion; of Condor, the father of Falcon; and of Lizard, all of whom had magical or supernatural powers and were responsible for fabulous occurrences.

There were also tales about the First People, quasi-human heroes who fought fierce battles with giants and took part in such daring exploits as the quest for fire. Just before Coyote created the ancestors of the Indians, he transformed the First People into birds, mammals, trees, rocks, rain, hail—even stars. The names of these First People and their distinctive traits were retained in their new forms: *To-to'-ka-no*'s piercing cry therefore became a marked characteristic of Sandhill Crane; *Oo-hoo'-ma-te*'s great liking for acorns was not lost when she was changed into Grizzly Bear; nor did *Ko-to'-lah* abandon the practice of jumping into water with every whisper of sound after he was turned into Frog. Myths about these transformed First People were legion. A favorite concerned Mouse, the skilled flute player who lulled the Keeper of the Fire with his music, then slipped some live coals into his elder-wood flute and got safely away. Sometimes the narrator, usually an older man, sang in conjunction with storytelling—songs that Coyote, Condor, and the First People sang in the beginning; songs that had come to him through dreams or visions.

Some tales explained the origin of lightning and thunder, of the rainbow and the echo. Echo was Lizard-Man talking back—Lizard who gave the newly created Indian people the gift of five fingers, knowing their worth, for he had five himself. All of these legends were concerned with deities, half-human heroes, and events in the very remote past. But other tales were local, such as the one about the *Ho-ha'-pe*, or Water Women, who lived in deep pools in that part of the Merced River which winds through Ahwahne. With their long hair, they were beautiful to see.

Yosemite Valley's fantastic rock forms, the very size of its steep towering cliffs, the thunder and roar of its waters, the mysterious rush of cold air that accompanied the falls—all appealed to the Ahwahneeches' imagination and seemed to demand an explanation. Each landmark suggested its name, and there was some story to be told about every one.

4

"THE WHITE SACHEM"

O<small>NE CLEAR, COLD MORNING</small> in January 1848, James Wilson Marshall, charged with building a water-powered sawmill on the banks of the American River at Coloma, in the Sierra foothills, took a walk to inspect a newly made tailrace. Seeing something glistening in the bottom of the ditch, he stooped to pick it up. He recalled: "It made my heart thump, for I was certain it was gold." It proved to be gold, and Marshall's discovery prompted the great rush to California in 1849.

The first parties of gold seekers who followed the rivers into the foothills were greeted by the Indians with friendliness and hospitality. But as more and more flocked in and the area was overrun—by the end of 1849 there were around 100,000 miners there—the natives found themselves dispossessed of their traditional territories and faced with the total ruin of their delicately balanced economy and their sacred relationship with nature. Villages in the way of mining operations were burned, and their inhabitants scattered. Oak groves, which furnished the Indians' staff of life, the acorn, were cut down, while the feverish activity in the hunt for gold drove off the herds of deer, elk, and bear, and disrupted fishing grounds. Precious plant foods and material were grazed away by horses and cattle.

Granted no rights, the Indian was without recourse. Starving, many were forced to raid mining camps, trading posts, and ranches to run off horses, which they butchered and ate. Exaggerated accounts of "massacres," for some white men were killed during these forays, and "outrages by the savages" were in constant circulation throughout the mines, feeding the fires of that implacable hatred—at best a deeply ingrained prejudice—held by most Anglo-American gold seekers. Many Indians were shot on sight solely because they were Indian, by men who believed along with California's governor that extermination was the only solution to the problem.

There were, however, a number of white men who disagreed, having discovered that they could profit from the Indian by inducing him to work in the mines in return for a cheap calico shirt or a handful of trinkets. One of the most successful of these men was James D. Savage, leader of the first party of white men to enter Yosemite Valley. He had come overland in 1846 and arrived just in time to be recruited for the California Battalion, organized by brevet-Captain John C. Frémont to seize the territory from Mexico, with whom the United States was then at war. The battalion supplied itself with horses, beef, meal, and other necessities by plundering the Mexican ranchos in its line of march. A fellow trooper remembered that Savage, who had "a special knack for looting trips," always volunteered for that service. After the company was disbanded the following spring, Savage was employed at various tasks by John A. Sutter, an energetic Swiss colonist who under the Mexican rule had established a small empire in the Sacramento Valley. Savage managed at the same time to carry on horse and cattle rustling, and by fall was devoting full time to it. He soon after became the leader of a gang of sixty to eighty white men who swept through the great central valleys, stealing thousands of head of horses and cattle.

For some months after the discovery of gold the concentration of prospectors was along the American River, its several forks, and those streams lying to either side of it. Not until August 1848 was there exploration in the region to be known as the Southern Mines. Then, on a small tributary of the Tuolumne River that rises among the peaks of Yosemite, a party of gold hunters that included James Savage found incredibly rich diggings. Using only picks and knives they were able to take out from two to three hundred dollars a day per man, for the rest of that season. Toward the end of the year Savage moved on to a camp called Jamestown, just a few miles distant, staked claims, recruited Indians, and taught them how to placer mine. Shortly he was seen sitting "under a brush-wood tent . . . measuring and pouring gold dust into candle boxes by his side. Five hundred naked Indians, with belts of cloth bound round their waists or suspended from their heads, brought the dust to Savage, and in return for it received a bright piece of cloth or some beads."

The following spring (1849), with his Indian work force, he located and opened placers where the gold camp Savage's Diggings (later Big Oak Flat) sprang up, about thirty miles west of Yosemite. Near his claims Savage put up a brush-bower store to supply the prospectors who flocked to the area. With the returns from his mines and his trade, his profits often amounted to twenty thousand dollars a day and he began storing his gold in pork barrels. He also continued his cattle rustling in order to maintain a constant supply of beef, a staple of the miner's diet.

To ensure this regular flow of wealth, he made conscious efforts to retain the Indians' goodwill and strengthen his influence among them by learning their languages, marrying the daughters of chiefs and headmen from several bands, adopting their customs, and protecting them from white aggressors. It was said that he had thirty-three wives ranging in age from twelve to twenty-two, but that only five or six lived with him at a time.

To avoid the inevitable clashes between miners and his Indian workers, he moved on after a time to an unpopulated region at Horseshoe Bend in the narrow canyon of the Merced River, just where Piney Creek enters it, about ten miles west of Yosemite Valley. There again he found rich diggings, but upriver Indians who considered him a trespasser—a capital offense—attempted a raid. With the help of his retainers, many of whom were not on friendly terms with the mountain tribes, he drove them off. But discretion prompted another move, this time to the less remote and more easily defended Mariposa Creek area, where he opened a trading post in conjunction with mining. His success suggested expansion, and he next established a branch store on the Fresno River, southwest of Yosemite, where gold camps were mushrooming, and worked placers there with his Indians. By that time his sphere of influence extended over a large number of Yokuts and Miwok people who regarded him as their friend and benefactor.

Sam Ward, the friend of Thackeray, the comrade of Longfellow, the brother of Julia Ward Howe, and the would-be gold seeker, met Savage—"the white sachem," he called him—at his height of power. Ward was struck first by the fact that Savage was clean-shaven, and his complexion sallow, a rarity among the bronzed and bearded population of the mines. He observed that Savage's face was round, his features even; his eyes were large and light blue. His hair, "fair as the golden locks of Achilles," hung below his shoulders in "ringlets like a young girl's." Of wiry build, he probably weighed no more than 138 pounds. Ward thought Savage resembled Peter the Great in features, stature, and bearing. He noted with interest that Indians, especially women and children, from an encampment near the trading post where the two men met thronged the store and pressed about Savage as he talked with them in their own tongue.

Other men have described Savage as "physically an Apollo" and "conversationally a polished, entertaining gentleman." Although he had little formal schooling, he managed to give the impression of having been well-educated. He had the reputation for being "magnificently generous," and many a man who had reached the mines destitute could vouch for that. Those who knew him well were aware of the "extraordinary hypnotic powers" that enabled him to manipulate white men to act to his advantage, and the "magnetic and almost mysterious influence" he held over certain Indians. But there were some who had found him "a blasphemous fellow" whose language was often "foul"; who saw him as a braggart, a liar, and "a dangerous man to have for an enemy." And there were a few men who realized that he had reduced his Indian workers to peons.

By the summer of 1850 many of his Indian subjects, as he liked to think of them, had learned the value of gold, had realized that he was growing rich at their expense, and were aware that he was protecting them only for selfish reasons. Through his wives he learned of this discontent, and of a possible coalition of tribes to drive miners and settlers from the foothills. In order to impress these Indians with the number of white men and their potential power he took with him to San Francisco, José Juarez, a headman whom he considered his most important Yokuts ally, and two of his Miwok wives through whom he communicated with their people. Another reason for the trip was to bank a pork barrel full of gold, which was worth nearly a million dollars.

They traveled by stage to Stockton, then on by steamboat to San Francisco, where, instead of stopping at a hotel, Savage set up camp in Portsmouth Square, attracting considerable attention even in a city inured to the unconventional. One night he caused a flurry of excitement in the gambling rooms of the Plaza Hotel when during a game of monte he leaped upon the table, and putting his foot on a certain card, wagered his weight in gold dust on it. With the turn of that card he lost close to $35,000. He settled part of the debt with gold allocated by the Indians for the purchase of goods, prompting José Juarez to berate him in public, and Savage to knock Juarez down for what he considered insolence.

During the trip home, Savage heard rumors that certain Yokuts bands were demanding tribute from white men passing through their territory, and that they were gathering in number near his Fresno River post. Going there directly, he saw nothing to alarm him; those Indians who were at the store had apparently come to trade. Still, he called a council, and addressing them in their own tongue said he knew that certain Indians did not want to be friends with white men. But this must not be: "I have just been where white men are more numerous than the wasps and ants; and if war is made and the white men are aroused to anger, every Indian engaged will be killed before they are satisfied." He stressed again the numbers and strength of the whites, and their superiority of arms, then turned to José Juarez for confirmation.

The Yokuts leader said that Savage had told them many interesting things, but that he had not said anything about gambling away all the gold to be used for their supplies, or about striking José Juarez and knocking him down. He no longer believed Savage was their friend: "He is ready to help the white gold diggers drive the Indians from their country." Juarez did not think white men living in faraway cities would come to help the miners fight Indians. But if they should, he said, "we will go to the mountains. If they follow, they cannot find us. Our country is now overrun with white people; we must fight to protect ourselves."

Angered, Savage withdrew and prepared to continue his journey to Mariposa Creek. "Now that you have spent the money, where do we get our food from?" an Indian asked. "There are plenty of horses," Savage retorted. In order to spy on Indian activities and avoid recognition, he exchanged his buckskins for "a tattered coat, corduroy pants, tarpaulin hat, horse hair beard, and a buffalo hair mustachio."

In Mariposa County, the center of the southern mining district, which bordered the future Yosemite National Park on the west and south, Indian troubles were brought to a climax by the so-called Mariposa Indian War, actually only a series of skirmishes. There a number of Yokuts bands, in response to dispossession, impending starvation, and white exploitation, commenced stock raiding. Reports were forwarded to the governor, who responded by sending Adam Johnston as his special Indian agent, to "reconcile differences." From his talks with chiefs Johnston became aware of disaffection, as he said, and "a restless feeling toward the whites," but foresaw no immediate danger. That was early in December 1850.

On the night of December 17, some three hundred Miwok and Yokuts who worked for James Savage left his Mariposa Creek camp quietly in a body, taking their families with them. On missing them, Savage immediately suspected a movement against him and organized a party of sixteen volunteers to follow their trail.

Around daybreak, after riding some thirty miles toward the Sierra, Savage pushed ahead to the top of a ridge to try and sight the Indians. Discovering them on an adjacent mountain, he hailed them in their own language and asked why they had left his post in secret. They were taking their women and children into the Sierra for safety, the chief replied, for Savage's store on the Fresno River had been raided and his storekeepers killed. Now they must prepare for the white men's retaliation.

Anxious to verify this report, Savage hastily retraced his trail, and increasing his party to thirty-five, set off three days later for his Fresno post. He found it in shambles, his horses and cattle driven off, and three of his clerks, "filled with arrows," lying where they had fallen. Then, upon his return within a week to Mariposa Creek, he discovered that *that* post had been plundered, and his six Yokuts wives taken by their own people.

Seeing in a war the chance to punish these Indians and to gain recognition (and possibly public office) within the white community, he proceeded to incite hostility between the races, chiefly through the circulation of false rumors. Responsibility for the ensuing trouble was mainly his.

At Savage's insistence James Burney, sheriff of Mariposa

County, raised a company of seventy-four. He appointed Savage its chief scout. This punitive party set off on January 6, 1851, heading once again toward the Sierra. Around two o'clock in the morning of the second day Savage rode in to report a nearby village, on a high point above the North Fork Fresno River: he had heard the Indians singing. Leaving a small guard with their animals, the sheriff and his men followed Savage's lead. By removing their boots as they neared the summit, they were able to crawl undetected to within a hundred and fifty yards of the settlement. There they lay shivering on the snowy slope, waiting for daybreak. With the first light the Indian sentinel discovered them, and yipping like a coyote, ran to give the alarm.

"Never did I hear before such an infernal howling, whooping and yelling as saluted us from the throats of six hundred savages, as they rushed down the hill," a participant wrote. There was utter confusion among those troops new to Indian fighting. When Burney gave the order to charge, they ran wildly about, firing at random. Shots from the rear began felling those ahead; one officer was killed, and several men badly wounded. Somehow a few in the lead managed to push through and enter the village. All was quiet, so they presumed they had possession and started hunting for loot. Suddenly there came the crack of a rifle from the brush below, and another man fell, victim of a comrade's haphazard shot. Believing, however, that the Indians were now attacking with firearms, the entire company panicked and began running down the slope— "running as if they never intended to stop," it was remembered. Burney and Savage had just managed to halt a few and persuade them to re-form when the accidental discharge of a pistol and the wounding of a young trooper sent the men on the fly again.

That night Burney ordered the camp moved six miles down the river, and a log fort constructed. In the morning, leaving thirty-five men under Savage to guard the fort and care for the wounded, the sheriff set off with the others for the mining settlements to get supplies and reinforcements.

Chagrined by their rout, those at the fort reorganized and drilled, and without waiting for Burney's recruits, started out to track down the Indians, who had pushed deeper into the wilderness. They were discovered encamped on "a round mountain covered with dense undergrowth . . . rocks and trees," a natural stronghold close to the North Fork San Joaquin, which, like Yosemite's

Merced River, rises at Mount Lyell. There were, Savage estimated, some five hundred warriors, Yokuts and Sierra Miwok, a
number no doubt greatly exaggerated, since an assault party of
thirty-five was able to scatter them. There were, according to the
official count, twenty-three Indians killed in the skirmish, and no
casualties among the volunteers.

Since this was not the decisive blow hoped for, Savage, who
was determined to administer it, rode north to call on the governor
and ask for a body of state troops to keep the Indians in "subjec-
tion," as he said. Legally, such an application could be made only
to the commander of the Army's Pacific Division, since Indians
were under federal jurisdiction. But Savage knew that he could
better influence the governor than a commanding general who
maintained that "the Indians have been more 'sinned against than
sinning' since the settlement of California by whites." They were
by nature unwarlike, the general believed, but "the germ of a hostile
spirit has been *created* in them." Only peaceful action could keep
that germ from growing into "a deadly hatred."

Savage insinuated to the governor that he had already applied
to the general and that little help could be expected from that
quarter. He stressed the threat of a widespread Indian revolt, and
the governor, thoroughly alarmed, authorized the organization of
one hundred state militia (a number he shortly doubled) to be
recruited by Savage and Sheriff James Burney. He followed this
order with a message to the federal Indian commissioners, appris-
ing them of an imminent uprising and asking for their cooperation.

On February 12, 1851, around one hundred and eighty volunteers reported to the Whittier Hotel in Agua Fria, the county seat,
and were mustered into what was called the Mariposa Battalion.
The men furnished their own horses, arms, and equipment; the
state paid for their provisions and baggage trains. James Savage,
owner of the only trading post in the area, was the supplier, bound
to profit heavily from such a campaign.

Although the sheriff was the logical choice for commander, he
pleaded press of business—his territory was of such size it was
later divided into six counties—and declined. Savage was voted in,
and shortly commissioned a major of the California militia.

Eager for action, he immediately sent out scouting parties and
led others himself, to hunt down Indians, a policy that drove them

ever deeper into the Sierra. But with the arrival of the federal Indian commissioners who had responded to the governor's call, this course of action was immediately suspended. The commissioners assumed full command over the battalion, and instructed Savage to stop all hostile demonstrations until further notice.

5

THE TRAIL
TO YOSEMITE

*F*ROM THEIR HEADQUARTERS camp established along Mariposa Creek, the federal commissioners sent out some half-dozen former Mission Indians who had a knowledge of Spanish and English and had been recruited by James Savage to act as interpreters and emissaries. It was their duty to meet with the chiefs and urge them to make treaties; and to explain that as a protection from the white men's aggressions they would be settled on land put aside especially for them along the Fresno River. Food and clothing would be provided. But the Yokuts and foothill Miwok were wary, and only a few responded. Those Miwoks who lived in the remote parts of the Sierra and had almost no contact with whites saw no reason for protection. One messenger reported that the band of Sierra Miwok called the Ahwahneeches (Savage knew them as Yosemites or Grizzly Bears), who lived in a deep valley hidden in the heart of the mountains, refused to consider any treaty that involved leaving their homeland. No white man had yet entered it, and they did not fear invasion, for it was a natural fortress, surrounded by high steep walls of rock; entrances were few and easily guarded. Another messenger added that the Ahwahneeches would roll down great rocks on any white men who ventured near. The valley was not safe to enter, he continued, for "there are many witches there."

This refusal to consider resettlement, which the white men interpreted as recalcitrance, was prompted by that strong sentimental attachment all California Indians held for the place in which they were born and had always lived. It was their cherished hope to complete the life cycle in that one spot. The commissioners, growing impatient, sent another message to the mountain dwellers, giving them eight days in which to report. If at the end of that time they had still not come, Savage had instructions to scout the region for them, and when he found them, to burn their houses and granaries. The eight days passed and nothing was heard from the mountain bands or those who had gone into hiding in the Sierra. On Saturday morning, March 22, Savage, with two companies and fifteen days' rations, rode off on a trail that was to lead eventually to Yosemite Valley. Each man was issued fifteen rounds of ammunition with strict orders to reserve it for Indians, not to waste it on squirrel-shooting and other sport.

Going by way of Chowchilla Mountain, the party soon encountered rain, which turned to heavy snow as they gained elevation, burying the trail and making it nearly impossible in places to bring the pack train through. After covering some ten miles, a rest halt was called on the slopes of Black Ridge. Savage announced his intention of pressing on, even though it was nearly sunset, to take by surprise a village (Nutchu) he knew was located along the Merced's South Fork.

Spirits rose as they made good time over a hard-packed trail, one trooper remembered. What lay ahead seemed a grand adventure; he and the others looked forward to prospects of an all-out war and discussed their chances with those three thousand well-armed Ahwahneeches rumored waiting in that impregnable valley.

Suddenly the terrain grew steep. Packs slipped off as mules floundered through snowbanks; there were frequent delays, and the summit of Chowchilla Mountain seemed ever more distant. But once they reached the top, the descent proved even worse, for the night was moonless and they had to grope their way over gullies and fallen trees in a forest of cedars and pines so dense not even the stars could prick the blackness. At around three in the morning camp was made in a grove about a mile below present Wawona, at the park's south end. Some of the men threw themselves in exhaustion on the snowy ground. Others hunkered about the small fires Savage permitted them to build.

Shortly he called for volunteers to take the village. "It may be a fight or a footrace," he told them. About seventy men responded, and with an allied Indian in the lead, they filed off on foot just as day was breaking. The villagers were completely surprised and offered no resistance. At Savage's order they packed their food and property and crossed the Merced to a site at the mouth of Bishop Creek, where he established a camp to serve as his headquarters. During the morning he sent Indian runners to find those bands still said to be hiding in the Sierra. Again the chiefs were to be assured land, food, clothing, and protection if they consented to make treaties; but if they refused, Savage would fight until he had destroyed them all.

Around a hundred Sierra Miwoks and refugees responded, but only a few at a time, cautiously keeping to the protection of trees and boulders until they had made sure they would not be shot on sight. But nothing was heard from the Ahwahneeches. Savage, not too anxious to battle the rumored three thousand warriors with the advantage of home ground, dispatched a special envoy to their chief, Tenaya.

Tenaya came in alone, perhaps from a desire to settle finally this demand for relocation, and stood "in dignified silence before one of the guard, until motioned to enter camp," Lafayette Bunnell, a young physician with the battalion remembered. He noticed that Tenaya was taller and had a better build and a lighter complexion than any California Indian he had yet seen. The doctor observed that he was also cautious, suspecting this might be a ruse of Savage's to get the Ahwahneeches in his power for personal vengeance, since they were suspected of having attempted the raid on his Merced River trading post.

Tenaya now asked why all the Indians were being taken to the plains "to be yarded like horses and cattle." Savage explained, stressing that the white man's government would give the Indians everything they needed, including protection.

"My people do not want anything from the 'Great Father' you tell me about," the chief countered. "We have all we need. We do not want anything from white men. . . . Go then; let us remain in the mountains where we were born; where the ashes of our fathers are. . . . My people do not want to go to the plains. The tribes who go there are some of them very bad. They will make war on my people. We cannot live on the plains with them. Here we can defend ourselves against them."

Savage told him his people must go to the commissioners: "If they do not make a treaty, your whole tribe will be destroyed; not one of them will be left alive." After a few moments Tenaya said that if he was allowed to go back to his home valley, he would bring the Ahwahneeches in. Savage agreed to his leaving, and the following day Tenaya returned with word that his people would come, but that they would be slow, for the recent snowstorm had left deep drifts, making it hard for the old women and the children to climb out of the valley—and he indicated its great depth with his hands.

When another day passed and the Ahwahneeches did not arrive, Savage called for volunteers to ride with him to their villages. Taking along five days' rations, fifty-seven men with Tenaya as their guide left camp around noon on Thursday, March 27. Each man was required to take the lead by turn to break a trail through the four-foot-deep snow. After they had traveled about half the way, they met Tenaya's people, a band of seventy-two. Among them was his granddaughter, To-tu-ya, a girl of about twelve, who never forgot the captain of the white soldiers, a man she came to hate, whose yellow hair hung to his shoulders and whose shirts were bright red. Years later she was to speak of him contemptuously as "no good. . . . ketch-um young girl." He did "all the tricks with the women the very first time he was with Yosemite Indians," she explained through an interpreter.

Looking over the band, Savage asked Tenaya: "Where are the rest of your people?" This was all who were willing to go to the plains, the chief explained. "Many that have been with me are from other tribes. They have taken wives from my band; all have gone with their wives and children to the Tuolumnes and the Monos." Savage expressed doubt.

After detailing an escort to accompany Tenaya and his party to the camp and selecting one young Ahwahneeche as a guide, Savage and his company pressed on. "You will not find any people there," the chief called after him. The Indian trail they were following led to an eminence (Old Inspiration Point) from which there was a general view of the Yosemites' home valley.

Domes, peaks, spires, and cliffs were capped with fresh snow, their walls and slopes dappled with it, marking in strong relief the various sculptured forms. Some were veiled in wisps of cloud; others seemed to rise from a deep blue haze, giving the whole a drifting, unreal quality, like a vision, young Dr. Bunnell thought. Of the party he alone was moved, and admitted that tears filled his eyes. To get a still better view and to be by himself, he rode off the trail. He was so absorbed by what he saw he failed to notice his comrades riding on. Savage, who brought up the rear, roused him with a shout and the advice not to straggle or he might lose his hair: "I don't believe Tenaya that there're no Indians about." Bunnell hastily joined him. By the time they reached the valley floor, cooking fires were blazing and camp was set up in a broad meadow lightly covered with snow. Just across the river towered the giant cliff that would shortly be named El Capitan. The date, March 27, 1851, was a memorable one in the history of Yosemite, for, as Tenaya told them later, they were the first white men to enter the valley.

After supper they gathered in groups about the fire, lighted their pipes, sat or stretched out on their blankets, and joked and told stories. The doctor alone was silent. When after a time the talk among those who were near him turned to the day's events and they spoke of the valley, the men's obvious indifference to its rare beauty and their inability to feel its spell troubled him. To divert himself and them, he suggested they think up a name for it. A number of possibilities—foreign, biblical, and romantic—were offered. As none satisfied the majority in his group, he proposed they give it an Indian name rather "than to import a strange and inexpressive one." Why not call it Yosemite and so perpetuate the name of those Indians whose home this was: "It was . . . euphonious, and certainly *American*." He was interrupted by a shout: "Devil take the Indians and their names! Why should we honor these vagabond murderers?" "I agree," another spoke up loudly. "Damn the Indians and their names! . . . Let's call this Paradise Valley." The attention of the rest of the camp was caught. What was the shouting about, they wanted to know. One of Bunnell's companions stood up and addressed the whole company. He gave the doctor's reasons for wanting to call it Yosemite, and before the whole camp could plunge into argument, announced that a vote would be taken right then. The ayes were nearly unanimous in favor of Yosemite.

In giving the valley this name—a corruption of the Miwok *Yo-ham'-i-te*—they were actually honoring only one band of Ahwah-neeches, who lived in a large village on the south, or coyote, side of the Merced River. Among these villagers had been some noted hunters of grizzly bear, called *Oo-hoo'-ma-te*, or *O-ham'-i-te*, from which their name derived.

After an early breakfast next morning, Savage and his men forded the Merced, "a raging torrent," to the north side, which they found free of snow. Riding along a well-defined trail, they came on a cluster of recently abandoned bark lodges near the base of El Capitan, where four small villages stood. Seeing smoke rising in the distance, they hurried on in that direction. Scouting parties were detached along the way to explore side canyons and follow divergent trails. Bunnell wrote that during their ride they were "on every side astonished" by the size of the cliffs and the number and height of the waterfalls, "which constantly challenged our attention and admiration." He spoke for himself; his comrades, interested only in tracking Indians, were not impressed. As one of them remarked later, had he known the valley was to become so famous, he would have looked at it. The general opinion held that it was "a gloomy enough place."

While wandering among some large rocks fallen from that massive shaft to be known as Washington Column, the doctor was startled to see some living object in a talus cave. It proved to be an old woman—"over a hundred"—seated close to the remains of a fire. This then accounted for the spiral of smoke seen earlier. She seemed neither alarmed nor curious at his presence. He replenished her fire, and then, hailing a comrade, told him to summon the major and bring some food. When Savage questioned her about her people, she told him: "Hunt for them if you want to see them." And when asked why she had been left alone, she said, "I am too old to climb the rocks."

No other Indians were found, even by those parties who scoured the valley east to its head in Tenaya Canyon and followed the Merced River to its heights, thereby becoming the first white men to see Vernal and Nevada falls and enter the Little Yosemite, a valley very like the great Yosemite in form and sculpture, lying beyond the head of Nevada Fall. Even though Savage was certain that some of Tenaya's people were in hiding not far off, he was forced to abandon pursuit, since rations were running low and it had begun to snow again. If he could not bring these Indians in, he would starve them out. Orders were issued to start firing the food caches and houses. When Bunnell came on him that afternoon near Tenaya Creek, he was supervising the burning of some large acorn granaries. The doctor recalled talking with considerable enthusiasm about the splendid views to be had from there of certain domes and waterfalls. Savage replied brusquely that to him the best views of all were the billowing clouds of smoke choking the valley.

The next morning, at "early dawn," the company started back from their camp near the mouth of Indian Canyon, east of Yosemite Falls. As they rode through the lower end of the valley, Bunnell noted that the acorn caches were still smoldering but the bark huts had been reduced to heaps of ashes. The expedition had failed in its main objective. Only for the doctor was there a sense of accomplishment: "During these three days absence from headquarters, we had discovered, named, and partially explored, one of the most remarkable . . . geographical wonders of the world."

Upon reaching their headquarters on the South Fork Merced, the officer who had been left in charge announced that they were "about out of grub." Savage therefore ordered that camp be broken. With those Indians who had agreed to settle on the reservation—some three hundred and fifty, including Tenaya's band—a move was made toward the federal commissioners' encampment on Mariposa Creek. But progress was slow, for the Indians were on foot. Since they did not seem disposed to run off, it was considered safe to leave them with a single officer, Captain John Boling, and a guard of nine, while Savage and the others pushed ahead to get rations and stand ready, if necessary, to send back relief.

Boling was delayed beyond all reason. The relief party was dispatched, and when after still more time not even a messenger appeared, the worst was presumed and a large detachment ordered back. Not far from Savage's camp they met the relief party, the guard of nine, and the chagrined Boling with one Indian. "Where are the rest?" Savage demanded when he came up. Boling flushed. "They have all escaped to the mountains but the one I have with me." Having learned from some Yokuts runners met along the way that they would all be killed by the white men when they reached the plains, the Indians had slipped off during the night. A fruitless search for them had delayed Boling.

Again the federal commissioners sent out their emissaries, this time to find the fugitives, quiet their fears, and persuade them to treat. Within a few days the messengers returned with about one hundred Indians; most of the others followed shortly, but Tenaya and his people were not among them, for they had gone back to Yosemite.

The joy normally felt at a return to their home valley was shattered. Tenaya's granddaughter, Totuya, remembered that they had discarded their deerskin cloaks during flight; now it was snowing, and their snug cedar-bark lodges were in ashes. They were hungry, but their stores of acorns, roots, dried meat, fish, and fruit had also been burned by the white soldiers. By digging beneath the top layers of charred acorns, however, they were able to reclaim some that were only scorched. The little girl remembered how carefully they sifted the ashes in the hope of finding something to eat. Spring harvest of greens and bulbs was more than a month away; until then they would have to live on whatever game their hunters might bring in.

Early in May 1851 a second expedition, headed this time by John Boling (Savage had convinced the commissioners that he was indispensable to their treaty-making, and they would not let him go), was organized to try to take the Ahwahneeches by surprise. If the surprise failed, they were prepared to search the High Sierra for them. When the advance rode into Yosemite Valley they saw no spirals of smoke from cooking fires or flashes of human activity; heard no voices of children at play, no dogs barking. Dr. Bunnell noticed some newly erected bark huts near Bridalveil Fall, but they were unoccupied. On looking inside he saw several bushels of scorched acorns, packed in carrying baskets. Tenaya had evidently received warning of their coming, but only in time to get his people away.

Riding on, the doctor's attention was fixed on the waterfalls, the oak trees in new leaf, and the meadows turning green. Suddenly his eye caught sight of some "shadowy objects" flitting past rocks and trees, beyond El Capitan. Pulling up, he saw with his spyglass that they were Indians, five of them, scouts, he suspected, watching their movements. Intent on their capture, he and six companions swam their horses over the river and gave chase, but in the talus at the base of a rugged mountain mass with three peaks, one above the other, fronting on the valley, the scouts vanished. Later they were persuaded by the company's Indian interpreters to give themselves up. Three of them proved to be Tenaya's sons, a coincidence which suggested to Bunnell, who had a penchant for naming, to call those triple peaks the Three Brothers.

When asked through an interpreter where Tenaya was, one of the captive scouts pointed to North Dome. In the morning Boling sent two of the prisoners, Tenaya's son-in-law and a son, to bring in the chief before noon the following day. The others would be held hostage until the chief came in. Dr. Bunnell was instructed to act as escort to protect them from those detachments searching for Indians throughout the valley. As further protection for the doctor's charges, Boling kept the men in camp. To help pass time, some of them tried target-shooting with bows and arrows taken from the captives. But most of their shots went wild, some narrowly missing comrades. Then they asked one of the prisoners to demonstrate and were amazed at his accuracy and at the ease with which he flexed a bow many of them could scarcely bend. A more challenging target was then set up at longer range, and since retrieval of the arrows became more difficult, the bowman was allowed to help find them.

While hunting among the rocks for one arrow that had gone far beyond the target, the Indian made a sudden dash toward a steep and craggy ravine. The guard, having left his rifle in camp, shouted for help, and the sentry on duty fired at the running man, but missed. Striking a trail that was used by his people to go into and out of the High Sierra, he was soon lost from sight. This was the route by which Tenaya's granddaughter and her family had left the other morning. The troopers, who were now nearly as anxious as Bunnell to give place names, called the gorge Indian Canyon, although it was known to the Miwoks as Le-hamite, meaning "arrow-wood." The Indian scouts with the party, joining the ranks of the name givers, now called the pinnacle between Yosemite Falls and Indian Canyon *Ummo*, the lost arrow.

Boling ordered at once that the two remaining prisoners, Tenaya's sons, be tied back to back and picketed to an oak tree in the middle of camp. Impatiently he waited for noon. It came and passed, but Tenaya did not arrive. The Mission Indian Sandino and his scouts were then sent out to discover the cause of delay. When Sandino returned, he reported that he had seen and talked with the chief, but was unable to reach him, for he was on a high ledge, accessible only from above. Tenaya was determined not to go to the reservation and would make peace only if allowed to stay in his own territory. Neither he nor his people would come down into the valley while the white soldiers were there. Boling sent Sandino back with orders to find a way to reach Tenaya. Accompanying him was a small band of volunteers, who were to climb to the heights beyond Mirror Lake and cut off possible escape.

Later that morning, as Dr. Bunnell was returning to camp, he came upon the lifeless body of Tenaya's youngest son, "the warm blood still oozing from a wound in his back." How had this happened, he wanted to know. Questioning the guards closely, he learned that they had stood by and watched while the brothers untied their bonds and escaped. Then, without reporting to their officer, they had made it their responsibility to fire at the running men while they were still within rifle range. The second son had only been grazed by a bullet that singed his hair. Uninjured, he succeeded in gaining the safety of Indian Canyon. Totuya, the granddaughter, who could look down on the white men's camp from her place of hiding, heard the shots and saw the gun smoke. Her family then decided to press on to the valley's rim and move as rapidly as possible over the Sierra to the east side.

In the afternoon Tenaya was brought in—a captive. Just outside the camp he saw the body of his favorite son, the one who resembled him in appearance, lying where he had fallen. The chief stopped and observed him in silence, his lips quivering with suppressed emotion. After a few moments he raised his head and stared at Boling with "a glaring expression of deadly hate." Then, lowering his eyes, he searched the ground for the body of his other son. Boling "expressed his regret," explained the circumstances, and gave permission for the body to be removed. The next morning evidence was found that it had been taken up into Indian Canyon. For several days afterward Tenaya did not speak. Normally he would have been able to express his grief in a mourning ceremony.

Then one day he escaped, but was caught by the guard just as he was about to plunge into the Merced River and swim across. When brought before Boling, a turmoil of emotions—disappointment at having failed to get away, anguish over the murder of his son, hatred of the man he considered responsible, and uncertainty as to his own fate now—made him break his silence and drop his usual reserve. He "burst forth . . . in a style of language and delivery which took us all by surprise," Bunnell remembered. He noted that Tenaya made use of many Spanish words.

"Kill me, sir captain!" he said. "Yes, *kill me*, as you killed my son; as you would kill my people, if they should come to you! . . . Yes, sir American, you can tell your warriors to kill the old chief . . . you have killed the child of my heart, why not kill the father?—But wait a little; when I am dead I will call to my people . . . to avenge the death of their chief and his son.

"You may kill me . . . but I will follow in your footsteps; I will not leave my home, but be with the spirits among the rocks, the waterfalls, in the rivers and in the winds; wherever you go I will be with you. You will not see me, but you will feel the spirit of the old chief, and grow cold. . . . I am done." A spirit was thought to announce its presence by a chill wind.

Tenaya was not punished, although his guard was reinforced, for his cooperation and influence were needed to get his people to the reservation. It was the commissioners' duty to settle Indians on those lands, and Boling had orders to conciliate and avoid bloodshed whenever possible.

6

TENAYA'S STORY

*I*T WAS A STORMY MAY. Deep snows kept Boling's scouts from penetrating the high country in search of Tenaya's people. Then the command's rations ran short, for they had overstayed their time, and the pack train had to be sent out to the settlements. While awaiting its return, Dr. Bunnell spent most of his time exploring the valley and learning from Tenaya the Indian names for the natural features and their meanings, which he carefully recorded. He was anxious to attach what he considered appropriate names before some of those chosen by his comrades—such as the Devil's Nightcap or the Giant's Pillar—became fixed. He sometimes kept the original name, but where that was difficult to pronounce or remember, he substituted an English or Spanish one conveying a close meaning. Others were the result of his own impressions. A few—Half Dome, Clouds Rest, Royal Arches—were given by battalion members, "but most were selected by myself, and adopted by our command."

Since that waterfall opposite their encampment was the highest and most prominent in the valley, and was known to the Indians as *Cho'-lock*, "The Fall," he thought it proper to call it Yosemite. For what is now known as Bridalveil Fall, he kept the original word *Po-ho'-no*, onomatopoeic for a puff or blast of wind. After sundown there is always a downward rush of chilled air from the gorge above, which billows the falls and agitates the trees and shrubs around its base. The gigantic cliff El Capitan was known to the Ahwahneeches as *To-to'-kon oolah*, derived from *To-to'-kon*, Sandhill Crane, a chief of the First People. Bunnell, failing to understand completely, interpreted it as Rock Chief. Not liking the English form, he substituted the Spanish El Capitán. The first great fall of the Merced River, nearest Yosemite Valley, he called Vernal because everything about it suggested spring—the "sun shining through the spray as in an April shower"—and the lushness of green growth—moss, grass, leafy trees and shrubs. The upper fall of the Merced, which reminded him of a "vast avalanche of snow," he called Nevada.

When he first told Tenaya that the valley had been named Yosemite, he said it already had a name. It was called Ahwahne. When the doctor asked him what that meant, the chief first indicated width and depth with his hands, then picked some grass and held it up. Bunnell interpreted this pantomime to mean "deep, grassy valley." Actually, Tenaya was trying to describe a large, wide-open mouth (*awo*). The grass was meant to make his meaning clear: a mouth ready to eat. Those who lived in the valley were called Ahwahneeches, and long ago had been numerous, the doctor understood the interpreter to say, but a sickness had killed many of them. If correct, this would have been some disease contracted around 1780 through contact with lowland or coastal Indians who, having no resistance to white men's diseases, caught them all. The survivors in Ahwahne fled and went to live with other tribes.

Bunnell gathered that Tenaya's family crossed the Sierra and joined the Eastern Monos, a Shoshonean people from the Great Basin, living in an arid, open valley along the eastern base of the range. His father, a chief or headman, took a Mono wife, and Tenaya grew up among her people. But existence in the desert was harsh, and of monotonous simplicity. Among the Ahwahneeches there were memories and traditions of a better life in that beautiful valley, well-watered and rich in game and plant food, across the mountains, and they talked about those other days.

When Tenaya was a young man, by then hereditary chief, he and a party of his people visited their ancestral home, the doctor was told. All vestiges of the plague were gone. The air was sweet, the meadows green, the streams and waterfalls full and rushing. There were many fish in the river and deer in the glades; and stands of pine and oak trees for nuts and acorns. An old shaman, a friend of Tenaya's father, was said to have urged the son to leave the Monos and reestablish his people here. With a following of around two hundred, Tenaya returned to settle in Yosemite Valley, perhaps about 1821. Shortly before his death, the old shaman stressed the importance of guarding against invaders, especially the "horsemen of the lowlands"—the Spaniards—for if any should come in, his people would be captured, his tribe scattered and destroyed. This was why, the chief explained to Bunnell, he wanted to drive out the seekers of gold who pushed up the river ever deeper into the mountains and threatened his stronghold. He would make peace, but only if the Ahwahneeches were left undisturbed in their mountain homeland, where they were content to stay.

Upon the supply train's return the doctor joined a party that set out on foot for the Yosemite highlands, to look for the Ahwahneeches. With them was Tenaya. Beyond Mirror Lake they followed an Indian path to the rim. Soon after gaining the summit, their Indian scout discovered a fresh trail leading to the heights, a trail that was obvious to no one else. He pointed out to the incredulous Boling occasional fragments of rock and bits of lichen that had been broken off by Tenaya's scouts. By keeping to the bare ridges they had avoided leaving tracks in the snow or soft ground, but it was impossible not to disturb something. From these signs he judged their camps were not far off, probably at the head of *Py-we'-ack*, lake of shining rocks. But if the Ahwahneeches were not there, it would mean they had crossed the mountains.

That afternoon as they were climbing a ridge they noticed their Indian scout waiting for them near the top. When they reached his side, he pointed out some wisps of smoke rising from the foot of a granite dome at Pyweack's head. Looking through the spyglass, the doctor discerned a cluster of bark huts. Since they appeared to be no more than half a mile away, the captain immediately began outlining his plans for a surprise capture. But he suddenly stopped short when he saw a group of his scouts pursuing a lone Indian who was racing toward the little settlement. Hoping to cut him off before he could give the alarm, Boling ordered his party to double-quick and charge. "Each man . . . stripped to his drawers . . . ran at full speed at least four miles," the captain reported, over and through snow that was ten feet deep in places.

When Totuya, the granddaughter, was an old lady, she was asked what she remembered about the capture of her people at that highland lake. "Oh, lots of red," she replied. The sight of all those men in bright red flannels floundering through the snow was never forgotten.

The Ahwahneeches were in no position to resist, for they were close to starvation. In their flight from the valley they had taken almost nothing with them, expecting to make a rapid crossing of the Sierra. But storm after storm had piled the snow ever deeper, burying the trails and passes. Now they were without hope. "Where can we go that you will not follow?" their spokesman asked, voicing a whole people's despair. "Where can we make our homes that you will not find us?"

After a hasty predawn breakfast, the company assembled for the return to Yosemite Valley, with their captives. After a march of perhaps half a mile they came to a rise, and Bunnell turned to look back at that beautiful, deep-blue lake where the Ahwah-neeches, now dwindled to thirty-five, had made their final stand. He suggested to Boling that they name the lake Tenaya. Boling had no objections, but when Tenaya was told, he pointed to the glacier-polished granite walls beside the lake and said to the doc-tor, as he had said so many times before, "It already has a name. We call it Py-we'-ack."

The party returned to the valley without incident, went into camp near El Capitan, and started the next day for the reservation on the Fresno River. Chief Tenaya was marched from his home-land at pistol point, a sight his granddaughter would never forget.

With the delivery of these people to the Indian agent, the Mariposa Indian War was considered ended and the battalion was soon disbanded. But for the Ahwahneeches, troubles were not over.

As Tenaya had foreseen, there were disagreements with those other tribes gathered on the reservation, who had been traditional enemies. The humid summer heat of the San Joaquin Valley proved unbearable for these mountain dwellers. Government ra-tions were not to their liking, and as soon as acorns ripened they made their customary soup, mush, and bread.

In gathering acorns some of the Ahwahneeches wandered farther and farther from the reservation, and once well out of sight,
slipped off and went back to Yosemite. Tenaya was worried about
his son, the one the trooper had killed, for there had been no
mourning ceremony.

"I am thinking of my child," he said, "about going back to him,
to see him and take care of him." He told this to his own people,
and to the white men in charge.

Tenaya and his family were finally permitted to return home,
and the chief held a "cry" for his son. Soon the rest of his band
quietly left the reservation, and no effort was ever made to bring
them back.

Little further thought was given to the Ahwahneeches or to
Yosemite Valley until the following May (1852) when a party of
eight prospectors made their way to it from Coarse Gold Gulch,
some thirty miles to the south. While the prospectors were encamped on a flat above the valley, a small party of Indians paid
them a visit. They were friendly, but made it clear that the white
men were trespassing on their territory. Most of the miners
thought it foolhardy to go on, but three of their number, Sherburn,
Tudor, and Rose, finally convinced them that their fears were
groundless.

After picketing their horses and setting up camp in a clearing
west of Bridalveil Fall the next day, five of the men started up the
valley on foot—one to chop firewood, a couple to hunt, and the
others to pan the Merced River for gold.

The circumstances, and whether all five white men were involved, will never be known; but an Indian boy was murdered not
long after the miners left their camp. The three who had stayed in
camp heard frantic shouts and rapid gunfire, and shortly one of
their companions, wounded in the neck and arm by arrows, came
running in, followed by another, who was unhurt. Sherburn, Rose,
and Tudor had been killed, they said—Tudor by his own axe. Now
the Indians were after them.

Snatching up their rifles, a sack holding a few pounds of flour,
and a tin cup, the five men fled with the others toward the trail by
which they had come in, "the savages in hot pursuit." Very soon,
however, they found escape cut off in front. Apparently surrounded—the valley seemed alive with Indians, "on rocks, behind
trees . . . shrieking their war whoops"—the miners headed for a

steep bluff and began scrambling up its face, all the while dodging rocks tumbled on them from above. They succeeded in reaching a high, recessed ledge, where they found protection from falling boulders, although "arrows whistled among us thick and fast." They managed to keep the Indians at bay with rifle fire until after dusk. Then, under cover of darkness, they crept to the valley's rim, found their old trail, and made their way back to Coarse Gold Gulch.

News of the killings—no mention was ever made of the Indian child's death, which had provoked them—aroused the southern mining camps, and a report was sent on to Fort Miller, a nearby federal army post. Soon a detachment under the command of Lieutenant Tredwell Moore was dispatched on a punitive expedition to Yosemite. Entering the valley by night, Moore surprised and captured a party of five Ahwahneeche men who were just escaping, for Tenaya had received advance warning of the soldiers' coming and had already gone into hiding with most of his people.

In the morning the bodies of Tudor and Sherburn were buried on the edge of a meadow near Bridalveil Fall; Rose's body was nowhere to be found. On examination of the prisoners, it was discovered that each was wearing some article of white men's clothing (a common practice), which was immediately presumed to have belonged to the three dead miners. With this as circumstantial evidence (and the only evidence), the Indians were formally accused of the murders, and according to the record did not deny the charge. If they spoke of retaliation for the little boy's murder, it was not written down, for they were quoted only as saying that the white men had been killed because they had no right to be there without the Ahwahneeches' permission.

Through his interpreter Moore explained to the Indians that they had sold their homeland to the Great Father, that it belonged to white men now, and that they had no right there, for they had signed a treaty and agreed to live on the reservation. The Ahwahneeches replied that Tenaya had never signed a treaty or agreed to the sale of his home; if it had been sold by others, it was without his knowledge or consent, and he had never received pay for it. Therefore it still belonged to his people.

What these Indians said was applicable not only to Tenaya but even to those tribes whose chiefs had signed, for the treaties were still unratified. A few weeks later, on June 5, 1852, the United States Senate rejected all nineteen of those treaties and filed them in the secret archives, where they lay forgotten for nearly half a century, a situation that allowed white men to settle and farm choice reservation lands, dispossessing the Indian and stripping him of even his birthright.

Moore, satisfied that he had captured the murderers, summarily sentenced them to be shot. From his covert, an Ahwahneeche scout witnessed the execution, then hastened to report to his chief. Tenaya, knowing that five Indian lives would never be considered sufficient payment for two white lives (for Rose, the supposed third victim, had meanwhile come in unharmed to Coarse Gold Gulch), started out at once with his people to cross the Sierra east.

As Tenaya had foreseen, Moore was determined to kill them all and scoured the valley before striking into the high country. In the vicinity of the talus caves at the foot of Washington Column, used for centuries as hiding places from enemies (their name, *Lah-koo'-hah*, means "come out") and as temporary winter shelters, he discovered a group of Ahwahneeches just making their escape. Giving chase, he captured several, whom he hanged from the oak trees fronting the talus. The rest fled into the first of these rock chambers, rolled a boulder in place to block the entrance, then climbed to the highlands by way of a "tunnel." Once safely on the rim, they rolled down rocks on those soldiers who tried to follow.

At Tenaya Lake, Moore picked up the Indians' trail. But spring had come early that year, and they had all been able to get through the passes and away before the troops could overtake them. Seeking refuge with kin among the Eastern Monos, the Ahwahneeches were welcomed and assigned a certain territory for themselves. There they supposedly stayed until the summer or fall of 1853; then, feeling it safe to return, they reestablished themselves in Yosemite Valley, setting up their bark lodges at the extreme east end, in a spot well screened by large boulders.

Late that same fall, the Eastern Monos made a successful raid on several southern California ranches and drove off a large band of horses. When this news reached the Ahwahneeches, they thought about getting horses, too, but dared not risk being trailed by white men and driven from Yosemite again. But some of their rash young men, without Tenaya's knowledge, went over the mountains, stole horses from the Monos, and brought them home by way of a little-known pass at the head of the San Joaquin River. Either their trail was discovered or the Monos had their suspicions, for they dispatched a war party that entered Yosemite Valley secretly by way of Tenaya Canyon and surprised the Ahwahneeches in the midst of a horseflesh feast. During the ensuing skirmish, Tenaya's skull was crushed by a large rock hurled at him. "As he fell, other stones were cast upon him by the attacking party . . . until he was literally stoned to death." Only eight young men succeeded in escaping. Those old people who survived were left behind, but the children and young women were taken prisoner and marched back over the Sierra.

This is the accepted version of Chief Tenaya's death, which has been repeated for a century. But Totuya, who was there and whose memory was keen, has said that the Ahwahneeches did not return to Yosemite Valley to live before her grandfather's death, and that he was killed among the Monos. There was a feast, she remembered, held by the Monos, and her people were invited. Afterward there were gambling games, and during the intense excitement that accompanied "hand," a quarrel broke out. In the fight that developed, Tenaya and five of his tribesmen were stoned to death. A number of Monos were also killed.

A Yosemite Indian who was present afterward cremated the bodies of the Ahwahneeches. Then he carried their ashes over the mountains to Hite's Cove on the South Fork Merced. There a two-week-long mourning ceremony was held for Tenaya, the last chief of the Ahwahneeches.

7

GRIZZLY ADAMS

*A*FTER THE RETURN of Lieutenant Moore's punitive expedition, a year passed before any white men dared go into Yosemite Valley. Then three miners, having heard Dr. Bunnell's glowing descriptions of it, ventured there out of curiosity. They brought back accounts of towering waterfalls and cliffs, and some good samples of gold-bearing quartz found along the Merced River, which induced five more prospectors to risk the trip. Although neither party saw any Indians or any signs of their habitation, they were unwilling to try mining either along the approach or within the lonely valley, where every thicket or boulder might be an ambush.

The next year, 1854, the only white men known to have entered Yosemite were James Capen Adams and a companion named Solon. Adams, a hunter and wild-animal trainer, was wintering alone in a little valley on a northern branch of the Merced River; his friend was from the gold-mining town of Sonora. Spring had come to the mountains, bringing with it those animals that had spent the winter in the foothills, when Solon stopped by Adams' cabin and asked him to go for a month's hunt in Yosemite. After getting pack mules at Howard's Ranch near the gold camp, Hornitos, and a stock of provisions in town, they started over the mountains with a Yokuts youth called Tuolumne, who had been one of Adams' two Indian hunting companions for several seasons. The other Indian, Stanislaus, was staying at the cabin to guard it during their absence. Also going with the party was Adams' tamed grizzly bear, Lady Washington, whom he had taught to carry loads, and a greyhound he had recently bought from Howard.

Three days' travel over country that Adams remembered as "rough and difficult" brought them to a clearing from which they could see into Yosemite Valley, a view "so impressive that we delayed a long time, as if spellbound. . . . But however grand the valley looked from above, it was not until the next day, when we descended into it and looked upward, that we obtained the grandest views." What Adams saw in every direction produced "impressions upon my mind that are ineffaceable." Who could ever forget the stupendous cliffs and waterfalls, the groves of tapering pines, the winding river, the green meadows bright with flowers? "We spent the entire day visiting the interesting points, and searching out the varied beauties of this inexhaustible valley."

The following morning they took an Indian trail to the high country above Vernal and Nevada falls where, in the Little Yosemite, they pitched camp in a grassy glen and hunted with success for several days, killing a number of deer and bear and drying the meat. At this camp the greyhound gave birth to a litter; one of the pups, which Adams named Rambler, became another of his noted animal companions. Moving on next to what he calls the "head waters of the Merced River," he discovered in a ravine whose slopes were densely covered with manzanita, chinquapin, and huckleberry oak, a huge heap of fresh earth, which he immediately recognized as the sign of a grizzly bear den. "No sooner had my eyes fallen upon it, than I forgot all other hunting; I thought and dreamed of nothing else but how to take it." He hoped there would be cubs he could capture and train. But he intended to be ready for whatever might be there, and spent his time in camp cleaning his rifle and pistol, sharpening his knives, and preparing muzzles and stout cords. Then one morning, packing provisions and blankets on his mule, he started off alone for the little canyon. Upon reaching it late in the afternoon, he climbed a tree to survey the entire ravine and to select the best spot from which to watch the den's mouth. He chose a well-concealed hiding place about a hundred yards from the burrow's entrance. Then going back to his mule, he built a small fire to protect her from night predators, and leaving her alone, took his blankets and walked back to his post. "It was an uncomfortable vigil; the ground was so steep that there was no level place to lie down, and the night was very cold." Several times during its course he thought he heard cubs whining.

At dawn he discharged his rifle, to put in a fresh charge, but mainly in the hope that it might provoke some action. As the echoes died away he became aware of a muffled snarling underground, which as it grew louder became a distinct growl. He took the precaution of climbing a tree, but the bear did not appear. In a few minutes all was quiet again, and he slipped back down. Around noon he returned to his mule, moved her to a new pasture, then took his first meal in many hours—dried deer meat "washed down" with spring water. Feeling much refreshed, he resumed his watch, sitting on the slope with his rifle ready for action. The afternoon passed slowly with no sign of bears, or any sounds other than the drone of insects and an occasional bird twittering in the thickets. Growing drowsy, Adams took a much-needed nap. At dusk he once more tended his mule, "but before dark I was at my post . . . , and there I remained, shivering, till morning."

At daybreak there were loud scuffing noises in the den, and Adams prepared for the grizzly's appearance; but again to his disappointment nothing happened. Soon growing impatient, he discharged his rifle again, and this time the bear came roaring to the den's opening, put her head out, looked around, but seeing no dangers, drew back. Adams heard distinctly the yelping of cubs. Certain then of their presence, he made plans for a direct attack. His present position being too distant, he moved to a point across the ravine some forty yards above the den. To reach it he had to make his way stealthily through the shrubbery, forced in many places to cut his way through, careful always not to attract the bear's attention by any unusual noise.

On the morning of the third day he was ready to rouse the grizzly: "There was some danger in this, for my plan would probably attract her directly to me . . . and give no time to draw an aim. Before putting my plan into execution . . . I stuck my cap full of green twigs, and stationed myself in such a manner in the bushes that it would take a nice eye to discern my form, even though looking directly towards me." Then, "cocking and drawing my rifle, I gave one of those terrific yells with which I had so often started the grizzly to his feet. It echoed like the roar of a lion up the cañon." A moment later "there was a booming in the den like the puffing and snorting of an engine in a tunnel, and the enraged animal rushed out, growling and snuffing." She rose on her hind feet—a monster in size, with "limbs of terrible strength." Looking all around but seeing nothing to attack, she soon sat on her haunches, her back toward Adams.

"During these few minutes I stood as motionless as a statue, hardly breathing, waiting and watching for an opportunity to fire. . . . As I watched, I saw her turn her head toward the den; . . . fearing she would retire, I gave a low sharp whistle, which brought her to her feet again . . . her breast fronting . . . me." Taking aim, he fired; the bear staggered and fell backward. Dropping his rifle, he drew his pistol, and taking his knife in the other hand, ran through the chaparral toward her. When he was within thirty feet, she rose and sprang at him, but had not the strength to push on through the undergrowth. Emptying all six chambers of his Colt, he felled her for the final time.

His next concern was the cubs. Approaching the entrance, he knelt and peered in, but all was dark and silent. He wondered what dangers lay within the den, if any. The presence of another adult grizzly crossed his mind, but that would be counter to all his experience. Still, he carefully reloaded his rifle and pistol. Then he took from his pocket a small torch of pine splinters, lighted it, and leaving his rifle at the mouth of the den, dropped to his knees and crawled in. The entrance tunnel, about three feet high and four wide, extended into the hillside nearly horizontally, and almost without a turn for six feet. There it opened into a chamber of some eight feet in diameter and five feet in height. The entire floor was carpeted with leaves and grass. At first it seemed to be empty, and Adams felt "grievously disappointed"; but then he heard a stirring in the dry carpet, and bending down with his torch, discovered two beautiful young cubs. Making certain there were no more, for he had sometimes found litters of three, he tucked the little bears into the bosom of his buckskin shirt and made his way out. Delighted with his prizes, he fairly "danced" his way down the slope and over to the grassy spot where he had left his mule.

Riding back to the dead grizzly, he cut off all the best portions of meat and packed them back to camp. There, taking the cubs from his shirt, Adams chose one for himself, naming it Ben Franklin, and gave the other to Solon, who called his General Jackson.

Ben Franklin was destined to become, in Adams' words, "the flower of his race, my firmest friend, the boon companion of my after-years." He was also his most famous trained grizzly. The problem of what to feed the cubs now arose, until Adams suddenly thought of giving them to the greyhound to suckle. At first she snapped and bit at them; within a few days she was tolerating their presence, and after a week or more, was licking and nuzzling them. To keep their long claws from scratching her, he and Solon made them little buckskin mittens. The milk proved nourishing, and they grew rapidly.

"Our success in hunting exceeded our expectations"; and Solon was able to make several trips out of Yosemite to the nearest mines, taking with him the horse and mules packed with fresh and dried meat that the miners bought readily, paying high prices. During these absences, Adams and Tuolumne would take Lady Washington on their hunts, in place of the pack animals. "I had made a kind of saddle of green hide, resembling a Mexican *aparejo*," Adams said, "and with this we could pack upon her loads of two hundred pounds' weight, which she would cheerfully carry." After one hunt she brought back to camp a large bighorn ram which Adams had taken among Yosemite high peaks, as well as a good-sized mule deer. At the month's end, the hunters returned to Adams' cabin with bales of dried meat and hides, and boxes and baskets of live animals—the two grizzly cubs, two wolf pups, and two fawns. Lady Washington carried a cage containing five mountain-lion kittens, whose mewing made her so nervous that Adams had at times to walk beside her until they quieted.

James Capen Adams was a shoemaker by trade, but a hunter and wild-animal trainer by choice. A Massachusetts man, he was born in the little town of Medway in 1807, and at an early age was apprenticed to his craft. But, being of "a roving and adventurous disposition, I no sooner attained my majority than I threw aside the pegging awl, and hired myself to a company of showmen as a collector of wild beasts"—panthers, wolves, and wildcats—which he captured in the woods of Maine, New Hampshire, and Vermont. Since he had a way with animals, his employers set him to "reclaim" one of their exhibits, a Bengal tiger that had grown unmanageable. "Not doubting my ability, I entered his cage a number of times." On the last visit the animal attacked, threw Adams to the floor, and "buried his teeth and claws in my flesh."

Adams was carried from the cage unconscious, and for many weeks his recovery was in doubt. When he was finally able to get about again, it was obvious to him that he could no longer tramp the wilds, and he returned regretfully to shoemaking.

During the next fifteen years he married, had a daughter, regained his health, and managed to save some eight thousand dollars. In the expectation of doubling or even trebling that amount, he invested in a cargo of boots and shoes which he shipped to the frontier town of St. Louis. But there a fire destroyed the entire stock. "In one short night I found myself a ruined man." That was 1849, the year of the great gold rush to California. In the hope of recouping his losses, he left his family and joined an overland party going by way of Mexico. After his arrival in California that fall, he tried mining, trading, stock-raising, and farming. "Sometimes I was rich, at other times poor. At one time, in 1850 . . . I possessed thousands of dollars' worth of cattle, most of which were stolen from me in a single night. . . . In the space of three years, I failed three times. . . . In the fall of 1852, disgusted with the world and dissatisfied with myself, I abandoned all my schemes for wealth . . . and took the road towards the wildest and most unfrequented parts of the Sierra Nevada, resolved to make the wilderness my home, and wild beasts my companions."

From the wreck of his fortunes he managed to salvage an old wagon and a pair of oxen; one Kentucky rifle, one Tennessee rifle, a Colt revolver, and several bowie knives; an axe, a saw, and a few other tools; some clothing and several blankets. He found the place he was looking for in that little valley not far from Yosemite. He made friends with the nearby Miwoks, who helped him build a conical bark hut like their own and showed him how best to dry the wild grasses to winter-feed his oxen, and which seeds to pound into flour. The Miwoks also taught him how to tan and sew deerskins so that he could make himself buckskin hunting shirts and trousers fringed at the edges and along the outer seams, and a deerskin cap lined with rabbit fur and decorated with a pendant foxtail; and how to fashion moccasins.

Just before the heavy snows came, his Miwok neighbors left for the foothills, and the little mountain valley was deserted. "Yet, strange to say, those months were among the happiest of my life." When his stock of food ran out, he made flour from grass seeds and discovered that roasted acorns made a good substitute for coffee. He had on hand an ample supply of dried deer meat which he varied by a little winter hunting. This solitary existence so appealed to him that he spent three successive winters there, and once expressed the wish that he could live out his life in that sequestered valley north of "Yo-Semite."

The following spring (1853), a brother who had preceded him to the gold fields, had found rich diggings, and was then ready to return East heard about James' misfortunes and traced him to his Sierra retreat. Before that, they had been lost to one another in California. Now William wanted James to join him, but he refused to go back to his family as poor as when he had left. William then made another proposal: he would advance the money for James to collect wild animals native to the West and ship them to menageries in the East and elsewhere, which he, William, would contract to supply. It was an irresistible offer. The brothers drew up an agreement, and William left for home. James packed his belongings, hitched up his wagon, and headed for Howard's Ranch, where he exchanged his oxen for mules and packsaddles and laid in a stock of ammunition and other necessities. At the ranch he met a young Texan, William Sykesey, who had some knowledge of Washington Territory, owned a good rifle, was a fair marksman, and being part Indian was skilled in woodcraft. Adams suggested that they make an expedition to the Northwest together.

From Howard's they moved on to Strawberry Ranch on the Tuolumne River, where Adams met and hired two Indian youths who spoke English and knew how to handle a rifle. The elder of the two Adams called Tuolumne for the name of his tribe (Yokuts), and the other, Stanislaus, doubtless for the area from which he came. This was the beginning of a close association that was to last through all the years of Adams' stay in the western wilderness.

That summer, somewhere in eastern Washington (or perhaps Montana, for Adams tells of hunting buffalo), he captured the yearling grizzly he named Lady Washington. Before the party started west again in the fall, he was able to lead her with a lariat, had taught her to carry small loads, and had taken her with a chain leash on a hunting trip, during which she helped him subdue a wild grizzly.

Adams described the caravan that made its way that autumn toward Portland, Oregon, where the live animals were to be sent off by ship. In the lead were five horses packed with buffalo robes; then four horses carrying bearskins; next, four more with bales of deer and antelope hides. Following was one horse laden with fox and other small pelts; seven horses with dried meat for the use of the captive animals aboard ship; one horse with boxes containing live bear cubs; two with cages of wolf pups; a mule with young foxes and fishers in baskets; another mule laden with tools, blankets, and camp equipment. "But the most remarkable portion of the train consisted of the animals we drove along in a small herd: these were six bears"—one of them Lady Washington—"four wolves, four deer, four antelopes, two elks," and an Indian dog, the gift of a chief.

Adams returned to find his Miwok hut in shambles, the work of passing hunters and miners who had removed most of the foundation poles and bark for firewood. With the help of Tuolumne and Stanislaus he built a substantial cabin and stable and put up several stacks of dry grass for feed. The two Indians then went to their own people for the winter, and Adams was alone except for his horse, the Indian dog, and Lady Washington, who was "the constant companion of all my little excursions. She accompanied me to the scenes of my labors, stayed by me while I worked, and followed me when I hunted. The kind and gentle disposition she had begun to exhibit in Washington Territory, improved with time and care."

It was in the coming spring of 1854 that Adams, Tuolumne, and his friend Solon made their extended hunt in Yosemite, and the hound pup Rambler and grizzly cub Ben Franklin were added to Adams' personal collection. Soon after the return from Yosemite he set off for the Rocky Mountains to hunt and live-trap. Stanislaus and Tuolumne were of the party, as were the Lady, Ben, Rambler, the Indian dog, and the greyhound. Being too young to travel afoot, Ben and Rambler rode in the wagon. From that expedition Adams came back with another large collection for the showmen and an addition to his own bear family: a grizzly cub he was to call Funny Joe, who came to stand "next in my esteem to Ben Franklin and Lady Washington."

Since grizzly bears were one of the most popular exhibits and brought the highest prices, that fall, with the help of his two Indian friends, Adams built three bear traps in the Yosemite region and concentrated on the capture of bear to keep pace with the demand. One afternoon while exploring a brushy glen in search of bear signs, he came on the largest paw prints he had yet seen, and determined at once to capture that bear "at all hazards." Before dawn the next day he was back, looking for the trails the animal frequented and for the best place to locate a trap. After lying concealed for half an hour, Adams saw the grizzly advancing, his head raised as he sniffed the air suspiciously. "I had never seen so large a bear before; he looked like a moving mountain, and my heart fluttered for fear of being discovered; but he passed on up the ravine, and disappeared in the chaparral." Sure that this was his regular territory, Adams returned to the cabin. Within a week he and the two Indians had cut and hauled logs and finished the largest, strongest trap they had yet built. Then they baited it with deer meat and waited for results; several weeks passed and they saw nothing more of the bear. They began to fear that he had left the area, for it was then mid-November, the first snows had come, and game was moving out of the mountains. But one morning on examining the trap, they found that he not only had been there but had gone inside; for some reason the door had failed to lower. After adjusting the trigger with the "greatest nicety," Adams decided to spend the next nights within hearing distance of the trap. He and Tuolumne pitched a small tent a short way down the ravine.

Two nights passed uneventfully; but in the middle of the third one they were suddenly awakened by "a terrific roaring. It was the awfullest roaring and echoing in the mountains I ever heard, with the single exception of an appalling thunderstorm in the Humboldt Mountains . . . the summer before. I jumped up at once and ran out to listen. It could be nothing else but the bear in my trap. The night was cold, with a light snow on the ground, but I called Tuolumne, and we at once lighted our torches." As they neared the trap Adams could see that the bear was "taking chips out of the white-pine logs faster than I could have done it with an axe." When the grizzly saw them, he made a "tremendous lunge," and for a moment Adams thought he would burst out. They immediately built a blazing fire and by its light proceeded to strengthen the trap with additional logs.

For over a week Adams watched the trap night and day, making his bed close by to accustom the animal to his presence and smell, snatching what sleep he could between the fits of "unearthly bellowing" and attacks on the log bars with teeth and nails. To divert him from tearing the trap to shreds, they threw in firebrands and whacked him with a rod. By the eighth or ninth day Samson, as Adams named him, seemed less savage, but it was not until spring that Adams felt it safe to shift him to a cage. Meanwhile the season advanced to mid-winter, and since game was growing scarce, Adams moved all his stock and wild animals except Samson (he hired four woodcutters in the area to feed him) to a camp on the Merced River below Yosemite. There he took still more live bears to sell.

In mid-April he rode to Sonora and bought a cage large and strong enough to contain Samson. Then he engaged a teamster with a wagon and yoke of oxen to haul it to the mountains. It took a number of days to get the grizzly from the trap into the cage, for he refused to stir. In the end they had to loop a logging chain around his neck, pass it through the front bars of the cage, and hitch it to the oxen. Then while the oxen pulled, Adams prodded Samson from behind: "So he advanced, inch by inch until he got to the doors leading from one to the other, when he suddenly bounded into the cage, and commenced tearing around, as if he were going to demolish it." But Adams was not concerned, for the door had been locked and the cage was of iron. Samson was left at Howard's Ranch that season while Adams, the Lady, Rambler, and Ben hunted mountain lions and grizzlies in Corral Hollow, near Livermore Pass in the Coast Range.

Once during the summer he made the long trip back to his Sierra cabin, "that favorite old spot." Thinking that it might be some time before he got there again, for he was considering exhibiting his menagerie, he revisited all his best-liked haunts. One day as he, Ben, and Rambler were following a trail through a thicket Adams heard the snap of a twig to one side, and turning his head, saw a huge grizzly, with three young cubs, ready to attack. With one forepaw she knocked his rifle aside, and with the other gave him a blow that laid open his scalp and pitched him face forward on the ground. Holding him down, she began tearing at his buckskin shirt, biting through to his flesh. Able to spit out the command "St'boy!" to Rambler and Ben, who were a few paces behind, these two rushed forward, Rambler sinking his teeth in her thigh and Ben grabbing at her throat. Her attention diverted, Adams was able to seize his rifle, jump aside, and climb the nearest tree. By this time the grizzly was "chewing and tearing [Ben's] head and neck fearfully." Adams then let out his noted "bear screech," and the old bear stood erect. Wiping the blood from his eyes, he took careful aim and shot her through the heart. She fell backward to the ground "like a log of wood." Ben, freed, went bounding off for camp, "yelling at every leap." Adams, seeing that the grizzly showed signs of revival, slipped down from his perch and finished her with his bowie knife.

On his return to camp he found Ben lying in the shade licking his bleeding sides. "The poor fellow had certainly saved my life, and I felt so grateful that I at once took him into the cabin and dressed his wounds before I dressed my own." Later he was to admit that this had been one of the narrowest escapes of his life, and whenever he told the story of that near fatal combat, he would point out the scars on Ben's neck and head, where he had been chewed and slashed by the old grizzly's teeth and claws.

As to Adams' own injuries, the most serious was the head wound. Putting the peeled scalp in place and trimming its ragged edges, he applied an herbal poultice that he renewed every few days. He was confined to his cabin a number of weeks on its account, and when the wound did heal, "it left a depression about the size of a silver dollar near the top of his forehead, which looked as if the skull underneath had been removed," a friend noted.

After he and Ben were able to travel, they went back to Corral Hollow for more hunting and trapping. As winter approached Adams planned to spend the season in his Sierra retreat, but he was delayed and diverted, and since it was then so late, decided to show his menagerie instead—first at San Jose, then at Santa Clara and Santa Cruz. Encouraged by the public's response, he enlarged his collection, taking some of the animals in his favorite Yosemite region. By September of 1856 he had opened what he called The Mountaineer Museum, in a large though dingy basement at 142 Clay Street in San Francisco. On the door was a placard announcing that the proprietor had just returned from the mountains with "THE LARGEST COLLECTION OF WILD ANIMALS ever exhibited on the Pacific Coast." Among them were "SAMSON, the largest Grizzly Bear ever caught, weighing over 1,500 pounds; LADY WASHINGTON (with her cub), weighing 1,000 pounds"; and "BENJAMIN FRANKLIN, King of the Forest."

A young newspaper reporter, Theodore Hittell, spotted the sign

soon after it was posted, and going down the stairs, "found a remarkable spectacle." In the middle of the room, chained to the
floor, were the Lady and Ben, "pacing restlessly in circles some ten
feet in diameter . . . and occasionally rearing up, rattling their
irons, and reversing their direction. Not far off on one side, likewise fastened . . . were seven other bears, several of them young
grizzlies, three or four black bears, and one cinnamon." Near the
front was an open stall in which were two large elk. Further back
was a row of cages containing wildcats and mountain lions; hawks,
vultures, and eagles. At the very back in a large iron cage was
Samson: "From his look and actions, as well as the care taken to
rail him off from spectators, it was evident he was not to be approached too closely." In the midst of this collection stood Adams,
dressed in fringed buckskins, moccasins, and a deerskin cap. "He
was a man a little over medium size, muscular and wiry, with
sharp features and penetrating eyes. He was apparently about fifty
years of age; but his hair was very gray and his beard very white."

Of the animals, the Lady and Ben were Hittell's favorites:
"Adams seemed to have perfect control over them. He placed his
hands upon their jaws and even in their mouths, to show their
teeth. He made them rear on their hind legs and walk erect, growl
when he ordered them to talk, and perform various tricks. He put
them to boxing and wrestling, sometimes with himself, sometimes
with each other; and they went through the performance with
good nature and apparent enjoyment of the sport." When the
newspaperman asked why the hair was worn off their backs,
Adams said it came from the packsaddles. This led him to tell
about his life in the Sierra and his capture and training of bears.
He had no packsaddles at hand, but to demonstrate how easily
the grizzlies could carry a burden, he unfastened Ben, jumped on
his back, and rode several times around the room. Later, after the
reporter came to know this bear well, he often rode on his back.
Adams spent most of his time with his animals, he said, even sleeping in the same room, on a buffalo robe spread in a corner.

Recognizing good copy, Hittell wrote a number of short pieces
about Adams and his bears for the *Daily Evening Bulletin*, with
the result that attendance at the museum so increased Adams was
enabled to rent more spacious and attractive quarters on the first
floor of the California Exchange, on the northeast corner of Clay

and Kearny streets. During the move it was reported that Samson "got out of his cage and took possession of the lower part of the city. A crowd of excited men and boys were soon at his heels, endeavoring to corral him, but for a long time without success. At length, tired of picking up damaged fruit from the gutters, upsetting ash . . . and swill-barrels, and frightening all the women and children on the street out of their several senses, he took refuge in a livery stable, where he was speedily surrounded and cornered."

The following year Adams renamed his collection The Pacific Museum, added monkeys, and hired a man to exhibit snakes and "a fine brass band" to play each evening. Although he continued to bring in a variety of creatures—a roadrunner, a South American vulture, a sea lion in a tank, even a gopher—the big grizzlies remained the most popular attraction, and Hittell lost no opportunity to keep them and Adams before the public. Throughout 1857 there appeared in his newspaper around a hundred such squibs as "Adams and his bears will growl and tumble about as usual tonight at the Pacific Museum"; or "Adams and his collection of California wild animals are no humbug . . . the visitor at every new visit, finds at the Museum, some new subject of instruction or amusement." Shortly Adams and his collection were recognized as one of San Francisco's institutions. Residents of the city never forgot the sight of Adams walking along the streets, accompanied by a troop of "monstrous grizzly bears, which paid not the least attention to the yelping dogs and the crowds of children which followed them, giving the most conclusive proof of the docility of the animals."

Not long after The Mountaineer Museum opened, the pioneer California artist Charles Nahl discovered it and made a number of drawings and paintings of Samson that were to have a celebrated future—first, to illustrate an article on the grizzly in *Hutchings' California Magazine*; then, as the trademark editor Bret Harte chose to appear regularly on the cover of the San Francisco literary magazine, *Overland Monthly*; and finally, as models for the grizzly bear on California's official flag. Nahl also made a drawing of Adams with Ben Franklin, which Hittell considered "excellent portraits" of both.

When, on January 18, 1858, Ben Franklin died from some sickness for which Adams knew no cure, San Franciscans in general

mourned the loss, and the *Evening Bulletin* published a long obituary under the heading, "Death of a Distinguished Native Californian":

> Ben Franklin, the grizzly bear, the favorite of the Museum
> man Adams . . . departed from this mortal existence on Sunday
> evening, at 10 o'clock. The noble brute, which was captured
> at the head waters of the Merced river in 1854, had been raised
> by his master from a cub, and during his life manifested the most
> indubitable indications of remarkable sagacity and affection. He
> was ever tame and gentle . . . although possessed of the size and
> strength of a giant. . . . He accompanied his master on hunting
> expeditions . . . and on two occasions saved his life in long and
> desperate struggles with savage animals in the wilds. He frequently
> carried his master's pack, provisions and weapons; frequently
> shared his blanket and fed from the same loaf.

Although, as the *Bulletin* noted, "attendance at the Pacific
Museum continues to be large," Adams expanded too rapidly—he
added a waxworks exhibit and an amphitheater and equestrian
ring over the next year—and gate receipts could not keep pace
with expenditures. In May of 1859 he was sued for one thousand
dollars in back rent. When, on January 7, 1860, he and his menagerie left San Francisco for New York, aboard the clipper ship
Golden Fleece, Hittell observed that Adams was just as "poor in
purse" as when he had first come to the city. However, he had no
sooner landed in New York than he called on P. T. Barnum. The
timing was perfect, for Barnum had just bought back his museum
and was looking for exhibits that would rebuild its reputation.
Here was Adams, as the great showman wrote, "with attractions
sure to prove a success." He had brought with him around the Horn
some thirty large grizzlies, among whom were Samson, Lady
Washington, and her son, General Fremont. There were also
some half-dozen black bears, as well as wolves, mountain lions,
elk, buffalo, and Old Neptune, the great sea lion from the Pacific.
In Barnum's opinion, the hunter "was quite as much of a show as
his beasts," dressed as he was in his buckskin suit and cap made
from a "wolf's head and shoulders, from which depended several
tails, and under which appeared his stiff, bushy, gray hair and his
long, white . . . beard. . . .
" 'Grizzly Adams' . . . was brave, and with his bravery there was

enough of the romantic in his nature to make him a real hero,"
Barnum felt. From his varied experiences in the wilderness he had
"acquired a recklessness, which, added to his natural invincible
courage, rendered him one of the most striking men of the age"—
qualities the entrepreneur was determined to use to best advantage. He and Adams formed a partnership.

During their first meeting the hunter had removed his cap and
pointed out to Barnum that depression above his forehead which
had resulted from his encounter with the old grizzly near Yosemite. "The skull was literally broken in," Barnum saw, and the
"workings" of the brain were "plainly visible." He told Adams it
might prove fatal.

"Yes," the hunter replied coolly, "that will fix me out. It had
nearly healed; but old Fremont opened it for me, for the third or
fourth time, before I left California, and he did his business so
thoroughly, I'm a used-up man." After a few moments he confided:
"I am not the man I was five years ago. Then I felt able to stand
the hug of any grizzly living. . . . But I have been beaten to a jelly,
torn almost limb from limb, and nearly chawed up and spit out
by these treacherous grizzly bears. However, I am good for a few
months yet, and by that time I hope we shall have gained enough
to make my old woman comfortable, for I have been absent from
her some years."

Barnum put up a canvas tent for Adams' show at the corner of
Thirteenth Street and Broadway, and on the morning of opening
day, a brass band led a parade down Broadway and up the Bow-
ery. Right behind the musicians was a flatbed wagon with Adams
in his mountaineer's buckskins, sitting astride General Fremont.
Flanking him were two other grizzlies he held by chains. For some
of the acts the bears were costumed: Lady Washington appeared
in bonnet, shawl, and long gown, with gold-rimmed spectacles
perched on her nose; escorting her was the General in military
coat with large epaulettes, trousers, sash, sword, and shako. In his
right forepaw he held a lighted clay pipe; in his left, a cane.

Adams was soon the idol of New Yorkers—"the prince of all
hunters," before whom Boone, Crockett, and Carson paled—and
they wanted to know all about him. *The New York Weekly*, taking
advantage of this keen interest, announced that it had "engaged
MR. JAMES C. ADAMS, the celebrated Californian, and 'wild man' . . .
to relate his experiences and adventures in the forest during the

period he was engaged in getting up his California menagerie. . . .
They will appear in a series of sketches . . . replete with fact,
thrilling incident and instruction." The first of fifteen articles with
such titles as "How I Was Scalped by a She-Grizzly," "How I
Captured the Grizzly Bear, Samson," and "A Snowstorm in the
Mountains—Five Days under a Snowdrift!" was published on May
31, 1860. Not long after, a purported autobiography, *Life of J. C.
Adams, known as Old Adams, Old Grizzly Adams*, was printed in
dime-novel form. In San Francisco, this same summer, Theodore
Hittell published *The Adventures of James Capen Adams, Mountaineer and Grizzly Bear Hunter of California*, with illustrations
by Charles Nahl. This first-person narrative by Adams was compiled from interviews the reporter held with him during the years
1857 to 1859. "As he talked, I wrote down what he said, usually in
his own language, but sometimes with changes to make it more
grammatical." At no time did he "appear to exaggerate, and told
nothing improbable." That September, while Adams was touring
New England, a Boston edition of Hittell's work was published.

After Adams had been showing his animals for ten weeks in the
tent on the corner of Broadway, the doctor who came daily to
dress his head wound advised him to sell out, for he was losing
strength rapidly. "I shall live longer than you doctors think," he
retorted; but, turning to Barnum, he said, "You must buy me out."
He named his price and the showman accepted. Adams then asked
if he would hire him to exhibit the animals during a coming tour
of New England. In addition to his weekly salary, he wanted traveling expenses for himself and his wife, who had come from her
Massachusetts home to take care of him. Anxious to keep Adams
as long as possible, Barnum agreed.

"What will you give me extra if I travel and exhibit the bears
every day for ten weeks?"

"Five hundred dollars," Barnum offered.

"Done! I will do it, so draw up an agreement . . . at once. But
mind you, draw it payable to my wife, for I may be too weak to
attend to business."

Although by the ninth week he was unable to lead in the bears,
he managed to show them through the agreed time, and on receiving the bonus remarked that he was only sorry Barnum was a
teetotaler, for he would like to stand a treat.

When it came time for them to part, Adams said, "I suppose,

Mr. Barnum, you are going to give me this new hunting dress?" and he pointed to a buckskin suit bought for his successor but worn by Adams a few times during the tour. Barnum explained that the new trainer would be wearing it the next day when he showed the bears. Anyway, what possible further use could Adams have for it?

"Now, Barnum, you have made a good thing out of the California menagerie, and so have I; but you will make a heap more. So if you won't give me this new hunter's dress, just draw a little writing, and sign it, saying that I may wear it until I have done with it." Knowing that Adams had at most only a few days more to live, Barnum consented.

Less than a week after Adams had taken to his bed at his wife's home, the doctor told him he would not last until morning, news which he seemed to accept calmly. Turning to his wife, he asked that he be buried in those new buckskins Barnum had agreed he could wear until he was "done" with them. Mrs. Adams promised to observe his request. "That dress was indeed the shroud in which he was entombed," Barnum confirmed.

The thought that he was catching at his own game the man who was a master at deception pleased Adams, and almost his last words were: "Won't Barnum open his eyes when he finds I have humbugged him by being buried in his new hunting dress?" One who was in the room stated that Adams' face "lighted with a smile as the last breath escaped him—and that smile he carried with him to his grave."

8

THE NEW BONANZA

THE GENERAL PUBLIC gave little further thought to Yosemite Valley after the close of the Indian campaigns in 1852, for it promised nothing in the way of fortunes, and gold was still an obsession with most Californians. It might have remained isolated (except for the occasional visit of a hunter) for a number of years yet had the attention of San Franciscan James Mason Hutchings not been caught by the mention of a thousand-foot waterfall, in a printed account of one of the punitive expeditions. Hutchings, a British-born forty-niner who had turned journalist, planned to publish an illustrated monthly devoted to California, and was in search of subjects of unusual interest: here was a waterfall over six times the height of the famed Niagara, and only a handful of white men had seen it. By June 20, 1855, he and a friend were on their way to find that valley. Going with them was the artist Thomas A. Ayres, whom Hutchings had hired to make drawings.

When they reached the gold town of Mariposa, some twenty miles as the crow flies west of Yosemite, it seemed for a time that they might have to turn back. Four years had passed since the principal members of Savage's battalion had set out from Mariposa on the expeditions against the Ahwahneeches, and mining populations being largely transient, most residents had by this time never heard of Yosemite. By diligent inquiry Hutchings man-

aged to ferret out a former battalion member, living some miles
out of town, but when questioned he admitted to having no sense
of direction and said he dared not attempt to point out the way.
He sent them to another former trooper who proved equally un-
satisfactory in his recollection of the region, but who gave them
the name of someone else who was sure to know. When night
overtook Hutchings and his friends, they were interviewing their
eleventh man, still without success. At this point they somehow
met Captain John Boling, who had led the second Yosemite expedition and was now sheriff of Mariposa County. But not even he
could be of any immediate help, for the trails, he explained, were
all overgrown with grass and brush and he could no longer pick
them out. Some thirty miles south, however, a few Yosemite Indians were living near John Hunt's trading post on the Fresno
River, and Boling believed that among them a guide could be
found. Undiscouraged, the Hutchings party rode off in the morning toward Hunt's, and hired not one but two Ahwahneeches who
led them unerringly through thickets and heavy forests where no
vestige of a trail remained. On the afternoon of the third day they
reached Old Inspiration Point, from which the view east through
Yosemite Valley was literally breathtaking. Thomas Ayres hurriedly unpacked his sketchpad and pencils and began work on the
first drawing of the valley by a professional artist.

That night they slept in a meadow not far from the south bank
of the Merced, and in the morning immediately after an early
breakfast began their explorations. Coming shortly to a waterfall
they had admired from the heights the previous afternoon, the
billow and drift of its mist clouds suggested to Hutchings a bride's
veil caught by a breeze. His companions thought the comparison
apt, and Ayres suggested they call it Bridalveil Fall, a name that
eventually replaced the Indian Pohono, which Dr. Bunnell had
decided to keep. When at length they rode out of the pine forest
into open grassland, they had their first view of the waterfall that
had lured them to Yosemite. It was more magnificent than they
had imagined, and seemed much higher than the original estimate.

They spent five days exploring the valley on both sides of the
river, reckoning the heights of cliffs and waterfalls, growing enthusiastic over each discovery and view, Hutchings taking copious
notes, and Ayres making numerous drawings. They rode east into
Tenaya Canyon, as far as the head of Mirror Lake, which Hutch-

ings claimed they named, a claim made also by Dr. Bunnell of Savage's command. Nowhere did they see any Indians or signs of recent habitation.

Upon their return to Mariposa, the editor of the newly established *Mariposa Gazette* asked Hutchings to write an account of their trip and of what they had seen. After publication this article was picked up by many leading newspapers throughout the country, and the general public read for the first time a detailed description of the remarkable sights to be found there. Locally it sparked great interest, and two tourist parties were soon on their way. Included in a group of seventeen from Mariposa, who hired Hutchings' Indian guides, was Galen Clark, who would become closely associated with Yosemite for almost fifty years. The second party from Sherlock's Diggings was, according to their chronicler, made up of "ten as fearless spirits and noble-hearted fellows as ever shouldered a rifle or gathered around a camp-fire." For their guide, they had by some stroke of fortune discovered perhaps the only living ex-battalion member who could find his way to Yosemite. They were not content to limit their explorations to the valley, as the Mariposans were doing, but scrambled up the steep slopes to the rim. On one of those excursions they rediscovered Vernal and Nevada falls, investigated the Little Yosemite, and climbed to the top of that peak to be named Liberty Cap.

A party led by a San Francisco clergyman who had learned about the valley from his friend, Hutchings, and had seen several of Ayres' sketches followed shortly. On his return to the city the minister acquainted a still wider circle, through lectures and newspaper articles. Then, that October, Ayres' drawing of Yosemite Falls was published, giving the public the first pictorial representation and prompting even more people to make the trip. At the end of 1855, the number of Yosemite sightseers stood at forty-eight.

So far, all the travelers there had been men. The following year marked the visit of the first white woman, a Madame Gautier, who worked as housekeeper in a Mariposa hotel. A few days after her excursion, Mrs. Jean Neal, also from Mariposa, and a Mrs. Thompson of Sherlock's Diggings undertook the strenuous horseback trip. There is no record of any other women going there until the next year, when two San Francisco teachers, Harriet J. Kirkland and Anna C. Park, joined a party headed by James Denman, the city's superintendent of schools. "After this," observed a pioneer in the area, "it ceased to be a novelty to see ladies in Yosemite."

The Mann brothers, Milton and Houston, two of those fearless spirits from Sherlock's Diggings, returned from their tour so confident Yosemite would soon become a tourist attraction that they undertook almost immediately the construction of a toll path for horse travel from the South Fork Merced to the valley, and opened it that fall.

The following spring (1856) Galen Clark, who had been with the first tourist group from Mariposa, had a severe lung hemorrhage, quit his job as packer and campkeeper for the Mariposa Ditch Company (it proposed to divert water from the Merced River to the foothill dry diggings), and moved into the mountains for a cure, settling on some lush meadowland near present Wawona. Since regaining his health was his first concern, he did little more that season than erect a shelter. But by the next one he was ready to fence acreage for an orchard and a subsistence garden and to put up a substantial log cabin close to the Mann brothers' trail, for he had noted the great number of Yosemite tourists who stopped at these fine grasslands to rest, cook their meals, and water and graze their horses. Soon he was catering to as many travelers as he could crowd into modest quarters. As these increased he was forced to expand, and the "long, rambling house, built under enormous sugar pines," became as noted for excellence as its host did for individuality. One visitor wrote: "Clark himself is . . . one of those men one frequently meets in California—the modern anchorite—a hater of civilization and a lover of the forest —handsome, thoughtful, interesting. . . . In his cabin were some of the choicest modern books and scientific surveys; . . . he knew more than any of his guests of the fauna, flora, and geology of the State; he conversed well on any subject, and was at once philosopher, savant, chambermaid, cook, and landlord."

The first issue of the illustrated monthly James Mason Hutchings planned to launch was published in July of 1856. Its lead article, illustrated with Ayres' drawings, was devoted to Yosemite Valley and aroused widespread interest not only among potential sightseers but among businessmen. This focus of attention on Yosemite at a time when a well-founded report was in circulation that John C. Frémont was about to develop the mines on his nearby grant, Las Mariposas, brought an influx of settlers into the

Mariposa region, and stimulated local capitalists to invest in what promised to be a double bonanza. A second ditch company was therefore organized to carry water from the foot of Yosemite Valley to the dry diggings, and a second horse trail was opened. Instead of approaching the valley from the south by way of Galen Clark's, it pioneered a route from the west, starting from Bull Creek, to which a wagon road had been built, and reaching the valley just north of present Arch Rock. A third company then hastened to construct yet another trail from Big Oak Flat (once Savage's Diggings), which joined the second trail between Crane and Tamarack Flat. Since the trip usually took about three days, the first night's camp was made at Deer Flat, the second one at Hazel Green, and the final encampment at still another meadow at Crane Flat. With the increase of travel over these routes, enterprising individuals set up blacksmith forges and opened little shops, while at the camping spots larger investors hastened to erect structures pretentiously called hotels, but described by tourists candidly as shanties.

For twenty-three years Yosemite Valley was accessible only by horseback, and contemporary accounts make it clear that those trails from the west over the high, rugged terrain were not for the timid. First, the string of saddle horses failed to inspire confidence: "On all sides you hear ejaculations from the people waiting. 'I'll never go on *that* horse;' 'nor on that;' '*that* horse will never live to go down again.' . . . Heads down, tails limp, legs out, abject, pitiable things." Once mounted "our sensations were not agreeable. We had seen how steep it looked when horse and rider disappeared over the hill-crest. It felt steeper. To an unaccustomed rider it is not pleasant to sit on a horse whose heels are much higher than his head. One's first impulse is to clutch, to brace, to cling."

Another traveler described the final descent from Tamarack Flat, the highest point on the trail: "We turn . . . into a sort of stairway in the mountain and cautiously tread the stony defile downwards; at places over loose boulders, at others around or over points of shelving rock, where one false step would send horse and rider a mangled mass two thousand feet below. . . . It is impossible to repress fear. Every nerve is tense; the muscles involuntarily make ready for a spring, and even the bravest lean timorously toward the mountainside and away from the cliff, with foot loose in stirrup and eye alert, ready for a spring in case of peril. The thought is vain; should the horse go, the rider would infallibly go with him. . . . At length we reach a point where the most hardy generally dismount and walk—two hundred feet in descent in five hundred feet progress. . . . I will not walk before and lead my horse, as does our guide, but trail my long rope halter and keep him before me, always careful to stay on the upper side of him . . . hugging the cliff . . . for now I am scared. All pretense of pride is gone. . . . At last comes a gentler slope, then a crystal spring, dense grove and grass-covered plat, and we are down into the valley."

When women's rights leader Elizabeth Cady Stanton reached Tamarack Flat, she balked. In spite of the guide's assurances that he had piloted hundreds of persons safely down that "fearful incline," she insisted upon walking the entire distance, equal to twenty miles on level ground. It was another story with Anna Elizabeth Dickinson, that slip of a Quaker girl who at nineteen had made her first speech for the abolition of slavery, and was at the time of her Yosemite visit, although only twenty-seven, known as the Queen of the Lyceum. She toured the country, speaking on behalf of "universal freedom, universal suffrage, and universal justice." She had come to California with the press corps on the first transcontinental train. Now, about to descend into Yosemite Valley, she asked for a man's saddle and rode astride, as she did at home. It was not long until other "strong-minded ladies" were not only riding astride in their bloomer suits over the steep trails into Yosemite, but throughout the valley as well, evoking male ridicule: "A grim Amazon in a short skirt, thick boots, large hat, and green spectacles, riding astride a horse or mule, is about as ludicrous—not to say ungainly—an exhibition as you could well contemplate."

For those who looked forward to making fortunes from the tourists, the next step was to provide places for them to obtain meals and beds within the valley. In the fall of 1856 four partners began work on a flimsy shedlike structure on the south side of the Merced, just east of Sentinel Creek. At the same time, a second partnership was formed by two miners from Bull Creek, Buck Beardsley and Stephen Cunningham, to build and operate a store and inn. Cunningham, the son of a New York judge, was described as "a gentleman of good education and general intelligence." He had, his acquaintance added, recently been adopted by a village of foothill Indians.

But winter came early that year, and Beardsley and Cunningham were unable to make a start on their buildings until spring. By mid-March they were at work, and soon completed a substantial shake-covered cabin, which they planned to use as a store. After buying out the four members of the other partnership, who had run short of capital or enthusiasm, Beardsley and Cunningham quickly finished that structure and opened it as a hotel.

The Virginia-born forty-niner Benjamin Harris, then practicing law in Mariposa, was preparing to visit Yosemite with a friend, James Bell, when Cunningham came into town. Finding the two packing food enough to last several weeks, he insisted that they take no more than was needed for the road, since after they got to the valley, they were to live on his hospitality. He would be offended if they did not, for he was amply supplied with provisions. On their first day in Yosemite, the lunch hour came and passed unmarked, and by midafternoon, seeing no preparations under way, and growing hungrier by the minute, they asked Cunningham when the meal would be ready.

"Why don't you help yourself?" he asked. "There's plenty to eat"—and he pointed to a large patch of wild clover in the meadow beyond, which some Indian women and children were picking and eating. "Help yourself, gentlemen; it's the best we have." Realizing that he was in earnest (later they learned he had not so much as an ounce of provisions on hand), they walked over to the meadow, but could "worry down" only a few mouthfuls. In the morning they "grazed" again. That was as much as Harris could stand: "I cut short my intended long stay . . . tightened my belt and headed for the settlements." Bell stayed on for two weeks more, but reached home, his friend reported, bloated and greatly emaciated.

That fall Beardsley and Cunningham separated, and Beardsley took another partner to help run a store and hotel in a blue tent. Meanwhile, he and the partner were at work on a wooden building of two rooms, one above the other, sixty by twenty feet, that would later be designated as the Upper Hotel. Because all boards had to be hand-hewn, and supplies packed in fifty miles by mule train, it was not open for business until May 1859.

Among its first guests was a party from San Francisco that included James Mason Hutchings. He had with him this time the pioneer landscape photographer, Charles L. Weed, whose picture of the hotel was the first photograph ever taken in Yosemite Valley. To get material for further articles, Hutchings explored the rim, and if they could recruit helpers enough, Weed accompanied him. The editor recalled the line of men who made the climb to the summit of Illilouette Fall: first, Buck Beardsley, who had volunteered to carry the heavy camera, which when inverted and strapped to his back resembled a hand organ; next, a man who carried the lunch hamper and a double-barreled stereoscopic camera, which in its turn looked like a small cannon; a third man with tripod, plate holders, and chemicals; still another with glass plates and lenses; and finally the photographer himself, packing his tent darkroom.

One day, when about halfway up the ladders Cunningham had built through the misty fern grotto to the cliff top at Vernal Fall, a young man in their party found a white petticoat. Picking it up, he folded it around his shoulders as protection from the penetrating spray. What had led this woman to discard so important a part of her apparel, they wondered. A lively discussion got under way as various theories were offered. Then the guide who had been in the rear tethering their horses caught up and gave the explanation: a few days before he had led a party that included Nina Frémont, the colonel's nineteen-year-old niece. In climbing the ladders she found the underskirt a nuisance, and slipping it off, had tossed it aside. The finder, an admirer of her uncle, carried it back to the hotel, and "reverently" fashioned an American flag from one "delicate fold" of Miss Nina's petticoat. When the party ascended Yosemite Falls, he took it along. At the summit Hutchings made his way up a pine tree and tied the flag to the top; the company then saluted it with a "triumphant three times three."

That same summer Horace Greeley, the distinguished editor of the *New York Tribune*, stayed at the Upper Hotel. Following his own advice, he had come west to appraise California's potential. Now he was a guest of Jessie Benton Frémont and her family at their cottage in Bear Valley west of Yosemite. On August 11, Greeley, perpetually in a hurry, ever dashing with his coattails on the wind, decided to make the strenuous sixty-mile trip from the Frémonts' to Yosemite without the usual overnight stop. Thirty-eight of these miles, from Clark's into the valley, were covered on the back of "one of the hardest trotting mules in America." Greeley, who had not been in the saddle for thirty years, was "utterly helpless" by the time he reached the hotel, and had to be lifted down. At his request he went to bed supperless. Close to noon the following day he was "assisted from his couch," and after a light breakfast—he was dyspeptic—helped into the saddle. He made a brief and uncomfortable tour of the valley floor before setting off on the return ride. He arrived at the Frémonts' "tired and cross," Jessie Benton remembered, with little good to say about Yosemite. Yosemite Falls were a "humbug"—a mere "trout brook" straggling down the cliff. As she handed the myopic editor his eyeglasses he had left behind on the dressing table, she suggested this might be the answer to his having seen "nothing to praise in Yosemite." A cold bath, fresh clothing, and a good night's sleep helped prepare him for the arduous stage ride that was to take him on to several speaking engagements. Some three weeks later James Hutchings met him hobbling along a sidewalk in San Francisco. When mention was made of his lameness, Greeley replied: "Oh! Mr. Hutchings, you cannot realize how much I suffered from this jaunt to Yosemite." Later he relented and wrote for publication that it was the most "unique and majestic of nature's marvels."

Two years later when Thomas Starr King, the noted Unitarian clergyman, lecturer, and author of many works on the beauty of American landscape, took a room at the Upper Hotel—"the Shanty-Hotel," he called it—he noted that the front was clapboarded, but the back wall was made only of "common cotton cloth. The hall upstairs is not finished into chambers, but has spaces of eight feet square divided by cotton screens, within which beds without sheets are laid upon the bare floor. There are one or two rooms below which have beds upon posts, and furniture for the ladies."

Having observed the great meadows of rich grass that in New England would be put to thrifty use, he did not think it unreasonable to ask the host, Charles Peck, that day at dinner: "Can you give us a broiled chicken, some bread and butter, and a cup of tea with fresh milk or cream?

"Peck replied: 'Gentlemen, I have no milk, for I do not keep a cow. There is no butter in the house, and chickens were never seen here.'

"What, O Transcript," King asked in a letter written for that Boston newspaper, "do you think our meal consisted of? Stewed oysters and lobster! Among these wilds of the Sierras we had on the table oysters and lobsters from New York with a bottle of Boston pickles."

From the start the Upper Hotel had a rival in Stephen Cunningham's Lower Hotel. In the spring of 1857 when he and Beardsley were still associated they had bought out the four original partners, finished their flimsy structure, and opened it as an inn. Heavy snows that winter leveled it, but Cunningham soon had it rebuilt more substantially and ready for guests the next season—a year ahead of Beardsley's Upper Hotel. Cunningham hired Mrs. Jean Neal, the second white woman to have entered Yosemite, and her husband, John, to operate it. Wrote one of Mrs. Neal's first guests: "I secured a bed, such as it was, for my wife, in a rough board shanty occupied by a family that had arrived a few days before to keep a sort of tavern, the woman being the only one within fifty or sixty miles of the place. For myself, a bed of shavings and a blanket . . . under some trees formed my resting place."

Over the next years few improvements were made. A British clergyman reported: "When G—— and I were shown to our bedroom . . . we found that it consisted of a quarter of a shed screened off by split planks, which rose about eight or ten feet from the ground, and enabled us to hear everything that went on in the other 'rooms,' which were simply stalls in the same shed. Ours had no window, but we could see the stars through the roof. The door opening into the forest was fastened with cow-hinges of skin with the hair on, and a little leather strap which hooked on to a nail. We boasted a rough, gaping floor, but several of the other bedrooms were only strewed with branches. . . . As a grizzly bear had lately been seen wandering about a few hundred yards from our 'hotel,' we took the precaution of putting our revolvers under our pillows. I dare say this was needless . . . but . . . it had the charm of novelty."

For ten years there were only two hotels in the valley, and at times just one, Cunningham's, for Buck Beardsley and his partner incurred a large indebtedness they could not meet, and had to assign the Upper Hotel to their creditors, who leased it or kept it closed as circumstances determined.

In 1861 Cunningham sold the Lower Hotel to Mrs. A. G. Black, who leased it to Peter Longhurst, "a weather-beaten round-the-worlder" who sang songs, recounted tall tales, and was skilled in the art of flapjack frying. "Scorning such vulgar accomplishments as turning the cake over in mid-air, he slung it boldly up, turning it three times, ostentatiously greasing the pan with a fine centrifugal movement, and catching the flapjack as it fluttered down, spanked it upon the hot coals with a touch at once graceful and masterly," wrote a guest. "I failed to enjoy these products, feeling as if I were breakfasting in sacrilege upon works of art."

Yosemite Valley was rapidly gaining the reputation of being not only California's greatest scenic wonder but one of the most remarkable in the world. Although travelers from all over the nation, Europe, and Great Britain were coming to see it, the aggregate was far less than anticipated, and no fortunes were made by the valley's businessmen. Over the nine-year period, 1855 to 1864, there were only 653 registered visitors; at the peak of the 1863 season, but a dozen. Many who would have liked to see it were reluctant to take the long, tiring transcontinental stage trip. Others were deterred by the expense of horses, packers, and guides for the excursion into the valley. Still others considered the charge of three dollars a day for meals at the hotels exorbitant. One might not even cross the Merced to reach the hotels without paying, a tourist wrote with some dismay, and told of arriving at the river ford just as Stephen Cunningham and helpers were "adjusting the last rope to a flat boat. . . . In fifteen minutes, they had earned the first fruits of their enterprise—one dollar from each of us ferriage."

A number of those men who had rushed to invest in toll bridges, ferries, and trails; in livery stables, blacksmith shops, stores, and hotels were unable to hold out until the anticipated bonanza materialized. One of the first enterprises to succumb was the Mann brothers' trail. Although it was the most scenic route, having the best initial view of Yosemite from a high clearing that was to be named Inspiration Point, and had the additional attraction of a grove of two hundred Big Trees, discovered in 1857 by Galen Clark and Milton Mann, who advertised it to draw trade, the brothers were forced to sell to the county at about one-third of the original cost. But the completion of the transcontinental railroad in 1869 brought a change, and the number of Yosemite visitors jumped in that one year to twelve hundred and twenty-two, giving impetus to a building boom.

Mrs. Black, who had bought Cunningham's Lower Hotel, razed the old barnlike structure and replaced it with an elongated shed to be known as Black's, architecturally no improvement over the original. George and Isabella Leidig, husband and wife, who had managed the old Lower Hotel for Mrs. Black, built a two-story guest house just west of her new inn. It stood in the shadow of Sentinel Rock and faced Yosemite Falls. Surrounded with porches, it was "a pleasant place to sit and contemplate the magnificence of the scenery." A woman visitor thought Leidigs' "the best in the line of hotels. Mrs. L—— attends to the cooking in person; the results are that the food is well cooked . . . and served." The beds were clean and comfortable, as well.

One winter visitor from England wrote that George Leidig "was glad enough to see us, for tourists are very scarce commodities at this time of year, and he determined to celebrate . . . by exploding a dynamite cartridge, that we might . . . enjoy the grand echoes. These were doubtless extraordinary, but I am free to confess I would rather have gone away without hearing them than have experienced the anxiety of mind, and real risk to body, which preceded the pleasure."

The climb to Vernal and Nevada falls became so popular the enterprising Vermonters Albert Snow and his wife, Emily—noted for her wit and cooking skills—packed in lumber and supplies and built a little inn on a granite flat between the two falls. From its veranda was an unobstructed view of Nevada Fall, considered by many to equal Yosemite Falls in grandeur. To facilitate travel to the hotel, Snow hired George Anderson, a Scotch sailor who had come to the gold fields but was now plying the blacksmith's trade in the valley, to survey and build a horse path.

Another improvement was replacement of the hazardous trail to Glacier Point, popular because of its unexcelled views of the entire valley and the High Sierra beyond, which seem to stretch endlessly and merge finally with the horizon. The new route, engineered by John Conway, who became the valley's master trail builder, zigzagged four miles up the 3,254-foot cliff to the summit. On its completion, James McCauley, who had financed it, brought lumber and other materials by muleback up the zigzags and proceeded to construct a two-story hotel facing the famed panorama. The Mountain House, as he called it, was to serve guests for almost a hundred years.

Although peering straight down into the valley from the rail at the cliff's edge, just beyond the hotel, caused "spiders of ice to crawl down one's spine," few tourists could resist. Next in popularity were experiments to determine the length of time the eye could follow various objects thrown over the brink. Wrote one of McCauley's guests: "An ordinary stone . . . remained in sight an incredibly long time, but finally vanished somewhere about the middle distance. A handkerchief with a stone tied in the corner, was visible perhaps a thousand feet deeper; but even an empty box, watched by a field-glass, could not be traced to its concussion with the Valley floor."

At about this point, it is said, McCauley would appear with "an antique hen" tucked under his arm, walk to the edge, and throw it over—"amidst the terrified ejaculations . . . of the ladies.

"The hapless fowl shot down, down, until it became a mere fluff of feathers no larger than a quail. Then it dwindled to a wren's size, disappeared, then again dotted the sight a moment as a pin's point, and then—it was gone!

"After drawing a long breath all around, the women folks pitched into the hen's owner with redoubled zest. But the genial McCauley shook his head knowingly, and replied: 'Don't be alarmed about that chicken, ladies. She's used to it. She goes over that cliff every day during the season.' —And sure enough, on our road back, we met the old hen about half way up the trail, calmly picking her way home!"

But the "greatest wonder of the Valley" at this time was The Cosmopolitan, which boasted a "saloon, billiard hall, bathing-rooms, and barber-shop"; full-length mirrors, pyramids of sparkling glassware; "the finest of cues and tables, [a] reading room handsomely furnished and supplied with the latest from Eastern cities." There was "a long writing table, with stationery ready to one's hand; and a small sitting-room, furnished with sofas and comfortable easy-chairs . . . exclusively for the use of ladies." The owner of this wonder was C. E. Smith.

The author Helen Hunt Jackson was particularly impressed with the five bathrooms: "The tubs shine; the floors are carpeted; Turkish towels hang on the racks; soaps, bottles of cologne, and bay rum are kept in each room; a pin-cushion stands under each glass, and on the pin-cushion are not only pins, but scissors, needles, thread, and buttons. Has anyone ever seen a public bathroom of this order? And Mr. Smith mentioned apologetically, that the button-hooks for which he had sent have not yet arrived." Although everything was still packed in by mule train, he told Mrs. Jackson that he intended next to bring in a grand piano.

Men visitors reported approvingly that in the bar, Smith was a master at concocting anything from Queen Charlottes, One-eyed Joes, Moral 'Suasions, and Stonewalls to gin slings and mint juleps.

9

EDITOR-INNKEEPER

IN THE SUMMER of 1863, James Mason Hutchings, the San
Francisco editor and author who had led the first tourist party into
Yosemite, took over the valley's financially faltering Upper Hotel.
The following April he, his wife, and his mother-in-law began
their careers as Yosemite innkeepers. Hutchings, who had succumbed to the valley's spell during that first visit in June 1855,
found in his wife's delicate health and her doctor's recommendation that she leave the coastal fogs for a drier climate a good
reason for a move to Yosemite, something he had been considering
for a long while.

In February 1860, Hutchings, then forty, had married Elvira
Sproat, the eighteen-year-old daughter of his landlady, Florantha
Thompson Sproat, whose father, Cephus Thompson, was a noted
American portrait painter; and whose brother, also named
Cephus, and sister, Marietta, were still more celebrated por-
traitists. Elvira had inherited artistic talent from her mother's side,
and literary tastes and inclinations from her father, a wandering
versifier who could never find his place in life and had left the
family's support chiefly in his wife's hands. Mrs. Sproat's long experience in operating boardinghouses led them to believe they
might succeed in the hotel business. There was one important
uncertainty: was it feasible to live in Yosemite Valley the year

round, or was it buried each winter deep in snow and cut off from the outside world? Early in March of 1862, Hutchings set off to find the answer. He could not have chosen a better time for such an investigation, as this was the worst California winter on record.

At Mariposa he was joined by Galen Clark and James Lamon, both interested in the results, for no white man had yet wintered in the valley. Lamon, described by a friend as a "fine, erect, whole-souled man, between six and seven feet high, with a broad, open face, bland and guileless," was a gold seeker from Virginia. Before coming to California he had lived along the Brazos in Texas, where he raised melons and hunted alligators for a living. "Right interestin' business," he told his friend, "especially the alligator part of it." While at work in Mariposa County he had heard from some of those first tourists about the wonders of Yosemite, and went to see them first in the summer of 1857 and again the following year. He decided then "to quit roving and make a permanent home" there. In April 1859 he returned, located a preemption claim at the east end along the south wall, and built the valley's first log cabin. Then packing in seed potatoes, berry plants, and young fruit trees on the back of a "contrary old mule," he planted a garden and orchard in sunny, open acres, expecting in time to produce enough for sale. He was told that he was foolish to try and raise crops in that climate, and that he would surely starve. But his vegetable garden, berry patch, and orchard became known to every visitor over the next thirty years, for their productiveness and the fine flavor of their crops. Today, after nearly a century and a quarter, his apple trees still bear bountifully.

Beyond Galen Clark's inn, the snowbanks that blocked the trail north to Yosemite, grew ever larger. After the three men had been breaking their way for several hours, Lamon and Clark announced that it was impractical to go on, since the drifts would increase in size with the constant rise in elevation, and finally become impassable. But Hutchings was determined, and finding that he could persuade neither man to continue, went on alone. It took him six days, "not merely walking in or over snow, but wallowing through it." The first view into the valley, however, was as "a look into Paradise," for it was nearly free of snow. Once he had reached the floor he heard frogs chorusing and found currant and gooseberry in bloom along the sunny north wall. Convinced that the valley was not only practicable for winter living but accessible after even such a prodigious snowfall, he began the return journey home. Stopping in Mariposa, he reported his findings and conclusions to James Lamon, who decided to pack in supplies and spend the coming winter in his cabin, alone.

Lamon's success—he was amazed at the gentleness of the season and at the number of sunny days when he could work in his garden—encouraged Hutchings, who went back to the valley in the summer of 1863 to locate. Rather than build, as he had at first intended, he decided to buy and refurbish the old Upper Hotel. He also took up two claims of a hundred and sixty acres each.

A young New England woman traveling with a small party stayed at Hutchings' hotel in June of 1864, not long after it had opened. In a letter to relatives at home, she described the accommodations:

> No partition between the dining and sitting rooms; no plastering, no chairs, except one rocking chair. We sat at table on long wooden benches, without backs, and at other times on ottomans or stools. Up stairs the rooms were only divided by pieces of cotton cloth, and were very small at that, containing a small bed, a small rough wash-stand, a rough bench, and no place to hang anything. The only choice being to go to bed with one's clothes on, or leave them under the bed, on the floor. Of course every word and movement were plainly audible and visible, and it required some little strategy to place the candle so that one's figure should not appear on the cloth partition, hugely magnified, for the amusement of one's neighbors. Fanny J——'s soap slipped from her fingers when washing, and flew down into the parlor, because the floor and the outside wall didn't quite meet.

A British journalist also took exception to this flimsy construction and declared in all seriousness that the building was so "airy" it was in real danger of blowing away in a moderate wind storm.

"The house was kept by some literary people, who were rather out of their sphere," the young New England woman continued. "We slept in unironed sheets, on rough, dry pillow-cases, and dried our faces on towels guiltless of attention, beyond a hasty washing." On the evening of her arrival she and her party were "ready to retire early, but a fiddler and guitarist being in the Valley, they were sent for; the guests danced, and there was singing with guitar accompaniment." On other evenings there was group singing beside the river; and there were walks to see the valley by moonlight, with Hutchings as their guide.

At this time a favorite joke with guides leading the horse trains into Yosemite was to warn the traveler not to leave his bedroom door unlocked because there were thieves about. On retiring to his room at night the guest was naturally amazed to find that his door was a sheet, as were the partitions between adjoining quarters.

In 1861 Hutchings published *Scenes of Wonder and Curiosity*, the first book in which Yosemite was treated exhaustively. It went into several editions, and did much to publicize the region and the author. Hutchings' reputation as a writer attracted the literati to his hotel, and many of them described him in their books of travel. The poet-novelist-historian Helen Hunt Jackson found him "an enthusiast, a dreamer, a visionary," with a keen awareness of the rare beauty of his surroundings. "All this is plainly to be seen in his mobile, artistic face, and in the affectionate ring of every word that he speaks of the Valley. But landlords are not made of such stuff as this. Artistic sensibility and enthusiasm do not help a man to order dinner." Breakfast, she noted, was "a freebooting foray, lunch a quieter foraging expedition, dinner a picnic. As soon as one learns the order or disorder of the things one can get on."

The philanthropist and author Charles Loring Brace, who thought Hutchings "a man of considerable literary abilities," a poet, and "a 'Guide' in the highest sense," for he "loves the wonderful region which he shows yearly to strangers from every quarter of the globe," gave details of the freebooting foray: ". . . we come down very hungry, to a delicious breakfast of fresh trout, venison, and great pans of garden strawberries; but, unfortunately, there are no knives and forks." Just as Hutchings' attention has been called to this oversight,

> a romantic young lady asks . . . about the best point of view for the Yosemite Falls. "Madam, there is but one; you must get close to the Upper Fall, just above the mist of the Lower, and there you will see a horizontal rainbow beneath your feet, and the most exquisite. . . ."
>
> Here a strong-minded lady, whose politeness is at end, "But here, Hutchings, we have no knives and forks!" "Oh, beg a thousand pardons, madam!" and he rushes off; but meeting his wife on the way, she gives him coffee for the English party, and he forgets us entirely, and we get up good-naturedly and search

out the implements ourselves. Again, from an amiable lady, "Please, Mr. Hutchings, another cup of coffee!" "Certainly, madam!" When the English lady from Calcutta asks him about some wild flowers, he goes off in a botanical and poetical disquisition, and in his abstraction brings the other lady, with great eagerness, a glass of water. Sometime sugar is handed you instead of salt for the trout, or cold water is poured into your coffee; but none of the ladies mind, for our landlord is as handsome as he is obliging, and really full of information.

Elvira Hutchings was also temperamentally unsuited for innkeeping. However, unlike her gregarious husband, who enjoyed crowds and adulation, she was withdrawn and preferred solitude. Slender and fragile appearing, she had "a Madonna cast of countenance, deep, pensive hazel eyes, a blush-rose complexion, and brown hair," a friend wrote. Resentful of having to give up time more rewardingly spent with her books, music (she composed for the guitar), and painting, and with her studies of local flora and Ahwahneeche customs, she performed her duties perfunctorily. That the hotel functioned as well as it did was due to the management of her mother, Mrs. Sproat; and that it made a profit was owing to the popularity of her husband.

Mrs. Sproat's sphere included the Hutchings household, which she also managed. In August 1864, not long after the hotel opened, Elvira had her first child, a girl, Florence or Floy, much of whose care was assumed by her grandmother, for motherhood was as foreign to Elvira's nature as keeping house or running an inn.

One winter spent on the cold south side of the valley—the sun did not reach the hotel until one-thirty and was gone again within two hours—particularly with a young baby, convinced them they should follow the example of James Lamon, who had built himself winter quarters under the Royal Arches on the sunny north side. With his help Hutchings put up a log cabin about three-fourths of a mile from Yosemite Falls, set out a hundred and fifty fruit trees, and planted an acreage to strawberries. A cow, some horses, sheep, poultry, pigs, and a vegetable plot completed the homestead.

"When shall I see another such cabin as that one—with its great fireplace, and its loft full of pumpkins?" mused the San Francisco poet and musician Charles Warren Stoddard, who spent a winter there. Reading aloud from a collection of about eight hundred volumes was a favorite pastime, he wrote, and after the evening lamp was lit and they had drawn close to the fire, the "gentle-voiced" Elvira would open a book—often Sir Walter Scott—and read. For variety they would sing to her guitar accompaniment, or play whist or euchre. Saturday nights, when their only neighbor, James Lamon, left his "hermit-like solitude" to join them, were regularly given over to cards and music.

"Baby was abed, of course," Stoddard went on, "the baby whom we knew as 'Squirrel'," a nickname Floy soon earned because of lightning-quick motions. "Dear little Squirrel! she knew nothing of the world but what she saw of it within her mountain-walled horizon; such an odd little child she was, left to herself and her fancies; no doubt thinking she was the only one of her kind in existence; contented to seesaw for hours on a plank by the wood-pile; making long, solitary explorations, and returning, when we were all well frightened, with a pocket full of lizards and a wasp caged in her hand—they never stung her." She knew no fears. When happy, she imitated the birds in song; when displeased, she growled like a bear. As she grew older she came to resent having been born a girl, for it was boy's play and boy's concerns she liked best. When old enough to have her own way, she put on trousers, freeing her to ride her horse astride at top speed over the grass-lands—a favorite pastime; to climb to the tops of trees and scramble up rocky cliffs, sliding down them if so prompted.

An English novelist who visited the Hutchings family in 1870 described her introduction to Floy at six. Catching the author's attention by a pinch on the arm, the girl then broke into a torrent of words: "Say! Listen! where do you come from, where are you going, what made you come; do you want to camp out? I'll go with you. We had better start before the moon goes down; have you plenty of blankets? It's only twenty miles to the top of Tis-sa'-ak [Half Dome]. I'll show you the trail. I've just come down today. . . . You are not afraid of rattlesnakes, I suppose; there is one just below here that has bitten me three times, but I always cut the piece out with my jack-knife, and it did me no harm. . . . Say! do you want a polecat skin? I'll go out and catch and skin one alive, and bring it to you."

The novelist was meanwhile observing Floy's appearance: face slender and oval; "eyes piercing black"; brow, Grecian, "broad and low"; complexion, "the richest brunette . . . with a pure vermilion tinge on the cheeks, which had little of the roundness of childhood"; mouth "small, with thin, compressed lips, but . . . chin of extraordinary depth and power"; hair, "dark and silky."

Beyond being taught to read and write, Floy was without formal schooling during the early Yosemite years. Her learning came from other sources: her varied experiences and observations out-of-doors; the evenings of reading aloud after she was old enough to participate; the association with adults eminent in many fields who stayed in the valley. From the Scotch naturalist and inventor John Muir, who worked for her father, she came to know much about plants, insects, animals, and mechanics. He spoke of her as "a tameless one," "a rare creature," "a smart and handsome and mischievous Topsy." Other adults who spent time with her noted her broad general knowledge and the precocity of many of her comments. Two more children were born to Elvira: a second girl, Gertrude, known always as Cosie—"a very precious darling," to Muir's mind—blue-eyed and fair, who also developed a fierce independence; and a boy, William, who had a spinal deformity.

Improvements at the hotel were in order. In spite of the amusement they afforded, especially in retrospect, the muslin doors and walls became a thing of the past. Lumber that had to be packed in by mule train was costly, so Hutchings decided to put up a water-powered sawmill to cut boards from the hundreds of pines and cedars felled throughout the valley by a gale the previous winter. But the first man he hired to build it knew nothing about the principles and could not get the waterwheel to turn. Not until Hutchings engaged John Muir, at the time a jack-of-all-trades, did the mill work. Muir rebuilt it entirely and installed the machinery. It was then not long until rooms were being partitioned with wood, and closed off with solid doors. Verandas were built around the hotel, and additions made that included a kitchen, storerooms, and a parlor—the latter known as the Big Tree Room, for it was constructed around a large, living incense cedar. It was planned and built mainly by Muir, as were several guest cottages. Hutchings' next major project was to run a causeway, as he called it, over the meadows from the hotel to make Yosemite Falls and other north-side attractions more accessible to his guests. The finishing touch to the causeway was an avenue of imported elms planted on either side.

Hutchings, like many others, failed to perceive any threats to Yosemite's unique beauty in the encroachment of civilization through commercialization or in attempts to improve upon nature. The conviction that the world had been made expressly for man's use and exploitation threatened all of this country's scenic sites and wilderness then, as now. In the mid-1850s a number of foresighted Californians had begun to worry about the destruction of the few existing groves of rare giant sequoia, for lumber, and by the beginning of the next decade, the misuse of Yosemite Valley was included in their concern. A new concept was evolving: Yosemite as a natural park, a wild park that man had no need or right to alter, preserved and protected by the state.

On February 20, 1864, Israel Ward Raymond, a San Francisco shipping magnate, wrote a letter to California's junior senator, John Conness, urging that Congress grant to the state, "for public use, resort and recreation," Yosemite Valley and the Mariposa Big Tree Grove. (All forest and public lands were held by the federal government.) Raymond stressed that the grant be inalienable. With forethought he included "Yosemite Views," a collection of photographs made by Carleton E. Watkins, to be given Congress with the bill. It is said that these pictures made their way to the White House, and that Abraham Lincoln studied them. Senator Conness, who was receptive to Raymond's arguments, shortly introduced the measure. It passed both houses with little or no opposition, but only after the senator had assured his colleagues that the land was "for all public purposes worthless." Lincoln signed the bill into law on June 30, 1864.

Mystery surrounds the identity of many of those "gentlemen of fortune, of taste, and of refinement," who were advocates of the state park. In addition to Raymond, designated as the "prime mover," Frederick Law Olmsted is most frequently mentioned. Olmsted, who with Calvert Vaux designed New York's Central Park, was at this time superintendent of Frémont's old grant, Las Mariposas, some thirty air miles from Yosemite. Galen Clark stated that the "gentlemen" included one woman—Jessie Benton Frémont—and that she was "among the most active" of the park's proponents.

Three months after the grant was made, California's governor issued a proclamation in which he announced the appointment of the eight commissioners who were to administer the park, without pay, as specified in the act. Olmsted was named chairman, and Galen Clark made a member of the board. Shortly, Clark was given the office of guardian of the grant, a resident superintendent.

In the fall, the commissioners notified Hutchings that since private ownership was no longer recognized, he must either accept a ten-year lease or vacate. He refused on the ground that title to his holdings had been legalized before Yosemite was made a state reserve, and he continued to operate his hotel and live in his cabin. Pioneer settler James Lamon took the same stand, as did those early innkeepers Mrs. A. G. Black and her husband. A year later a suit of ejectment was filed against Hutchings as a test case for all parties involved. When the suit was decided in Hutchings' favor, the commissioners appealed to the California Supreme Court, which reversed the decision. Hutchings then brought an appeal before the U.S. Supreme Court, which likewise upheld the commissioners. Defeated, he, Lamon, and the Blacks then asked to be reimbursed for their improvements. In 1874 the state legislature, influenced by a strong ground swell of public support for the well-known and popular Hutchings, and with the approval of the Yosemite commissioners, who were eager to end a protracted legal battle, appropriated $60,000. Of this amount Hutchings received $24,000, Lamon, $12,000, and the Blacks, $22,000, out of which they were to pay a silent partner.

Forced to move, Hutchings and his family returned to Mrs. Sproat's house in San Francisco. Not long afterward, Elvira left him for another man, furnishing Hutchings with grounds for divorce. Her mother, however, continued to manage the household and superintend their annual summer encampments in Yosemite. Freed from the responsibilities of the hotel, Hutchings spent those seasons climbing the Yosemite peaks, usually with Floy and Mrs. Sproat, and often with resident landscape painter Thomas Hill and the botanist Dr. Albert Kellogg. Meanwhile he was at work on his *Yosemite Guide Book*, which was published in 1877.

Three years later a new board of commissioners appointed Hutchings guardian of the grant, and he returned to live in Yosemite with Mrs. Sproat, the children, and his new bride, Augusta Sweetland, a landscape painter and newspaper correspondent. John K. Barnard, who had leased his property, "placed the dear old cabin indefinitely at my disposal," Hutchings wrote.

For Floy, then sixteen, it was a joyous return, a release from city life and formal schooling, both of which were confining and oppressive to her. A nonconformist with whom her teachers had no

sympathy, and ever scornful of disapproval, she had been expelled. Hers was a disposition that was always chafed and restless,
and she found outlet in Yosemite—racing her horse over the
meadows, always astride and usually bareback, with only a piece
of scarlet braid for a bridle; exploring the high country; and camping alone in the wilderness. But there was another side to her: "a
warm and generous temperament, always ready to do an act of
kindness"; a capacity for close friendships; and a sympathetic
understanding of little children. Unhampered by scholastic regi-
mentation, she was an original thinker. She became very popular
as a "ladies' guide," for she was competent, fearless, patient with
their questions, and ready with her knowledge of the environment.

The following winter Augusta Sweetland died suddenly. The
faithful Florantha Sproat carried on as she had in all other domestic crises, continuing to act as "homemaker, doctor, cook, spinner
of yarn, knitter of stockings, in our homes as long as she lived—in
Yosemite and in San Francisco," Cosie recalled. Although no longer
guardian after 1884, Hutchings continued to occupy the cabin
where most, if not all, of his book *In the Heart of the Sierras* was
written. It soon became the classic work on the Yosemite region, the
Big Trees, and that territory contained in the several approaches.

10

ICE SCULPTURE

YOSEMITE IS DOUBTLESS the only mountain valley in the world
to have prompted so much speculation and controversy over its
origin and evolution, to have puzzled laymen and baffled scientists
for so long, and to have suggested so many diverse theories of
creation—flood, earthquake, volcanism, water and wind erosion,
lightning, and avalanches. Because of its unusual configuration
and the number and variety of distinctive rock forms, for it contains a greater collection than any other known area of equal size,
it seemed to defy interpretation. Many observers believed that it
was "an exceptional creation . . . accomplished by violent and
mysterious forces."

One noted geologist advanced the theory that during uplift of
the Sierra Nevada Range, or possibly just afterward, "the bottom
of the Valley sank to an unknown depth, owing to its support
being withdrawn from underneath during some of these convul-
sive movements." Its domes were formed during the upheaval as
great bubbles of liquid granite. "The Half Dome seems, beyond a
doubt, to have been split asunder in the middle, the lost half having gone down in what may truly be said to have been 'the wreck
of matter and the crush of worlds.'" Another scientist wrote that
an immense volcanic convulsion had caused the Sierra to be "reft
asunder, and a fissure formed," creating Yosemite Valley. Still an-

other scientist speculated that the valley floor, once level with the top of Yosemite Falls, was dropped by earthquake; while yet another found the whole answer in stream erosion, the peculiar rock structure being responsible for the unusual cliff formations and domes.

But it was James Mason Hutchings' sawyer and handyman, John Muir, who found the answer. Muir, who had studied geology during his last two years at the University of Wisconsin and was what might be called an intuitive scientist, found himself in direct disagreement with the cataclysmic theory of Yosemite Valley's origin. In 1868, the summer before going to work for Hutchings, Muir had herded sheep in the alpine meadows above the valley. He had observed many evidences of glacial action in the high country, had investigated what were obviously ancient glacier channels, and had discovered the basin of that great ice stream whose overflow branches he later traced into the valley by way of Tenaya and Merced canyons. To these he would attribute Yosemite Valley's final form, having been broadened, deepened, and sculptured by the movement of that vast glacier which filled nearly to its rim the original narrow gorge cut by the Merced River. Their forces had been "rigidly governed and directed by the peculiar physical structure of the granite."

After being hired by Hutchings, Muir spent all of his time off studying the evidence of glaciers throughout the valley and in the high country to the east of it—the direction from which the ice streams had come. At length he was ready to refute those explanations crediting violent forces. "Nature chose for a tool not the earthquake or lightning to rend and split asunder, not the stormy torrent or eroding rain, but the tender snow-flowers noiselessly falling through unnumbered centuries. . . . Laboring harmoniously in united strength they crushed and ground and wore away the rocks in their march," he wrote.

Eagerly he "preached" (as he said) his glacier theory to all who would listen; and to those who wanted to see, he showed the evidence in the valley and the highlands. He soon became the recognized proponent of this explanation of origin.

Clarence King, a member of the California State Geological Survey, which was headed by Josiah D. Whitney, had during exploration of Yosemite in the 1860s observed "ample evidence" of a glacier at least a thousand feet thick having once filled the valley.

However, since King agreed with his chief's subsidence theory, he did not credit the ice with any part of the valley's excavation, only with scouring and polishing after it was formed. But Whitney dismissed King's report by stating: "There is no reason to suppose, or at least no proof, that glaciers have ever occupied the Valley or any portion of it."

John Muir was soon attracting an audience, and by mid-1870 had gained the support of the famed scientist Louis Agassiz (Muir sent him details of his conclusions regarding Sierra glaciation) and the backing of Agassiz's pupil, the noted geologist Dr. Joseph LeConte, then professor at the newly established University of California. Feeling threatened, members of the State Geological Survey publicly branded Muir as "an ignoramus" and "a mere sheepherder"; Whitney announced that the glacier theory, "based on entire ignorance of the whole subject, may be dropped without wasting any more time upon it."

On the other hand, when John D. Runkle, president of the Massachusetts Institute of Technology, came to Yosemite late in the summer of 1871, he was fully convinced of the truth of Muir's readings. They spent five days examining the evidence of glacial erosion and discussing Muir's conclusions. Runkle urged him to write them out for the Boston Academy of Science. Muir told him that he intended to write his findings and thoughts for his own use, that he would send him the manuscript, and that if Runkle thought it of sufficient interest, the society was welcome to publish it. Actually Muir was undecided about whether to write for publication at this time, or wait until he had gathered more evidence and "say it all at a breath."

He decided to furnish Runkle with material (in letter form) and also to write an article, "Yosemite Glaciers," which he sent on to the New York *Daily Tribune*. This first published statement crediting glaciers with the creation of Yosemite Valley appeared in December 1871, just in time to establish Muir's claim. It was fortunate he had determined not to hold his "wheesht" [silence], as he had first thought he might, for his views and discoveries were hardly in print before Professor Samuel Kneeland of MIT read a paper before the Boston Society of Natural History, giving Muir credit "for all of the smaller sayings and doings" and reserving for himself "the broadest truth," Muir complained.

The State Geological Survey had also made the pronouncement

that there were no longer any glaciers in the Sierra Nevada. Muir was quite sure that many of their so-called snowbanks were actually glaciers, which were continuing on a modest scale the work of their vast and ancient predecessors. In August 1872, with the help of Galen Clark, Muir set stakes in an ice field on the slopes of Yosemite's Mount McClure. When he returned forty-five days later, Muir found that all five stakes had been carried downstream, and that stake number four, placed near the middle, close to the point of maximum velocity, had moved on the average an inch a day. Earlier, he discovered still more conclusive proof of living glaciers when he came on a stream carrying "mountain meal"— glacier mud. He traced it to its source in a "shadowy amphitheater" lying between Black and Red Mountain, two peaks in the Merced group. News of his findings that he sent to Joseph LeConte, in the form of two huge lumps of ice from the glaciers, brought the doctor to see for himself. Convinced, LeConte made in 1872 the first published announcement of the discovery of active glaciers in the Sierra, giving Muir full credit.

Again, a number of scientists were scornful. One of them, Clarence King, warned: "It is to be hoped that Mr. Muir's vagaries will not deceive geologists who are personally unacquainted with California, and that the ambitious amateur himself may divert his evident enthusiastic love of nature into a channel, if there is one, in which his attainments would save him from hopelessly floundering."

The debate over Yosemite's origin, often rancorous, continued for seventy years. Not until 1930, with the publication of an exhaustive study, "Geologic History of the Yosemite Valley," by the distinguished French geologist François E. Matthes was it settled, and Muir's theory of glacial erosion upheld. Matthes' project was commenced in 1913 for the U.S. Geological Survey, at the suggestion of the Sierra Club. To ascertain correctly the valley's origin and evolution, he found it necessary to make a preliminary investigation of the entire range.

Some sixty million years ago, that region where the Sierra Nevada mountains were to stand was still a coastal lowland with a warm, humid climate and luxuriant vegetation, which included hardwood forests of laurel, maple, sycamore, magnolia, and beech. Early in the Tertiary period there began a series of upthrusts which would be responsible for the range. Although the newly elevated block had only moderate altitude and a gentle westward slope, the old drainage system was largely replaced by a new set of master streams that flowed prevailingly to the southwest. The Merced River, one of these master streams, began trenching a broad valley that sloped gradually toward the sea which then occupied most of California's Great Central Valley. In its middle course, where Yosemite Valley developed, the river meandered leisurely. It was bordered on either side by rolling hills and occasional ridges averaging less than a thousand feet in elevation. One of these hills was El Capitan, which rose in gradual slopes to around nine hundred feet. Only the summit of Half Dome, "a bulky, irregularly shaped mass" of some fifteen hundred feet whose northwest face was furrowed by wooded ravines, and Clouds Rest stood well above the others. All sharp or angular contours were absent from the landscape. Even those peaks comprising the crest of the range were rounded mountains whose sides inclined gently to the base. In the valley that was to be Yosemite, there were as yet no waterfalls or cascades, for all of the Merced's tributaries joined it on its own level.

Late in the Tertiary period there came another series of uplifts, attended by intense volcanic activity, which raised the Sierra block and the country east of it, steepened the Merced's incline, and hastened its flow. So rapidly did the river work that within a relatively brief time it had cut itself a narrow, steep-sided inner gorge. During the long subsequent period of stability, it trenched its gorge into a rugged V-shaped canyon more than a thousand feet deep.

About a million years ago there were still greater upthrusts and tilting movements, and the range was raised to its present altitude, the summit peaks almost double their previous height. Mount Lyell, whose snows, glacier, and springs are the Merced's source, was lifted to over thirteen thousand feet, and the river, its course greatly steepened, became torrential. The augmentation of the river's volume by spring floods (the result of increased snowfall on the greatly elevated crest) so enlarged its cutting power that it produced a new, steep-walled inner gorge fifteen hundred feet deep, a chasm in which it still flows and which it continues to deepen as it leaves Yosemite Valley at the west.

High mountain ranges are climate makers, controlling in great measure their own weather conditions and those of adjacent areas.

The Sierra Nevada, lying parallel to the Pacific Coast, forms a lofty barrier over which moisture-laden winds from the ocean must pass. Forced to rise high, they are chilled and release their condensed water vapor. In winter, this falls chiefly in the form of snow. The final elevation of the Sierra coinciding with the arrival of a colder climate brought snow in such quantity to the heights that the summer sun was no longer able to melt it all. With successive winters, more snow was added to the residual fields, collecting into great masses of compacted snow which turned into ice and eventually into glaciers. These glaciers superseded the Sierran streams as cutting and erosive agents.

The glacial period in the Sierra Nevada was distinct from the vast continental ice sheet that covered most of Canada and the northern United States east of the Rocky Mountains, since it originated on the range itself. It was not a mantle, for the bulk of snow and ice lay in ravines and canyons, where it reached depths of hundreds, sometimes thousands, of feet, while the highest peaks were spread with but a thin layer or were often bare. However, in that region stretching from Lake Tahoe to Yosemite's Mount Lyell, where the crest of the range rises progressively to an altitude of well over thirteen thousand feet, it received huge amounts of moisture-laden air from the Pacific, a climax of glaciation was reached, and a true ice cap formed.

Glaciers entered the Yosemite chasm at least three times, a fact of which John Muir, Joseph LeConte, and other early advocates of the ice theory were unaware. During the earliest of these glacier invasions, the ice was three to four thousand feet deep, filling it to the rim. Only the summits of El Capitan, Boundary Ridge, Clouds Rest, Half Dome, and Sentinel Dome stood above the frozen mass "like islands of silver catching the thin fountain light of cold sunshine," as Muir described them. These successive periods of glaciation—particularly the earlier ones, which were heavier and of longer duration because of a colder climate—transformed the narrow, strongly winding river gorge into a deep, wide, and only slightly sinuous valley. The great ice mass, quarrying sideways as well as downward, ground, plucked, and trimmed the jutting spurs and craggy side walls characterizing the mountain valley stage. As Muir recognized, Yosemite's distinctive sculpturing was due to its varied rock structure, the closely jointed granites being worked into sharply pointed, many-faceted forms, while the unfractured rocks became sheer, smooth cliffs. Ice, however, was not alone responsible for Yosemite Valley's present depth, for as with all glaciation, there were periods hundreds of centuries long when the climate moderated, the glaciers melted back to the heights, and the Merced continued its downcutting.

Although the earlier ice invasions were responsible for extensively remodeling the landscape into the valley we know today, much refinement of cliff sculpture was accomplished during the last and least of the glacial periods, when the Yosemite chasm was filled to only one-third its depth. Then the exposed granite walls and spires were subject to intense frost action and other weathering, and to wear by frequent snow avalanches, which created their final form.

Yosemite's distinctive domes do not owe their roundness to overriding ice, as Muir believed, but to exfoliation—the casting off of successive shells or scales of rock arranged concentrically about one another very much like the layers of an onion, although not always convexly curved. These layers burst loose from the core of a dome because of expansive forces in the granite (as yet not thoroughly understood by geologists). Half Dome's sheer front, to which it owes its name, is also the result of exfoliation (shed here in plane sheets), and is not due to some catastrophic destruction of the mountain's front half.

With the departure of that final glacier, a great basin was left in the valley floor. At its west or lower end was a large glacial moraine that served as a dam for the lake which shortly occupied the basin. Although the filling of the lake began as the ice melted, the main work was done by the Merced River and Tenaya Creek. This ancient Lake Yosemite, which mirrored El Capitan and Half Dome on its placid surface, was five and a half miles long, and from one to three hundred feet deep. Each of its tributaries, carrying loads of sand and gravel, began gradually to build a delta at its point of entry in the lake. On the solid parts of this fill pine trees took root, and along its outer edges, willows. Over thousands of years the alluvial deposit, with its forest growth and other vegetation, spread toward the moraine; and Lake Yosemite, growing ever smaller, was at length extinguished. The Merced River, free once more, then began to trench a new bed through the delta plain and eventually breached the natural debris dam.

Yosemite Valley's unusual scenic character is due not only to its rock forms but also to its number of rare, free-leaping waterfalls. Few falls anywhere in the world plunge down sheer rock cliffs of such great height without being broken in their drop by projecting ledges—making them, properly speaking, cascades. With the first series of uplifts and tilting of the Sierra block, and the resultant acceleration of the Merced River, many of its tributaries, being of smaller volume and therefore less cutting power, were unable to keep pace. Others, having courses running northwest and southeast inherited from the old mountain system, were unaffected by the tilt and continued their meandering flow at right angles to the Merced. All of these tributaries, having their gorges cut off and left hanging above the vigorously trenching Merced, were forced to join it by means of cascades. Later, as the gradient leveled and the Merced cut more slowly, a few of these streams were able to catch up. But with the final upthrust, when the Merced was reaccelerated to torrential flow, those streams which had joined it at its own level were once again left far behind, and Yosemite acquired a second and lower set of hanging valleys. The display of tumbling cascades was then the valley's most distinguishing feature. With the coming of the glaciers and the cutting of craggy walls into smooth cliffs, the cascades were transformed into free-leaping waterfalls.

Since the end of the Ice Age, frost, heat, rain, wind, and running water have continued the work of shaping rock forms. Although most of Yosemite's great cliffs retain their glacial profiles, weathering, erosion, and dismantling have modified the austerity of ice sculpture and given the valley a less forbidding grandeur.

11

JOHN MUIR:
THE ALLURE
OF YOSEMITE

CHANCE BROUGHT about John Muir's startling discovery regarding the importance of glaciers in Yosemite Valley's origin and evolution.

In the fall of 1867 he completed a thousand-mile walk from Indiana to the Gulf of Mexico. It was his plan, he said, to explore next the mountains of Cuba, then go on to South America, land somewhere along its northern coast, push southward through the wilderness until he reached the Amazon, and float by raft or skiff down the great river to the sea. Had he been able to do so, he would have devoted much of his life to a study of that continent and might never have come to California.

He was penniless when he reached Cedar Keys on Florida's west coast that October after the long walk, and took work at a sawmill. Shortly he came down with a fever and lay in a coma for many days. He would have died had the mill owner not taken him into his home and his wife nursed Muir through the long illness.

After he left his bed he held to his plan, sailing for Havana in spite of his feebleness, but found himself too weak to venture into the mountains; instead, he spent his days botanizing outside the city. A month later, debilitated but still determined to drift down the Amazon, he looked about for a ship that would take him to South America. Unable to find one, he postponed that expedition and decided to go to California. Since it was not possible to make the voyage from Cuba, he had to sail for New York and there arrange a passage by sea to Panama, a crossing of the isthmus, and connection on the Pacific side with a steamer going up the coast.

Muir landed in San Francisco on March 27, 1868. Twenty-four hours in the city was enough for this man who disliked crowds and human bustle. Early the next morning he stopped a man he met on the street and asked the nearest way out of town. "But where do you want to go?" the man asked in turn.

"To any place that is wild" was the reply. Startled, and fearing that Muir might be crazy, he directed him to the closest exit— the ferry to Oakland.

Aboard ship to California Muir had met a cockney adventurer named Chilwell—"a most amusing and faithful companion"—and to him he now proposed that they take the ferry and find their way to Yosemite Valley, about which he had read. He suggested they travel light, going on foot, living on tea and flour-and-water cakes baked on the coals, and sleeping out in their blankets wherever night overtook them. Chilwell was agreeable, and he and Muir were soon heading south to the Great Central Valley.

It was spring and the air was spicy with the fragrance of millions of wildflowers; these covered the land so thickly that the hills and fields seemed to be enameled blue and orange and yellow— the "floweriest" part of the country Muir had yet seen. From the summit of Pacheco Pass he had his first view of the Sierra Nevada, edging a vast plain solid with shimmering yellow blooms—like a lake of gold.

Crossing the San Joaquin River at Hill's Ferry, they met the Merced, which Muir knew drained the Yosemite, and followed it into the foothills until they struck the Coulterville Trail. After several days spent in pushing over its rugged terrain, making their way across ravines and ridges and snowbanks—Muir in the lead, always at top speed—they reached a point from which there was a first view into Yosemite Valley. Muir was awestruck, but Chilwell was worried. Looking at the chasm floor nearly a mile below, then at the sheer, towering walls opposite, the little Englishman exclaimed: "Great God! have we got to cross *that gulch, too?*"

The eight days Muir spent exploring the valley, making sketches, collecting flowers and ferns, and observing birds and mammals cast a spell. Determined to go there again as soon as he had earned money enough to keep him in bread and tea for some while, he took a job as a ranch hand at Hopeton, on the Lower Merced River, breaking mustangs and helping with the harvest. After harvest, Chilwell who had also been hired, moved on, but Muir stayed to operate a ferry at Merced Falls, then to work as a sheep shearer for rancher Pat Delaney, near La Grange, on the Tuolumne River. After shearing was over, a neighboring sheep man, John Connel, known as Smoky Jack, hired Muir as a shepherd for thirty dollars a month and board. He accepted what Connel assured him would be a "foin aisy job" only because of the opportunities offered for studying flora, wild creatures, and weather.

By the end of May 1869, he was trying to plan a summer's excursion to Yosemite, wondering how he would be able to carry food enough to last that long, and whether he could learn to live like the birds on seeds and berries. In the midst of his quandary Pat Delaney came by with the solution: he wanted him to go with his flock to the headwaters of the Merced River, in the highlands above Yosemite Valley—not as a herder, for he had one, but as an overseer. College-educated, Delaney was interested in Muir's nature studies and assured him he would be free to continue them; all he wanted was a trustworthy person about camp to see that the shepherd did not neglect the flock. To further ease Muir's responsibilities, Delaney would ride with them to select their main Sierra camp and would afterward make periodic visits to renew food supplies and see that all was going well.

On June 3, the start was made—in a great cloud of dust churned up by the flock—Delaney, "bony and tall, with a sharply hacked profile like Don Quixote, leading the pack horse," among whose burdens was Muir's plant press. With his notebook tied to his belt, Muir brought up the rear. Trotting beside him was Carlo, a St. Bernard, lent him by an acquaintance, who had said, "I think I can trust you to be kind to him, and I am sure he will be good to you."

By mid-July the flock had eaten its way to the high pastures above Yosemite's north wall, and camp was made in a fir grove at the head of Indian Canyon Creek. Eagerly Muir anticipated his explorations of new mountains, canyons, forests, wild gardens, lakes and streams.

There was but one excursion into Yosemite Valley that summer, made under strange circumstances. Late one August afternoon as Muir sat on the summit of North Dome, sketching, he was suddenly overcome by a strong feeling that his friend and teacher from university days, Professor James Davie Butler, was in the valley below. Forgetting all else, he jumped up, ran along the canyon wall, and with Carlo at his heels, started down the first side ravine that promised access. Then realizing that he could not possibly reach the hotel until long after everyone was asleep, he turned back, resolved to make the trip in the morning. There was no real reason to believe Butler was there, for he had written Muir there was only a possibility he might come to California that summer.

The next morning Muir put on clean overalls, a cashmere shirt, and "a sort of a jacket," the pick of his camp wardrobe, and tying his notebook to his belt, started with Carlo down Indian Canyon. At Hutchings' hotel, Elvira responded to his question by saying she rather believed Professor Butler was there, but to make sure she would get the register. Muir soon picked out the familiar handwriting among the last entries. Learning that he and a companion, General Benjamin Alvord, had gone up the valley, probably to Vernal and Nevada falls, Muir hurried after them. In a little more than an hour he saw his friend, hot and tired, groping his way through brush and rocks, searching for the trail to Liberty Cap. Seeing Muir approaching and mistaking him for a valley guide, he asked the way. Muir pointed to the little cairns marking the route, and Butler called to his companion that the trail was found. As he prepared to go on, Muir asked, "Professor Butler, don't you know me?" "I think not" was the reply. But looking closely into his face there was sudden recognition: "John Muir, John Muir, where did you come from?"

Muir then told the story of his experience the previous afternoon. Instead of continuing his climb, Butler turned back with Muir toward the valley, the two talking constantly of school days and Madison friends; pausing every now and then to admire the great cliffs, hazy and mysterious in the gloaming; and reciting poetry. It was a "rare ramble," Muir noted. He had dinner at the hotel with Butler and Alvord, and was embarrassed by the attention called to him when Alvord introduced him to the dozen or so guests at table by telling the story of his having *felt* Butler's presence. "This is the queerest case of Scotch farsightedness I ever heard of," the general remarked.

After dinner Muir and Butler talked long together, alone, and Muir tried to persuade him to return with him to the highland camp for a ramble among Yosemite peaks; but the professor planned to leave the next day. In the morning, as he and Carlo scrambled up Indian Canyon, Muir was overcome with pity for his friend and the general so bound by "clocks, almanacs, orders [and] duties."

Because of attacks by bears, the sheep camp had to be moved east toward the upper Tuolumne region, where Muir was to discover so many evidences of glacial action and to begin building his theory for their part in the creation of Yosemite Valley. He learned all the geological lessons he could within the limited time available: climbing the peaks; noting the importance of cleavage joints in their sculpturing; investigating moraines and glacier-made lakes and meadows; mapping the pathways of ice streams; constantly observing, sketching, and describing everything he saw. Flora, birds, and mammals were included in these studies. When the day came for a return to the lowlands, he told himself that he would surely be back, for no other place had so "overwhelmingly attracted" him.

After eight weeks spent in building fences, plowing, and breaking horses for Pat Delaney, he could no longer resist Yosemite Valley's allure. "I am bewitched, enchanted," he told a friend, and must start at once for the "great temple" to hear its "winter songs and sermons."

In November he and Harry Randall, a friend and fellow ranch hand, "laden like pack animals," set off on foot for Yosemite. They passed a week in and around the valley, climbing, sketching, and plant collecting, before selling themselves, as Muir said, to James Mason Hutchings to reconstruct the sawmill, feed livestock, build hen roosts and laying boxes, and watch over Elvira and her mother, since Hutchings was going to Washington on business relating to the state's eviction suit. Although he and Randall would board at Hutchings' house, the day after being hired they started work on a cabin of their own along Yosemite Creek, not far from the foot of the falls. When finished, Muir declared it the handsomest structure in the valley. By means of a ditch he diverted water from the creek and led it along one inside wall, not only for the sake of convenience but for its music as well. With the coming of spring, ferns pushed through the cracks in the slab floor, two of which, growing vinelike because of the lack of light, Muir trained around the window that faced the falls, to frame his desk. Little tree frogs often climbed the ferns and sang with the water at night. To afford themselves moonlit views of Yosemite Falls, he and Randall hung their hammock beds from the rafters.

Muir established a warm relationship with the women and children of the Hutchings household, and with Elvira in particular he shared a deep interest in flora. Cosie Hutchings recalled him holding her or Floy on his knee as he patiently taught them the parts of wildflowers, and remembered following him through the woods and meadows on flower hunts. She also had a mental picture of this gentle man talking to her little crippled brother as he sat in his bath—typical, she felt, of his "kindly understanding for helpless things." Often the two girls would come to Muir's cabin and beg for food (Elvira was a diet faddist, and the children never got quite enough to eat). Then Muir shared his bread and contrived with Harry Randall, who milked the cow, to take them to the barn and give them as much as they could drink.

With Hutchings it was another story. The class-conscious innkeeper was resentful of his handyman's superior knowledge in many fields and considered it effrontery for him to publicly disagree with the state geologists' subsidence theory, to which he, Hutchings, subscribed and which he expounded to his guests. For six years he had been the authority on Yosemite—the center of attention as a journalist, poet, and philosopher. He had been mentioned in the writings of his literary guests and was greatly admired and flattered by women tourists. He now had a rival in his handsome hired man, whose popularity as a guide, a duty into which he was pressed during Hutchings' absences, soon matched Hutchings' own. Fortunate was the tourist who could have John Muir show him or her about the valley, observed the journalist and poet Sarah Jane Lippincott. She was delighted by his "quiet, quaint humor" and "simple eloquence"; admired his "clear blue eye . . . firm, free step, and marvelous nerve and endurance" in high places; and was impressed with his "serious air and unconventional ways," the result of long communing with nature in "her solitary, grand places."

An ever-lengthening procession of eminent scientists, writers, painters, and other notables began arriving at Yosemite with introductory letters to Muir from Jeanne Carr, wife of his chemistry and natural science professor at the University of Wisconsin. The Carrs were perhaps Muir's closest friends in Madison, particularly Jeanne, a pretty little woman with "tawny hair, a sweet expression, and a charming voice" who shared his preoccupation with botany (a subject she taught); who developed a maternal interest in his welfare, and ambitions for his future. She was ever a sympathetic listener to his soul's outpourings (she had sons of her own), and to her he wrote his finest letters. At this time Ezra Carr had accepted a professorship at the University of California, and the family had moved to Oakland. Mrs. Carr was anxious for Muir to have the stimulation of kindred minds and an ever-wider audience for his glacier theory. She had made her first visit to Yosemite Valley in 1869, when Muir was in the highlands with Pat Delaney's flock. She had stayed at Hutchings' hotel, and through her interest in local flora, became a close friend of Elvira. Afterward they corresponded regularly, and Elvira supplied her with bulbs, roots, and seeds of Yosemite wildflowers for the Oakland garden. James Hutchings realized that Mrs. Carr's requests for Muir to guide her friends were not to be ignored; a practical consideration was that most of them stopped at his inn. Although not always gracious, Hutchings did allow Muir to leave his work and conduct them about the valley and into high country.

Muir was grateful to Jeanne Carr: "I owe all my best friends to you." But for the ordinary tourist he had little tolerance: "All sorts of human stuff is being poured into our Valley . . . and the blank, fleshly apathy with which most of it comes in contact with the rock and water spirits is most amazing." Except when called on by Hutchings to act as guide, he was able to avoid "*the world* and his ribbony wife," since he, Muir, kept mainly to "pathless places" where they had no wish to go.

One of these places was a ledge he called Sunnyside Bench, on the valley's north wall. It was approached by way of Indian Canyon and was once used by the Ahwahneeches as a lookout. Muir used it as a place of study, since the entire valley was spread before him like a map. He often spent the night among the ferns and flowers in this high rock garden to note the action of the falls at different times—they had an ebb and flow similar to tides; to observe dawn and sunset, temperature changes, storm patterns, and shadows. It was here he discovered the important role of shadow in glaciation: seeing that the valley's shaded south wall was quarried and eroded far more than the sunny north cliffs, he reasoned that the protective coolness of shadows not only gave birth to glaciers but prolonged their lives and therefore their erosive power. He found that shadows on the valley floor coincided with forest growth on moraines, and that there was a definite relationship between these shadows and the meadows, groves, and river bends.

No one has made a more intensive, prolonged, and reverent study of Yosemite Valley and the high country than John Muir. No one understood it better. Nothing was too insignificant for notation; nothing overlooked: a grasshopper's trail in the dust; the lisp of a snowflake alighting; fern fronds uncoiling; the distant calls of Canada geese winging high above the valley on winter nights; the silence following each big storm; the lunar bows in Yosemite Falls at full moon; the night shadows of trees and rocks cast by Venus' light.

To comprehend Yosemite it was not enough to observe it scientifically: he must feel it, become a part of it: "I sail softly through the canyons . . . like a wind full of thistledown." He wished for clothing the color of granite so that he might merge with his surroundings. He must exult in its triumphs: "I shouted until I was exhausted and sore with excitement" as Yosemite Falls, at the height of flow, seethed "like a maddened onset of all the wild spirits of the mountain sky." He must find spiritual affinity: "I have been bathing in the Ganges," as he called his sacred Merced. "I wonder if I will ever know another river like this." He must lie on the rocks, as the ice had done, to arrive "at the truths which are graven so lavishly upon them."

One April afternoon he took his blanket and a piece of bread to Fern Ledge, intent on spending the night communing with Yosemite Falls. As he saw the stars shining through the mist clouds, watched the moon turn the waters silvery and irised, he was tempted to venture behind the torrent, and in a kind of trance he followed a little seam extending from the cliff face. As he looked up the falls to the brow of rock above, everything suddenly grew black, and he was struck by masses of water driven against the back wall. He crouched low and held his breath, expecting each moment to be swept away. When it grew light again as the fall swayed outward, he retreated rapidly along the rock shelf to a "snug place." There he built a fire, and at midnight, while drying out, described his "baptism" in a letter to Jeanne Carr: "I am in the upper Yosemite Falls and can hardly calm to write." It was an adventure, he admitted later to his sister, that had "nearly cost all."

By October, Harry Randall was tired of chores and millwork, and decided to return to Pat Delaney. Muir, who wanted to extend his glacier studies into the foothills and was therefore anxious to explore the lower Merced gorge, went with him. They were probably the first white men to travel over this route, today one of the main entrances into the valley. Muir intended to return to Yosemite almost at once, to trace some of the upper stream courses before snows buried them, but the Don, as he called Delaney, asked him to plow his fields first. Hutchings, irked at Muir's delay, wrote that he was going to let his sister use Muir's cabin (which stood on Hutchings' claim). Muir was in turn annoyed at Hutchings for "jumping my nest after expressly promising to keep it for me." Homeless or not, he was determined to go back and continue the tracing of glacier pathways. Further, he had left his notebooks and sketches behind; and finally, Hutchings owed him money.

It was evidently not until February that he started back to Yosemite, with Carlo the St. Bernard, and a young man he had talked into walking with him over the snowy mountains. He seems to have had use of his cabin for some part of this season, for Jeanne Carr wrote, "I think with delight of how the winter home looks, of little brown 'Squirrel' in the glow of the firelight." But by April he was sleeping in the mill, enjoying the "murmuring hush" of the stream beneath him, and had suspended from the building's west gable a boxlike room, a "hang-nest" for a study and retreat. On either slope of the nest's pitched roof were skylights, the one commanding a view of Half Dome; the other of Upper Yosemite Fall, while a window in the west end surveyed the valley's stands of cedars and pines. Access was by way of a set of rough, sloping planks with slats nailed horizontally, like a hen walk. It pleased him that only those people he disliked were afraid to climb it.

Many of Muir's friends, failing to comprehend the depth and scope of his studies, were urging him to leave the mountains and broaden his sphere. Jeanne Carr was the most persistent in pressing him to abandon solitude, join waiting society, and turn to books for further knowledge. No scientific book in the world could tell him how Yosemite granite had been formed or taken down, he countered. Only patient observation and ceaseless brooding over the rocks for years could furnish the answers. As to the refining influences of society which she stressed as necessary, they were "gross barbarisms" when compared to the purity and wonder of nature. In every act of nature—in earthquakes, in storms, in the movement of glaciers—there was reason, beauty, and harmony.

Tired of the uncongenial millwork and the increasingly irksome relationship with Hutchings, Muir quit his job early in July 1871. Free to devote full time to his mountain studies, he was soon ready to start for the high country, a blanket and some flour and coffee tied behind his saddle. First he would cross the Sierra by way of the old Indian trade route, through that country in which he had followed Delaney's flock, to the volcanic region around Mono Lake to resolve some problems; then on his return read "new chapters in glacial manuscript" around the slopes of Yosemite's Mounts Dana, Gibbs, and Lyell. When deep snow brought his work to an end, he would make himself a nest of moss and leaves in some sheltered nook and doze until spring. Mid-November, however, found him settled in a cabin at Black's hotel as its winter caretaker, enjoying such creature comforts as plenty to eat, long warm sleeps in a soft bed, and a roof to keep off the snow. There was no one left in the valley, though, with whom he could exchange a thought, for Elvira Hutchings, the only permanent resident who was entirely sympathetic with his pursuits and one of the few who did not consider him a little crazy, was going to Washington with her husband, who was still fighting the eviction suit. Before leaving, she gave Muir the pick of their library—a poor substitute for company to a man who regarded most books as mere "piles of stones set up to show travelers where other minds have been." Although he appreciated solitude, recognized its importance to his work, and scorned the "Babylonish mobs," he was no hermit, and often hungered for companionship of the right sort. A brilliant talker, he relished nothing better than an appreciative audience— even an audience of one. "If allowed to talk on interruptedly, he regales his hearers with a monologue of exceptional range and raciness," a friend noted.

But there was enough to occupy him that winter, what with working up his sketches and outline glacier maps, filling out his notes, keeping up his wide correspondence, and writing articles, which friends were urging him to do. His first, "Yosemite Glaciers," appeared in the New York *Daily Tribune* that December (1871), and was followed by a second and third, "Yosemite in Winter," and "Yosemite in Spring," both printed in the same paper the next year. As much as he disliked the mechanics of this form of writing, he now described a storm he experienced and sent the manuscript —"Yosemite Valley in Flood"—to Jeanne Carr, who placed it with the *Overland Monthly*.

That winter he watched the making of the great ice cone formed each season by frozen spray at the foot of Upper Yosemite Fall. The entire body of the fall plunges into its gaping mouth with "deep, gasping explosions of compressed air," and rushes out through arched openings at the cone's base. After it had reached its maximum height—some 250 feet—he grew anxious to examine its structure and interior, but all of his first attempts to even approach it were frustrated by blinding, suffocating blasts of wind and water. At length, one calm day he was able, by cutting footholds with an axe and hugging the surface so that most of the choking currents passed over him, to creep nearly to the apex. While he waited for the fall to be blown aslant so that he could crawl onto the opening and peer inside, he was aware of the thundering throbs beneath him, the ice hill vibrating like a giant drum in response to the pounding water. Suddenly a mass of frozen spray, tons in weight, broke from the wall high above and struck the cone, narrowly missing him. With it came another smothering blast of wind-driven water, forcing him to retreat.

Weeks passed before another opportunity came. Then one morning he saw his chance when a windstorm blowing from the east swung the fall aside for as long as half an hour at a time. Taking advantage of one of those periods, he scrambled to the summit of the cone. He saw that the mouth was black, and broken and ragged like a crater. He estimated its diameter at a hundred feet north and south, and around two hundred east and west. Looking down into the sparkling chamber, he watched briefly the maddened thrashing of the entrapped waters and the frenzied swirl of silvery mists.

At two-thirty in the morning of March 26, 1872, he was awakened by a severe earthquake. Knowing that he would be learning new lessons in mountain-making, he ran out of his cabin, shouting excitedly, "A noble earthquake!" He found the shocks so heavy and continuous that he had to balance himself in walking, as though on the deck of a storm-tossed ship. Then, for a minute or two, the convulsions grew yet more violent, and it seemed as though every Yosemite wall must tumble. But before a single rock fell, he was convinced that earthquakes were in great measure the talus makers. As if in confirmation, there came a tremendous roar, and Eagle Rock, on the south wall not far from Moran Point, gave way.

Muir watched entranced as it poured in a free curve, "luminous from friction . . . an arc of glowing, passionate fire . . . as true in form and as steady as a rainbow." Racing toward it in the moonlight, he was in time to leap upon the new-born talus before it had come to rest, hearing its groanings and whisperings as the boulders settled in place.

With the coming of daylight he walked around to see what other changes there were. On reaching Hutchings' hotel he found the white residents in a little group in front, all frightened and considering flight. As they talked in hushed tones, there came another series of jolts of such intensity as to make the cliffs and domes tremble, to cause the great oaks and pines to wave their branches uncannily, and to settle the minds of most winter residents about escaping to the lowlands. To one of them, a firm believer in the subsidence theory, Muir could not refrain from remarking that his "wild tumble-down-and-engulfment" explanation might soon be proved, for the valley floor could well drop double its depth, leaving the ends of the trails and wagon roads dangling thousands of feet in midair. Then, seeing that the man was completely unnerved, Muir tried to make light of the situation by telling him to smile and clap his hands now that "kind Mother Nature is trotting us on her knee to amuse us." But his acquaintance was in no mood for banter. Hastily handing Muir the keys to his store, he started out of the valley with a companion who shared his views. As Muir walked off he overheard some in the group calling him a fool, and others saying he was crazy.

There were earthquakes every day for over two months, and Muir kept a bucket of water on his table to learn what he could of their movements. During this time he studied the results: the most numerous and obvious changes were in the streams. Their channels, filled or half-dammed by fallen boulders, forced waters that formerly flowed smoothly to roar and surge in rapids; and where their beds were entirely choked by debris, they took new courses or were turned into ponds and lakes. While still at the peak of excitement over this "sublime" earthquake and over his good fortune in being able to witness this form of mountain-, canyon-, and stream-making, he wrote his observations and experiences and sent them to the *Daily Tribune*, which printed them; a similar account was given the Boston Society of Natural History.

April found him at work on a cabin for himself just opposite the Royal Arches, in the angle formed by Tenaya Creek and the Merced, about fifteen or twenty yards from the creek bank. There in July, at this new home (which was never finished) he welcomed Harvard's Asa Gray, the country's leading botanist and exponent of Charles Darwin. Gray came to Muir's door bearing an introductory note from Jeanne Carr. The two men, often with Gray's wife, spent a week botanizing in the valley and among its immediate high places. During their rambles he urged Muir to come to Harvard and teach. Muir explained that he could not leave his mountain work unfinished; moreover, he had been wild too long "to burn well in their patent, high-heated, educational furnaces." After Gray reached home, full of enthusiasm for his Yosemite jaunt, he sent a list of plants he wanted Muir to gather for Harvard's Botanic Garden. His special interest was the carmine-red Sierra primrose. Late one day after he had taken some measurements on Half Dome, Muir sped on to Clouds Rest for the primula. He described for Gray his return: "I ran in the moonlight with your sack of roses slung on my shoulder by a buckskin string —down through the junipers, down through the firs, now in black shadow, now in white light," through the "spiry pines of the open valley, star crystals sparkling above, frost crystals beneath."

The botanist's visit gave new impetus to Muir's study of Yosemite flora, for earlier he had been handicapped in determining species by the lack of proper keys. Now Gray not only sent him his own texts but offered to identify specimens. As Muir pursued his geologic calculations he also hunted for plants. One unfamiliar high-country flower he forwarded, Gray found to be a "wee mouse-tail Ivesia," which he named *Ivesia muirii*. An advocate of Muir's ice erosion theory, he wrote: "Get a new alpine genus, that I may make a *Muiria glacialis*!"

That summer (1872) Jeanne Carr tried determinedly to pry Muir from Yosemite. "This is what you are going to do," began a letter programming his activities for the coming fall and winter. She set up his headquarters at her home and had him spend his time writing, studying in libraries, and exchanging thoughts with kindred minds. For variety, he was to explore the Coast Range. Her approach had exactly the opposite effect. He had no intention of abandoning his work in the mountains, nor was he a man who could be forced. Almost immediately after receiving her letter he set off to plant glacier stakes. Upon his return he wrote her that he and his horse were ready for still more "upward." It was impossible to put into words the glow that lighted him at this thought: "I feel strong to leap Yosemite walls at a bound. Hotels and human impurity will be far below. I will fuse with spirit skies."

Failing to draw Muir into company, Mrs. Carr sent the company to him. On coming back from this expedition he found three of her painter friends—William Keith, Benoni Irwin, and Thomas Ross—looking for him. She had instructed Irwin to sketch Muir in his "hay-rope" suspenders, tattered trousers (the waist "eked out with a grass band"), and ragged shirt, with the sprig of greenery or flowering sedge he customarily wore in his buttonhole—against the day when he had become famous and had a string of degrees attached to his name. What impressed the three artists was not his dress, but his striking resemblance to classic renditions of Jesus.

Muir and Keith (both Highlanders, born in Scotland the same year) became friends at once, and were soon calling each other Willie and Johnnie. Keith now told Muir what he had in mind to paint: did he know of any such place? Only yesterday Muir had seen the very thing at Mount Lyell where he was setting glacier stakes, and would take him there. Late the next afternoon they reached the spot. Saying nothing, Muir reined his horse aside and waited for the reaction. Keith "dashed ahead shouting and gesticulating and tossing his arms in the air like a mad man." "It was the grandest thing I ever saw," he said later. Over the years he and Muir took many another high-country excursion in search of picture subjects. "There's naebody like a Scotchman to see beauty," Muir felt.

Once Muir began to write regularly for publication he found he rather enjoyed it. There was considerable satisfaction, too, in having the public read everything he wrote, as well as getting paid for it, he admitted to a sister. All of this writing was being done, he told her, with a quill he had made from a golden eagle wing feather found on the slopes of Mount Hoffmann. That December (1872) he made a hurried trip to Oakland and San Francisco to further publication plans by a meeting with the *Overland Monthly*'s editors, and to consult with Jeanne Carr, who was acting as his literary agent. His friends took advantage of this rare opportunity and swept him into a vortex of social activity—dinners, receptions, and introductions to such literary lights as Ina Coolbrith, Edward Rowland Sill, and Charles Warren Stoddard, Robert Louis Stevenson's close friend. They even rushed him to the photographer for a portrait. Homesick for Yosemite and depressed by the cities— "wastes of civilization"—he made a sudden break for freedom.

Once back in the valley he bathed in his sacred Merced to remove the taint. But afterward, still feeling "muddy and weary," he knew he must seek further purification among the heights. Stuffing some hard bread in his pocket, and taking along barometer, chronometer, and notebook, he started for the highlands by way of Tenaya Canyon, then as now, "accessible only to determined mountaineers." After passing the fine conifer groves that stretch for a mile above Mirror Lake, and scrambling around Tenaya Fall, he began the ascent of a steep rock face.

Although footholds were firm, he suddenly stumbled and fell, for the first time since he had come into the Sierra, and rolled head over heels down the cliff. When he regained consciousness after an hour, he found himself wedged among some short, stiff bushes, uninjured beyond a head bruise and some minor abrasions. He saw that if he had rolled only a bit more his climbing days would have been over. He felt worthless and angry with himself. "There," he said, sternly addressing his feet whose separate skills he had come to rely on night and day on any kind of mountain, "that is what you get by intercourse with stupid town stairs and dead pavements." Determined to discipline his body, he led himself into the "most intricate and nerve-trying places." That night, "no plush boughs did my ill-behaved bones receive . . . nor did my bumped head get any spicy cedar-plumes for a pillow. I slept on a naked bowlder."

When he awakened in the morning he knew that the last of the "town-fog" had been dispelled. Around noon of the third day he made his way out of the canyon, after "accomplishing some of the most delicate feats of mountaineering I ever attempted." At the canyon's head lies Tenaya Lake, which Muir found frozen solid, the ice so clear and unruffled that every peak and lofty pine was reflected as sharply as in "the calm evening mirrors of summer." He spent a number of days in the Tuolumne Basin studying and reaffirming the evidences of the vast and ancient ice sea that had once filled it; then he started for home. He returned from this excursion restored—resurrected, it seemed to him, from some "strange and half-remembered death."

By the next September Muir knew that Yosemite Valley was "the *end* of a grand chapter," which could be understood only by reading what had come before. This meant carrying his glacier researches into the Sierra Nevada Range itself. Early in the month he started off on horseback with Galen Clark—"the best mountaineer I ever met, and one of the kindest and most amiable of my mountain friends"—for an exploration of the Sierra from the southern tip to Lake Tahoe.

His discoveries of still more living glaciers, and his botanical and wildlife observations during this trip of over a thousand miles, furnished him with enough material for a series of articles, "Studies in the Sierra," which the *Overland* agreed to publish. In spite of his previous unhappy experience in the Bay Area cities, and his present misgivings, he yielded to Jeanne Carr's persuasions to winter in Oakland. There he spent ten months in spiritual exile, chafing over his physical confinement and becoming increasingly disillusioned with the "metallic, money-clinking crowds" who saw the world as having been made solely for their exploitation. He despaired of ever gaining a hearing with them on behalf of nature as he saw it, but hoped to win converts among scientists.

By the following summer he had completed seven articles, but lack of exercise and depression had undermined his health. Unable to ignore Yosemite's call any longer, he set out one day for the mountains, in such a rush that he forgot to conclude important business. At Turlock his impatience overcame him; he left the train and headed for the Sierra on foot. Feeling "wild" once more, strength and endurance miraculously returned as he hastened over the sweltering plains. At the ranch where he had put his sturdy little mule to pasture, he rested until the cool of evening; then mounting Browny, cantered across the fields of fragrant tarweed to Pat Delaney's, where he was welcomed in that "good old uncivilized way, not to be misunderstood," and pressed to spend the night.

In Yosemite he once again found physical and spiritual renewal. After sleeping four nights at Merced Lake, along the upper reaches of that river, he declared himself "hopeless and forever a mountaineer." He knew he could not stay in the region that entire season, for there were glacier studies to continue in the ranges beyond, to fill out Yosemite's story. But he constantly postponed departure day, meanwhile seeking out all his favorite haunts. One morning in late October, after a month of lingering, he reluctantly started on his way to hunt for active ice fields and ancient glacier channels on Mount Shasta.

12

CAPTAIN YELVERTON'S CURSE

THE HONORABLE THÉRÈSE YELVERTON arrived in Yosemite Valley unheralded. Although she was a friend of Jeanne Carr, she brought no introductory note to John Muir. That was the way she wanted it. She was trying to keep her movements secret, for she had an ever-present horror of being tracked by Captain Yelverton. A century later almost no one has heard of Thérèse Yelverton, but among those who have, there is a disposition to belittle her accomplishments and say nothing about her beauty and charm. In 1870, when she went to Yosemite, it was impossible for her to remain inconspicuous, for she was one of the most noted women of her day, and newspapers reported her every activity. Her name was a household word, for her story had been carried to all parts of the English-speaking world not only by the press but by such noted novelists as Wilkie Collins; by playwrights; and through her own speeches and writings.

As soon as she signed the register at the hotel, Hutchings recognized her. Delighting in celebrities, he invited her to become a member of his household, which meant that she took her meals and spent evenings at their cabin; he also suggested that she rent a cottage viewing the river, rather than a room.

Into thirty-four years she had already crowded a lifetime of experience and adventure. To those of her friends who asked, she told how as a child she had fled, with her mother and older sisters, the tyranny of an eccentric father, a prosperous silk merchant of Manchester, England, who was a religious zealot; how to escape persecution they were forced to live in hiding, like criminals. She related the story of that day when, as an orphaned schoolgirl in France, she saved the life of Napoleon III, who had been shot in a skirmish not far from the convent where she was a pupil, and was left untended; he would have bled to death had she not discovered him and bound a cloth tightly above his wound. In recognition of this act, while in her teens she was chosen by the Empress Eugénie to serve as her maid of honor at court. She recounted her experiences as a nurse during the Crimean War and spoke of the time when after a battle, a ship came into Galata with a thousand Russian prisoners, many of whom had cholera. Her compassion for the wounded and dying overruled the warnings to stay away, and she was the first to board and bring relief. She told, too, how it happened that while she was still in her twenties she spoke four consecutive days in the House of Lords, where no woman but the queen was ever heard.

In the summer of 1852 the sixteen-year-old Thérèse Longworth, as she was then, left France for England. Her escort on the voyage was an Irish officer in the Royal Artillery, an older man, Captain William Yelverton, the son and heir of the impecunious Viscount Avonmore. Upon reaching London he saw her safely to the house of a relative, the Marchioness de la Belline, and the following day paid a courtesy call. He admitted later that he was impressed by the rank and style of living of his young charge's kin, and wished for some excuse to become better acquainted. But shortly he was stationed in Malta, and there was no further contact until just before the Crimean War, when they began a correspondence that grew from her request for help in a business matter into a regular exchange of love letters. At the war's outbreak in 1854, Yelverton was dispatched to the front, in command of a battery of siege artillery, and Thérèse, then studying music and painting in Naples, joined the French Sisters of Charity as a lay member.

At Galata she and the captain met again. He declared his love and spoke of marriage, and she accepted him as a fiancé. Then one day he confessed that he was under "pecuniary difficulties" and had promised his father never to marry any woman who could not pay his debts. Three thousand pounds would cover his needs. In that case their engagement would have to be broken, Thérèse said, for her modest inheritance was in trust, and the interest was her only income. She asked him not to come again, but a week later he was back, with the proposal that they be married secretly at the Greek church in Balaklava. She refused, since she was a Roman Catholic, as he also claimed to be.

After the war she went to stay with a friend in Edinburgh. Yelverton, who was stationed in nearby Leith, called with the suggestion this time that they be married in the Scotch fashion: he had only to read aloud the ritual in the presence of a witness, then acknowledge her as his wife. Over her protests he called in a neighbor and read the rite, but she refused to live with him. Agreeing at length on a Roman Catholic ceremony, they met in a remote village in Ireland and were married on August 15, 1857, by the parish priest. Yelverton, however, withheld his surname from the church records. A few weeks later Thérèse supplied it.

Following a wedding tour of the Continent, the captain returned to his post at Leith, leaving Thérèse at Bordeaux, sick and pregnant. Before going he extracted a promise that she keep their marriage secret: "If you break your faith with me . . . be prepared for disgrace and humiliation," he warned. To register a child's birth in France it was necessary to present proof of marriage. Thérèse therefore obtained from the priest a copy of the certificate, on which Yelverton's full name now appeared.

After recovering from a stillbirth, Thérèse wrote that she was ready to come to Leith. In his reply the captain told her to "go to the ends of the earth" and hide herself—to save him from ruin. She returned to the house of her Edinburgh friend, and while there heard the news of Yelverton's marriage to a Mrs. Forbes of that city, a widow of "large fortune."

Thérèse immediately sued for alimony, and the captain, denying that he had ever married her, instituted the first in a series of court actions that were to take her from England to Scotland to Ireland and back to England, submitting her to seventeen trials, which he expected would break her spirit—a tactic that failed, for she once said that she liked nothing better than "the rush and strife of battle."

Public sentiment was on her side, and "sympathizing strangers and titled men" deposited large sums of money to help her meet expenses. Newspaper correspondents had been won early in the proceedings by her charm and candor, and by the indisputable proofs furnished by the marriage certificate and the witness to the Scotch rite that she was Yelverton's lawful wife—twice over. Reporters described her appearance and her apparel. She was about twenty-five years old and under middle height. Her figure was "admirably proportioned," and there was a "perfection of grace in her simplest movements." Her complexion was fair and her eyes were blue and "indicative of mental vigor and great tenderness." Her golden hair, "rich and glossy," was worn brushed high in the "French style." Although her features were not perfectly regular, with animation she became "wondrously handsome." She appeared in court on her first day in a "black silk moiré antique dress," a black velvet mantilla, a fashionable French bonnet in white, and mauve-colored gloves—proof, in one reporter's eyes, of "flawless" taste.

During cross-examination she exhibited "marked self-command, wit, and coolness." Her responses demonstrated "an intelligence, a quickness of comprehension, and a power of language rarely met with in a lady, even in the present intellectual age, when the education of females receives so much attention." A lovely young woman maligned by a blackguard (much of his testimony was too scurrilous for print) was an ever-popular theme, and readers the world over avidly followed the developments in what was known as "The Great Yelverton Marriage Case," heralded as "the most extraordinary trial of modern times."

Once during the progress of a court action, she met Yelverton in a railroad car. They were alone, and he immediately broached the subject of the marriage certificate. He tried at first to get it from her by persuasion, then bribery, and finally threats. Furious at his failure, he laid on her a curse: might she know every sorrow and misery during her lifetime, and die an agonizing death alone and far from help.

After the seventeenth and final trial, held in Dublin in 1861, firmly established the legality of both marriages, the captain vanished, to escape the bigamy suit that would automatically follow. This left Thérèse unable, according to British law, to collect interest from her own property. The public, angered over her plight, burned Yelverton in effigy.

One hope remained: to outlaw him and recover her inheritance.

It was for this purpose that she appeared before the House of Lords in 1864. By choice she was her own counsel and prepared her plea in the House library. She opened her case and spoke from ten o'clock in the morning until four in the afternoon, with only half an hour's intermission. One who heard her wrote that her voice was "almost trumpet-toned at times, then cadenced to . . . liquid melody that touched the depths of the heart." Her speech took four days to deliver. Each night as she sat in her hotel room reviewing her notes, she heard the shrill cries of the newsboys running through the streets with extras carrying the full text of her day's talk.

When the eminent attorney Sir John Ralt rose to reply, he spoke in Latin, hoping to confuse her. Coolly she asked for a translation, then read his text line by line, refuting errors in fact. Although the legality of both marriages was established once again, the majority in the House of Lords refused to sanction the outlawing of William Yelverton, who was heir to their distinguished title.

Robbed of her inheritance, Thérèse turned to writing books, lecturing, and giving dramatic readings for support. Meeting with considerable success, she was encouraged to go to the United States. In the fall of 1869 she arrived in San Francisco after a profitable tour through the eastern states. On learning from the newspapers that she was in town, the young poet Charles Warren Stoddard sent a note to her hotel, offering to help publicize her appearances. He had read her first novel, which was autobiographical, had been impressed by its "superb descriptions" and "recital of thrilling adventure," and "longed very much to meet this lady . . . take her by the hand and call her friend." This he told her, and she responded by return post, asking him to call. Over the months (she stayed in California nearly two years) they became close friends, and he noted characteristics others who were to write about her either failed to see or neglected to mention.

There was a good deal of the Bohemian in her, he found, and she fitted well into his circle. When in company, her repartee was brilliant. She was a lonely woman, he realized, appreciative of affection and lavish with her own for those who offered friendship. She was, however, sometimes suspicious of those who paid her marked attention, fearing they might be spies or even assassins in the pay of Captain Yelverton, whose curse haunted her. As she and Stoddard walked beside the bay or roamed the hills of Sausalito, where she retreated for the winter, he became aware how very much "a child of nature" she was.

From Stoddard, who had spent six months in Yosemite Valley, she learned much about it. It should be approached only at sunset, he told her: "Then the magnificence of the spectacle culminates. . . . One should sleep on the brink of that Valley, dream of it all night, and drop down into it on the wings of morning." The following spring she was there, going in by way of the Mariposa Grove and Galen Clark's.

She was charmed with the Hutchings cabin and gave details of its main room: on the wood-paneled walls hung engravings of the old masters and oil paintings of Yosemite scenes. On one side was a bookcase holding the eight hundred volumes; and opposite, a fireplace formed of four huge granite slabs. "Great logs, five or six feet long, raised on antique irons, blazed and crackled." The furniture was chiefly rustic: an easy chair made of gnarled manzanita branches; tables and writing desk to which were attached acorns, fir cones, hazelnuts, and pine bark in such a way as to resemble elaborate carving; a broad divan covered with wild animal skins. From the rafters hung moss baskets of native ferns, and in a deep glass frame was a large bouquet of dried Yosemite wildflowers. Every window ledge was a conservatory of blooming potted plants.

Elvira, whom she now met, appeared to be little over twenty and was at first taken for Hutchings' daughter. Six years of innkeeping had not changed her: "She moved dreamily, as if under a spell; and as she stood speaking to me, plucked meditatively the remains of a flower she seemed to be studying botanically."

Although Thérèse's presence caused a sensation in the valley, for everyone knew her story—even the recluse James Lamon and the unworldly Galen Clark—she kept as much as possible out of the public eye, spending her days working on a travel book, playing with the Hutchings girls, walking and riding over the valley, and boating on the river. She found a friend in California journalist Mary Viola Lawrence, who was there for the summer, and they made many excursions together. Mrs. Lawrence wrote: "For her my admiration was unbounded, being, without exception, the most interesting woman I ever knew. Others think likewise; so this is not alone the impression of enthusiasm and partiality."

On many of her walks and rides Thérèse had John Muir as a

The first general view travelers had of Yosemite Valley was photographed by Carleton E. Watkins between 1866 and 1874, from Old Inspiration Point. One of those early travelers wrote: "Our dense leafy surroundings hid from us the fact of our approach to the Valley's tremendous battlements, till our trail turned at a sharp angle and we stood on 'Inspiration Point.'" The scene was revealed with such startling suddenness as to suggest unreality—as it does today.

By 1000 B.C. Indians were establis[h]
in Yosemite Valley, living in all
essentials as their ancestors had fo[r]
thousands of years; weaving fine
baskets—their most highly develo[ped]
art; and celebrating a round of cer[e]
monies that called for special dres[s]
and adjuncts. Here Leemee is see[n]
traditional cape of great horned o[wl]
feathers; flicker-quill headband; a[nd]
face paint. In his right hand is a sp[lit]
stick clapper; in his left, a butterfl[y]
cocoon rattle, also used by shama[ns]
during rites. He is standing besid[e]
one of his people's conical bark
dwellings.

LEFT: Although the basket above was woven as a cooking basket, great care was taken to make it an object of beauty as well. The design is worked in bracken root on a foundation of scraped willow shoots. RIGHT: In Yosemite where little evidence remains of ancient occupation, these striking pictographs were found, hundreds of them in dark-red pigment, on a granite wall protected from weathering by overhanging ledges.

On the shore of Tenaya Lake, named for the Ahwahneeche (Yosemite Indian) chief, the Indians were overtaken by members of the Mariposa Battalion in May 1851. "Where can we go that you will not follow?" their spokesman asked. Too few to resist, they allowed themselves to be marched to a reservation. This photograph is by Eadweard J. Muybridge.

These well-preserved glacier-polished pavements north of Tenaya Lake "reflect the sunbeams like calm water," wrote John Muir. When Chief Tenaya was told that the lake had been named for him, he objected: "It already has a name. We call it *Py-we'-ack*"—lake of shining rocks.

Grizzly Adams, the former New England shoemaker, and his famed bear Ben Franklin, caught as a cub in Yosemite, near which Adams had a cabin. This drawing by pioneer artist Charles Nahl was made from life in Adams' San Francisco museum, and was considered an excellent likeness of both man and bear.

James C. Lamon, described as "a fine, erect, whole-souled man, between six and seven feet high," by his friend John Muir. Before joining the gold rush to California Lamon had hunted alligators along the Brazos in Texas— "right interestin' business," he said. He took up a claim in Yosemite Valley's east end, planted an orchard and berry patch, built the valley's first log cabin, and settled there in 1859. His apple trees still bear abundantly.

Galen Clark first visited Yosemite in 1855. Joining the group of conservationists who worked for Yosemite's preservation, he was appointed first guardian of the park. Also an early innkeeper, he was described by a guest as "handsome, thoughtful, interesting...he conversed well on any subject, and was at once philosopher, savant, chambermaid, cook, and landlord."

Frederick Law Olmsted, landscape architect and conservationist, and co-designer of New York's Central Park, saw Yosemite Valley as a new kind of park, a "wild park," which man had no right to alter. He, too, was prominent in the movement to preserve Yosemite. Olmsted presented this photograph to Clark "as a token of gratitude for his kindness."

James Mason Hutchings, editor, author, and leader of first tourist party to Yosemite Valley (1855), became highly popular landlord of the Upper Hotel (*below*). I reputation as a writer attracted the literati to his hot many of whom were aghast to find bedroom doors a walls made only of muslin. "It required some little str egy to place the candle so that one's figure should appear on the cloth partition, hugely magnified, for amusement of one's neighbors," a woman guest report This picture of the hotel, the first photograph ever tal in Yosemite Valley, was made by Charles L. Weed 1859.

Florence (Floy) Hutchings, bright, daring, fiercely independent, was born at the Upper Hotel in August 1864. Growing up in Yosemite without formal schooling, she rode her horse bareback at top speed over the valley, climbed the heights, and camped alone in the wilderness. John Muir spoke of her as "a tameless one"; "a rare creature." She died tragically at seventeen in Yosemite, where she is buried. Mount Florence was named for her.

LEFT: In 1869 John Muir was hired by James Mason Hutchings to rebuild and operate a sawmill near the foot of Yosemite Falls. By December of 1872, when this photograph was taken, Muir, already recognized as a geologist, was being urged to write articles about his Yosemite studies. BOTTOM: Muir built himself "a small box-like home" under the west gable of Hutchings' sawmill, he wrote his sister, for whom he made this sketch, the only surviving pictorial record of his "hang-nest." There he entertained Ralph Waldo Emerson with accounts of his mountain rambles and showed him his herbariums and drawings. RIGHT: The painter William Keith as he appeared when he and John Muir first met, in Yosemite Valley. Telling Muir what he wanted to paint, Muir led him to Mount Lyell. On nearing the scene, Keith "dashed ahead, shouting and gesticulating and tossing his arms in the air like a madman."

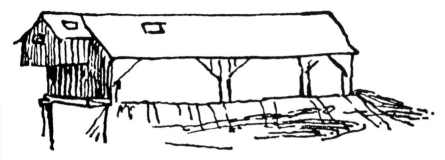

During the winter of 1871 John Muir watched the building of a similar ice cone formed at the base of Yosemite Falls each winter by frozen spray. He noted that the entire fall plunges into the cone's mouth with "deep, gasping explosions of compressed air," and rushes out through arched openings in its base. Anxious to climb to the top, Muir made a number of attempts before succeeding, each time driven back by blinding, suffocating blasts of wind-driven spray. The inset view, photographed from across the valley, shows the cone's relation to the cliff and falls.

Dr. Joseph LeConte, geologist, botanist, author, professor, came under Yosemite's spell when he first visited it in 1870. John Muir, who met him then, wrote: "It was delightful to see with what eager, joyful enthusiasm he reveled in the sublime beauty of the Great Valley." The doctor returned to Yosemite summer after summer, and attributed his continuing physical stamina and mental vigor to these excursions.

Thérèse Yelverton, Viscountess Avonmore, was one of the most noted women of her day. Brilliant, witty, talented, she was a popular author and lecturer. During a six-month stay in Yosemite Valley, she and John Muir, finding much in common, became warm friends. This drawing was made in court during action to establish the validity of her marriage to a British peer.

Mirror Lake with a perfect reflection of Mount Watkins, named for Carleton E. Watkins, who took the photograph. In early days before the lake's reduction by silting, tourists not only enjoyed the images and near views of Half Dome but also boated and swam, and from mid-lake tried the canyon's fine echoes. Here on a ledge projecting over the water, Thérèse Yelverton sang for a party one moonlit night. Here on the shore Ralph Waldo Emerson and his friends rested, watched cloud shadows race over peak and dome, and recited poetry.

For Carleton E. Watkins, in this self-portrait seated in the cave at the foot of Upper Yosemite Fall, the valley's moods and points of view seemed limitless. Year after year he returned for months at a time, leaving no part unexplored in his search for the photographic; venturing into places where it seemed impossible to carry the cumbersome camera equipment of the day. On August 5, 1867, possibly the date of this photograph, a hot and tired tourist who had made the steep and often dangerous climb to the Upper Fall recorded amazement at finding Watkins there with his heavy "photographic apparatus," taking "pictures at the foot of the Fall."

LEFT: A party of Yosemite tourists of the early 1880's, in mountain-climbing attire. BELOW: Sally Dutcher, an assistant to photographer Carleton E. Watkins, was the first white woman to reach the thirteen-acre summit of Half Dome.

At two o'clock on the afternoon of August 15, 1905, the Yosemite-bound stage was brought to a sudden halt by a young man in a ragged linen duster, battered slouch hat, and handkerchief tied around his face. After he had robbed the passengers, one of them, Anton Veith, asked permission to photograph the scene. "I guess my makeup is all right," the highwayman said. "Nobody would recognize me. Go ahead." This is the picture. The road agent is standing center background. The two men at right, with hands behind them, are stage-company blacksmiths, also passengers.

Around a hundred years ago John B. Lembert, a dreamer, a lover of mountain solitude, and a student of nature, built himself a log cabin in Tuolumne Meadows. Lembert passed the long summer evenings creating stories peopled with characters living in an imaginary realm of which he believed himself the king. His days were spent collecting rare alpine species for museums, since he was also an entomologist and botanist. This photograph by George Fiske was taken with Yosemite Falls as background.

This poignant picture, taken by a passing photographer at the time of the San Francisco earthquake and fire of April 1906, stresses the tragedy of Carleton E. Watkins' final years. Here the famed artist with a camera—old, ailing, and almost totally blind—is being led from his studio, where most of his life's work would soon be destroyed by flames.

On May 17, 1903, President Theodore Roosevelt and John Muir posed for pictures on the Overhanging Rock at Glacier Point, with its sheer drop of 3,200 feet to the valley floor. The night before they had camped in a little hollow behind the point, and had awakened at dawn to find their blankets covered with five inches of snow. Roosevelt was delighted. From Muir's lapel hangs the sprig of greenery that he customarily wore—his one personal vanity, he said.

Early one April morning in 1909, John Burroughs *(left)* and John Muir set off on foot for Yosemite's Vernal and Nevada Falls. "What beauty, what grandeur attended us that day!" Burroughs wrote. The acquaintance who snapped this picture of the two resting along the trail to Nevada Fall said they were sharing a laugh over Burroughs' witty retort to Muir, who had just pointed out some stupendous work accomplished by glaciers. Burroughs felt that Muir gave glaciers too much credit for the creation of Yosemite Valley.

Totuya, Chief Tenaya's granddaughter, returned to her native Yosemite after an
absence of seventy-seven years. She was by then the sole survivor of that original
band of Ahwahneeches who had been driven out in 1851. Still strong and agile,
she gathered several bushels of acorns, cracked them with a hammer-stone, and
pounded them into meal. As her white friend, Rose Taylor, helped her with this
work, Totuya talked about her people's history and her own life. Mrs. Taylor
noted that often when Totuya relived a scene, a faraway look would come into
her eyes and her fingers would stop their work.

guide and companion. At first his "tatterdemalion style of a Mad Tom" prejudiced her against him, and she wondered why that sedate Bostonian Mrs. Robert Waterston (Josiah Quincy's daughter) had been so anxious to introduce them. Thérèse must meet that young man who was "so fond of flowers" and had talked with her so earnestly about "the beyond," the old lady had said. But once Muir began to talk, Thérèse forgot his ragged clothing in her absorption with that "bright, intelligent face . . . shining with a pure and holy enthusiasm," those "open blue eyes of honest questioning," the "glorious auburn hair," and the gist of that poetic flow of words. As he raced ahead in their climbs to the heights, she admired his "lithe figure . . . skipping over the rough boulders, poising with the balance of an athelete . . . never losing for a moment the rhythmic motion of his flexile form." He was, she admitted, like no one she had ever met. She began studying him, noting down his opinions, his mode of expression, his mannerisms, even his "joyous and ringing" laugh.

Writers on Muir tend to make this relationship ridiculous by picturing Thérèse Yelverton as a silly older woman infatuated with the youthful Muir, who, embarrassed by her brazen and unremitting pursuit, tries to avoid her and finally runs away. Such a concept is unfair to both. First, Thérèse was only two years his senior (Muir was thirty-two); second, she was far from foolish. Muir's friend, the scholarly William Frederic Badè, who after Muir's death edited his unpublished journals and letters and wrote the first life, has stated that Thérèse and Muir became "warm" friends. It is only reasonable to suppose they did, for he would have admired her intelligence, candor, and courage, and the talents that set her apart as a remarkable woman. He would have relished her repartee (for he was witty himself) and appreciated her unconventional attitudes; he was surely not indifferent to her personal charms. Stoddard wrote of her at this time: "She might have stepped back into a 'Book of Beauty' and put some of her rivals to shame." She and Muir would have found a strong common bond in the appreciation of nature and in her ability to find spiritual solace by wandering through "rosiny pine woods or in gentian meadows." Further, he would have discovered what might be least expected—that she was a good listener. Accepting his ice erosion theory, she made notes on his explanations and examined with him the proofs. They even planned to ride one day across the Sierra through Yosemite high country to see the evidence there, and the wonders of the east side and Mono Lake. With his help—he lent her his herbariums—she studied local plants, and proved apt. Once, when returning from a collecting expedition in the late fall, she was seen "bearing bunches of autumn ferns, and trailing vines, and frail blooms, looking like Flora gathering her truant children from the coming winter storm."

"You had an existence in my heart," she once told him. They shared confidences and had their private and often unflattering names for some permanent residents in the valley. He was openly attentive enough to arouse jealousy in one of Thérèse's admirers, who thought Muir's eyes "too bright blue" when he talked with her. She was inspired to make him the leading male character in a novel set in Yosemite.

"I was finishing my book on America with a chapter on Yosemite, when I was suddenly seized with the desire to write a story," she explained to Charles Warren Stoddard. "It was like a possession. I at once set to work, and have written two hundred and fifty pages in four weeks." To flesh out her hero—thinly disguised under the name of Kenmuir—and lend reality to his dialogue, particularly his expressions of reverence for nature, she worked from his journals and her own records of his conversations. Muir read some of the manuscript and admitted that she had a "little help" from him. Since she was perceptive and a capable reporter, the book that was published the following year contained an accurate portrayal of Muir, although before reading the completed work he expressed the opinion that she perhaps did not know enough of "wild nature" to correctly depict the complete man.

Other characters were members of the Hutchings family, James Lamon, Galen Clark, the Snows, and Tom, the local Indian who worked for Hutchings and carried the mail. Even Carlo the St. Bernard appears, as Rollo. Florence Hutchings, in whom Thérèse was particularly interested, was the heroine, who during the course of the tale reached young womanhood. With remarkable prescience she had Floy meet a tragic death in Yosemite, a fate that overtook her nine years after the book was published. At that later time, September 1881, while Floy was guiding a party up to Glacier Point, she dismounted in front of Sentinel Rock and climbed to a ledge to pick some ferns for one of the women in the group. A large boulder, accidentally loosened on the trail above, came hurtling down and struck her. Fatally injured, she was carried back to the cabin and died the following day, having just turned seventeen. She was buried in the little pioneer cemetery beneath the oaks, to the east of Yosemite Falls. Benjamin F. Taylor, an author and family friend, proposed: "Let us give the girl . . . some graceful mountain height, and, let it be called 'Mt. Florence!' " The 12,561-foot peak west of Mount Lyell was shortly named for her, and as further tribute to this rare and free spirit, a nearby lake and stream.

Thérèse wrote Stoddard that she intended to winter in Yosemite, finish the one novel, perhaps complete another, then return to San Francisco and prepare them for publication. But by late August she had changed her mind, although she was not anxious to go. When in October, Muir was preparing to leave for the lowlands with Harry Randall, she told him that she expected to be at Oakland within two weeks; he therefore made up a packet of lily bulbs, ferns, and cones for her to take to Jeanne Carr. Thérèse wanted him to wait and guide her out, but he was unwilling to miss this chance to explore the Merced River gorge and carry his glacier researches into the canyon and beyond. When they parted, he was impressed by "the grand bow with which she bade me goodbye." It proved a final leave-taking. They never met again, although they corresponded regularly.

November found her still in Yosemite, where she felt at ease and safe from her nemesis. The beauty of her surroundings brought inner peace. "I can not tear myself away from the purple rocks, the golden ferns, the rosy sunsets on South Dome," she wrote Stoddard. Then one day she received letters from England announcing the death of Viscount Avonmore and Captain Yelverton's succession to the title, although his whereabouts were still unknown. An earl who was in the valley with a party of peers and had known the old viscount urged her to hasten to England and claim her rights and title. He and his friends, who would be leaving soon, offered to escort her over the mountain trail, and invited her to share their private carriage to Mariposa. She accepted, and dressed in a "blue-cloth bloomer suit," took her place with the party of horsemen one overcast morning in mid-November. She had ridden only a short distance when she decided to turn back and exchange her saddle for a more comfortable one.

"Ride along, gentlemen," she told them. "I will overtake you at

Inspiration Point in time for luncheon." A superb horsewoman who was well acquainted with the trail, she knew she could easily catch up. By the time the saddle was replaced, a light snow had begun to fall, and Elvira and Hutchings did their best to persuade her to stay. Fearing, however, that this might be the start of winter in earnest and the blocking of the passes until spring, she set off at a canter across the meadows. Once she began to climb, the snowfall grew heavier, the wind-driven flakes became almost blinding, and progress was slow. When she reached Inspiration Point, no one was there. Her escort, having expected to be overtaken long before, decided that she had either turned back or not started out at all. Fearful of being stormbound, they waited only a few minutes before riding on.

Although it was by then snowing harder and dusk was approaching, Thérèse was reluctant to retreat and risk the steep, hazardous trail in the dark. Holding some hope that she might still overtake the party, she pressed on. Twenty inches of snow covered the trail, but her horse followed instinctively. However, when they came to some marshy meadows, the animal balked. Thérèse was by then wet to the skin and shivering. Knowing that she must keep active to avoid freezing, she dismounted and, leading her horse, began retracing her steps. As she walked, she hunted for a shelter in which to spend the fast-approaching night. Although able to distinguish only vague shapes under cover of snow and dusk, she sighted a hollow tree. Removing the saddle blanket, she wrapped it around her shoulders, and keeping a firm hold on the bridle, crawled into the hole. She then drew the horse's head inside and rested her cheek against his for warmth and comfort.

The night seemed endless. Hungry, exhausted, cold, and desolate, she thought of Yelverton's curse. In the morning a bright, cloudless sky brought hope of finding the way back into Yosemite Valley, but when she started out, she found that snow had transformed the familiar landscape. Every identifying mark was gone; even the blazes on the pine trees were covered with blown snow. At a loss as to which way to go, she tried every direction, uphill and down; she stumbled and slid through the brush and around rocks, all the while tugging her horse and occasionally crying for help. Once she heard footsteps and a rustling from behind some large boulders, and thinking it might be Hutchings, who was supposed that morning to go into Mariposa, she called his name and hurried in that direction. Rounding the rocks, she came face to face with a large black bear. Her horse bolted and started for the heights while the bear, equally frightened, turned and fled. Thérèse started to run, broke through the snow, fell, and rolled twenty feet down a cliff. Bruised, cut, and bleeding, she got to her feet and started to climb back up, but growing suddenly weak, slipped down again. Certain that her end had come, and thinking once more of Yelverton, she lost consciousness.

The Yosemite innkeeper George Leidig, on his way out that morning, noticed the trail of footprints in the snow. Aware that she was the last person to leave the valley the day before, he knew at once that she must have missed her escort. Following the prints to the cliff's edge, he saw her lying motionless below. Climbing down, he was able to restore her, and with the help of Hutchings, who had by then come by, got her up the slope and back to the hotel.

A few days of rest restored her. During that time she wrote a long letter to John Muir, who was still at Pat Delaney's ranch, recounting her experience. He was puzzled; it seemed strange "that I should not have known and felt her anguish in that terrible night, even at that distance." He felt guilt at not having waited to guide her out. The press made much of this latest adventure of the Viscountess Avonmore, as they called her, and vivid stories, illustrated with artist's concepts of the most terrifying moments, appeared in newspapers throughout the world.

Upon her return to San Francisco, she was in no hurry to leave. She finished the Yosemite novel, which was accepted by the same Boston publisher who later issued Muir's books. She completed the narratives of travel and sent them to her London publisher. She wrote an article for the *Overland Monthly* and arranged with the editors to contribute to it regularly, as she did with the San Francisco *Daily Evening Bulletin*. Not until the fall of 1871 did she set sail—at midnight and in the midst of "a dreadful storm and fog"—for Canton rather than England. She stayed there a month, "reveling in Orientalism" and making notes for a projected book, and then moved on to Hong Kong. From there she wrote Muir in care of Jeanne Carr:

My dear Kenmuir

How I have wished for you, and sometimes longed for you avails not to say. It is sufficient to make you comprehend that I never see a beautiful place or a fine combination of nature without thinking of you and wishing you were here to appreciate it with me. I am sure you would enjoy this country immensely. The grandeur of the rocks and the luxuriance of the vegetation is superb.

He would find pleasure in "weaving" among the soaring peaks of mountainous islands, "wild and startling." She described the abundance of mosses and ferns: "I wish I could send you all the specimens I have gathered, but can only compress a few into my envelope." She spoke of the watercolor sketches she was making of blue sea and islands of red rock. Sometimes she "yearned" for sympathetic and appreciative souls, "but there are none here—all money-getting men and drawing-room ladies" who lay idly on divans, fanning themselves and complaining. At first they had welcomed and feted her as "a great world's wonder," but then dropped her after finding that the very characteristics which distinguished her were alien to them. "They don't understand me and I certainly do not comprehend them." She hoped Muir would find another valley as beautiful as Yosemite, but one without snow. If he did, she would come and see it, and "pitch my tent for a time." She pictured him in Yosemite, reading her letter "in some quiet spot with all nature as calm and still as your own heart. I used to envy you that, for mine will not be still but is restless and unquiet; yet I have enjoyed a great deal lately."

She was leaving shortly for Saigon and Bangkok, where she expected "to meet wonderful things" about which she could write. Then she would return to England by way of the Cape of Good Hope. She asked him to write her in South Africa, since she would be spending some time there.

"And now good-bye for a time but remember that your letters and proceedings have always a deep interest for me." She signed herself, "Your sincere friend, Therese Yelverton." Muir must have treasured her letters, for he carefully kept them.

Her adventures were by no means over. The sailing ship taking her to Saigon was dismasted in a typhoon and nearly foundered. Thérèse again narrowly missed death or serious injury when at the peak of the storm she was thrown violently about the cabin, which was partially broken in and awash. She was rescued under the most dangerous conditions. The story of that latest brush with death also received international news coverage and made its way to her friends in California.

Eventually she got back to England, but when she found that her rights and title were still withheld, and that to claim them would require further litigation whose outcome was uncertain, she did not remain long. Her wanderings took her all over the world (she seems never to have gone back to Yosemite) and ended in New Zealand. There, at the age of forty-three, she died of a fever contracted along the way. She was not alone and untended, as Yelverton had conjured, but at the home of a brother who was in government service at that outpost of empire.

13

TRANSCENDENTALISTS ON THE TRAIL

A HIGH POINT in John Muir's life was his meeting with Ralph Waldo Emerson, the poet, prophet, essayist, and great teacher. With a party of ten Emerson set off from San Francisco for Yosemite Valley on May 2, 1871. Included were his wife, Lidian; his daughter Edith; her husband, John Forbes, whose father, a railroad magnate, had provided a private Pullman car for the transcontinental trip; Wilkinson James, a younger brother of novelist Henry James; and the lawyer, author, and future Harvard professor James Bradley Thayer.

Their guidebook to Yosemite stressed that luggage be light—only the necessities. Even if it meant carrying it himself, Emerson was determined to take the purple satchel that he always kept at his side. It contained a copy of Wordsworth; Goethe's *Sprüche in Prosa* and a German dictionary (for train travel afforded an excellent opportunity to study his German, Emerson had found); the manuscript of his own "Parnassus," on which he worked at times with his daughter; and his journal. The trip to Yosemite via the Coulterville route would take three and a half days.

They were eager sightseers, and even on the barren plains of the San Joaquin Valley observed much worthy of noting—ground squirrels in profusion and little burrowing owls, numbers of jackrabbits, flocks of yellow-headed blackbirds, and magpies—none of which they had seen before. When they reached the fertile Tuolumne River region with its fine stands of wheat and oats, there was a welcome touch of the familiar in the meadowlark's plaintive notes, which reminded them of their wood thrush at home.

Emerson was talkative during that first day's drive. Someone broached the subject of immortality, and he discussed his own concepts and spoke of the Over-Soul. "The soul feels that it is in communication with the source of things; and it knows," he said in his slow, pausing way. He quoted at length from Goethe, through whose writings transcendentalism was communicated to such New England thinkers as Henry Thoreau and himself. By evening, however, he was content to simply sit on the hotel veranda at Roberts' Ferry, listening to the brawl of the Tuolumne just beyond, puffing his after-dinner cigar, and letting the others talk.

On arriving at the ferry they had been pleased to find one of their own people, for John Roberts, the proprietor, was a "Boston boy" who had come to the gold fields in 1849, and was now ferryman, rancher, and innkeeper. The next afternoon at the hotel in Coulterville, they discovered yet another transplanted Bostonian, David Clark, a "Franklin-medal scholar" who had been a gold miner, too, but was now teaching school. Innkeeping was only a temporary occupation in the landlord's absence.

After tea that evening Emerson sat outside, his tartan about his shoulders, smoking with some of the party. When alone, he said, he rarely cared to finish a cigar. But in company it was different. To one who found it as difficult as he did to meet people, the effect of a cigar was agreeable. "One who is smoking may be as silent as he likes, and yet be good company." Nathaniel Hawthorne had told him that he also found this true. One by one the party drifted off to bed, but Emerson was in a reflective mood, and unwilling to break it: "To me, *this* is delightful; I enjoy the passing hour."

Their first view of Yosemite Valley on that final afternoon reminded the party of a famed bit of New England scenery—the White Mountain Notch. But Yosemite, they admitted, was more impressive because of the chasm's depth and its towering walls. Once on the valley floor they noticed the "odd littleness" of their whole cavalcade and realized that these cliffs were mountains in size. At home there was nothing that could compare.

They made their headquarters at Leidig's Hotel, having been

struck with its beautiful setting and its neat appearance—white clapboard, reminiscent of Concord. Its "arrangements," however, proved "simple indeed," wrote one of the party after being awakened in the morning by a cackling hen walking over his bed in search of a good place to lay her egg.

That day they set off on horseback (Emerson riding a pied mustang) for Tenaya Canyon to see the reflections in Mirror Lake. Along the way their attention was caught by pine trees evenly riddled, and each hole plugged with an acorn—the work of woodpeckers, the guide explained. Emerson doubted that this was the work of any bird. In Acton Woods and around Walden Pond where he walked at home with Henry Thoreau, it was only squirrels who stored acorns. Not until after he had asked John Muir and was told that the scarlet-crowned California woodpecker did indeed eat acorns—"I have seen them eating them," Muir said. "During snowstorms they seem to eat little besides acorns"—was Emerson convinced.

By the time they reached Tenaya Canyon a breeze had sprung up, ruffling the water and distorting the images. Still they sat there a long time, admiring the little lake ringed with willows and conifers and listening to the sweet notes of the redwing, which nests among the tules and tall sedges, and the robin singing in the grove. Absorbing it all, Emerson remarked gravely: "This valley is the only place that comes up to the brag about it, and exceeds it."

Early the next morning as they watched Vernal Fall pouring down its rock face in a thick milk-white mass of foam, one of the party quoted from "The Wreck of the Hesperus": "She struck where the white and fleecy waves/Looked soft as carded wool." It was apt, Emerson thought; he gave a pleased nod and asked that it be repeated. When he got back to the hotel, he wanted to read it for himself—one of them had a copy of Longfellow in his bag.

Leaving their horses, they made the steep climb to the foot of Nevada Fall. The general tumult of its waters brought to mind the painting entitled "The Queen of the Night" by their own Vermont artist William Morris Hunt.

After an excellent noon dinner at La Casa Nevada, the inn kept on the flat between the two falls by those other Vermonters Albert and Emily Snow, the Emersonians sunned themselves on the porch in full view of Nevada Fall and discussed the Italians, praising them for their ardor and "elevation of sentiment." Emerson demurred. Dante was cited. "Yes, oh yes, Dante!" he remarked, as if he were an exception and not to be counted. Michelangelo was then brought up, and Tasso. "Yes, yes," Emerson granted, but he liked better what he found among the English Puritans—Lucy Hutchinson's life of her husband, for instance.

When it came time for a return to the valley, several of the young men were unwilling to go until they had climbed the Liberty Cap, for liberty was dear to the New England heart. Why tease the mind, Emerson objected. It is capable of holding only so many impressions. But they were reluctant to forgo the opportunity and hurried on up the trail. The others did not wait.

The following evening an "admiring and enthusiastic" letter from John Muir was handed to Emerson. In it Muir wrote that he had read Mr. Emerson's books and was now eager to come to him. Emerson had already heard about Muir from Jeanne Carr, and had in the purple satchel an introductory note. In the morning he mounted the pied mustang, and inviting Thayer to accompany him, rode over to the sawmill, where they found Muir alone. "Why did you not make yourself known last night?" Emerson asked. "I should have been very glad to have seen you." Muir perhaps did not say that he had been too shy to do more than hover about the edges of the crowd that pressed forward to be introduced and shake Emerson's hand. He now invited them into his hang-nest, and Emerson "bravely climbed up." Muir showed them his herbariums, and "hundreds of his own graceful pencil-sketches of the mountain peaks and forest trees," which he begged Emerson to accept. But he declined, asking only that he might bring his friends to see them. "He came again and again, and I saw him every day while he remained in the Valley."

On one of those days Muir told about his rambles over the mountains, during which he often camped out for weeks; "and he urged Mr. Emerson, with an amusing zeal, to stay and go off with him on such a trip," Thayer wrote. Emerson appeared anxious to go but worried about his party. Never mind them, Muir told him, "the mountains are calling; run away, and let plans and parties . . . all 'gang tapsal-terrie.' We'll go up a cañon singing your own song, 'Good-by, proud world! I'm going home.'" But his family and friends, who were unable to see "the natural beauty and fullness of promise of my wild plan . . . held Mr. Emerson to hotels and trails."

On their final day in Yosemite various members of the party did different things. Emerson spent time with Muir. Those wanting to see the famed view from Inspiration Point, which their out-bound trail would detour because of fallen trees and snow, rode there. The last traveler to have been that way, Thayer noted, was the "well-known Englishwoman, Mrs. Yelverton, who . . . was lost in a snow-storm, and with difficulty rescued by Leidig, our land-lord."

Every Yosemite wonder had suggested to these pilgrims from the wellspring of American intellectual activity some counterpart or allusion in poetry, prose, or painting. Now looking from Inspira-tion Point (which they considered an *uninspired* name) up through the valley, "set like a jewel among these magnificent heights," John Bunyan's Delectable Mountains came to mind.

The next morning, May 11, their departure day, there was, among other things on the breakfast table, an apple pie. Pie for breakfast was one of Emerson's weaknesses, and a pie now stood before him. Eager to try it, he offered to serve first one, then another, and still another of his companions, each of whom de-clined. Turning to a fourth, he asked to cut him a slice, but this man also declined. "But, Mr.——," Emerson remonstrated with a twinkle in his eye and an exaggerated thrust of the knife into the crust, "*what is pie for?*"

They were on the trail before seven o'clock, and Muir was with them at Emerson's invitation. When Emerson had first proposed that they ride together to the Mariposa Big Trees, Muir had said: "I'll go, Mr. Emerson, if you promise to camp with me in the Grove." At the suggestion he became as enthusiastic as a boy: "Yes, yes, we will camp out, camp out"; and Muir looked forward to at least one "good wild memorable night around a sequoia camp-fire."

As they rode along Thayer listened with interest to Emerson sound out Muir on literary points. He was not strong there, the Harvard graduate thought; he preferred, for instance, the poet Alice Cary to Byron. "He was an interesting young fellow, of real intelligence and character," Thayer observed, but a "botanist mainly."

Lunch hampers were unpacked in the woods. Everyone ate avidly but Muir, who preferred talk to food. "Place a sandwich close to his hand, or shell an egg for him and a courteous 'thank you' is forthcoming, but more often than not a mere nibble is all the attention he pays your efforts, and the talk flows on." After lunch some stretched out on the soft brown pine needles and slept; others lay on their backs and stared at the leaf patterns against the sky, listening to Emerson recall his student days at Harvard and then, with one or two others, recite Sir Walter Scott's verses. On the trail again, someone asked him about Coleridge, whom he had called on in England. Well, he looked just like his portraits. But that visit had been disappointing, for the talk never came to anything profound.

At length they reached Clark's, "a plain country tavern," and Muir was surprised to see all the party dismount. Were they not going to ride on to the Mariposa Grove to camp? he asked. That "would never do. Mr. Emerson might take cold; and you know, Mr. Muir, that would be a dreadful thing." Colds were caught only in houses and hotels, Muir countered. There was not "a single cough or sneeze in all the Sierra." Further, there would be a big "climate-changing inspiring fire," which he intended to build. Come, he urged, "make an immortal Emerson night of it!" But the "house habit" was too strong, and they all slept indoors. Muir blamed Emerson's family and friends. Actually, Emerson himself when faced with it, was opposed to sleeping alfresco, he told Thayer.

At first Muir was going to camp alone; then, realizing how soon Emerson would be gone, he decided to risk the inn. Although Emerson did little talking that evening, Muir was happy just to sit, "warming in the light of his face as at a fire."

The following morning they were off by eight o'clock for the grove. Galen Clark—"a solid, sensible man from New Hampshire," two of whose brothers were Unitarian clergymen—went as their guide. No white man knew more about the Big Trees than Clark, who had discovered this stand in 1857. As they rode along, Muir identified the various trees they came to, "and we grew very learned," Thayer wrote, "and were able to tell a sugar pine from a yellow pine, and to name a silver fir, and the 'libocedrus,' which is almost our arbor-vitae."

Suddenly Muir called out that he saw the sequoia ahead—"the king of all the conifers in the world, 'the noblest of a noble race!'" At first they did not seem so large, but after the Emersonians were among them for a while, they realized what company they were in. On passing one fallen tree, Thayer became suddenly aware that the trunk was higher than his head as he sat on horseback. With the help of his companions he was soon running a tape around the boles of the largest, pacing off the prostrate giants, and riding up the length, as through a tunnel, of one fire-hollowed sequoia. They encircled the Grizzly Giant with their horses to determine circumference, but found that thirteen animals were not enough: it would require six more. It was not the height they found so amazing, for there were rivals in many of the surrounding forest trees, but the size of trunks and limbs. Galen Clark pointed out a lower branch on the Grizzly Giant that was six feet seven inches in diameter. There was nothing like that in all of New England. This single branch was as big as the trunk of the largest elm in the Connecticut Valley, those great trees which their poet Oliver Wendell Holmes had immortalized. They saw that there were many young sequoias. "That is good! they are not then a mere decaying thing of the past," one of the philosophers remarked. This was a form of immortality. Muir pointed out how perfectly proportioned they were—"so firmly planted . . . so straight, with so clean a stem and so shapely a foliage."

Occasionally he and Emerson were able to leave the others and saunter quietly through the stands, Emerson as if under a spell. "There were giants in those days," he remarked.

To commemorate his visit, Galen Clark asked Emerson to select a sequoia and name it. He chose one that was vigorous and handsome, but not remarkably large, measuring only fifty feet in circumference, two and a half feet from the ground. He called it Samoset—"after our Plymouth sachem," Thayer noted.

As they ate their picnic lunch under the trees, Muir protested their going so soon: "It is as if a photographer should remove his plate before the impression was fully made." To Emerson he said: "You are yourself a sequoia. Stop and get acquainted with your big brethren." But Emerson had lecture commitments that were binding.

Around three o'clock they rode away, retracing the trail through stands of fragrant ceanothus and thickets of dogwood, up the slope of the sequoia basin, and over the divide to Clark's to board stages for the return to San Francisco. Emerson, reluctant to leave, rode in the rear. When he reached the summit of Wawona Ridge, he turned his horse, took off his hat, and waved Muir a final good-bye.

Muir stood for some while gazing at the spot where Emerson had vanished, then turned and slowly made his way back into the grove. There he selected a camping spot, gathered sequoia branches and ferns for his bed, and collected firewood. Around sunset he built the big fire he had hoped Emerson would share, "and though lonesome for the first time in those forests, I quickly took heart again—the trees had not gone to Boston, nor the birds; and as I sat by the fire, Emerson was still with me in spirit."

On May 18, after a final speaking engagement in Oakland, Emerson groped his way through the fog and dark to Jeanne Carr's back door, to thank her for John Muir, "a new kind of Thoreau . . . browsing upon the cedars and sequoias of the Sierra instead of the scrub-oaks of Concord."

The following day the transcendentalists were on the trail again, bound this time for Lake Tahoe. After a few days spent in sight-seeing there, the private railroad car caught up and the party headed homeward.

Emerson and Muir corresponded throughout the closing decade of the essayist's life (he died in 1882). Muir often included pressed flowers, incense cedar blooms, and other reminders of Yosemite, while Emerson sent books and urged Muir to roll up his sketches and herbariums and come to Concord. After he tired of that company, he could go on to Cambridge, where at Harvard he would find Louis Agassiz and Asa Gray.

14

CLIMBING THE HEIGHTS

THE SIERRA MIWOK were the first to climb Yosemite peaks and domes. Their shamans acquired power on mountaintops at night. Those who undertook vision quests scaled the heights to fast, thirst, and pray in solitude. Their hunters sought the bighorn and grizzly bear about the summits.

The first white men of record to ascend these mountains were members of the California State Geological Survey, the Whitney Survey, so adamant in their opposition to John Muir and his glacial erosion theory. In the summer of 1863, after six days spent in examining Yosemite Valley, which they decided was one of the most remarkable natural wonders in the world, the geologists and botanists followed the old Miwok-Mono trail through its high country. From their camp at Porcupine Flat in Yosemite uplands, they could see the craggy Sierra peaks. They marveled at their height, and grew so excited by the thought that no white man had ever scaled them or knew anything about them that they could hardly sleep.

The next day, June 24, they made a first ascent: William H. Brewer, the survey's botanist; Charles F. Hoffmann, its topographer and artist; and Josiah Dwight Whitney, their chief, reached the summit of a 10,850-foot peak they named Mount Hoffmann for their associate. From the top more than fifty peaks were in view, most of them higher still and many mere pinnacles of granite streaked with snow. There was the inevitable comparison with the Swiss Alps, made by most early visitors to Yosemite, and the conclusion that the scene lacked their "picturesque beauty" but possessed a desolation and starkness which imparted a "sublime grandeur." Four days later Brewer and Hoffmann made their way up one of those mountains, standing 13,853 feet above the sea, and called it Dana, in honor of the eminent American geologist Charles Dwight Dana. The air was particularly clear that day, and hundreds of snowy peaks could be seen this time. "All north, west, and south was a scene of the wildest mountain desolation." To the east, at their feet, lay Mono Lake, and south of it the chain of extinct volcanic cones that merges with the barren plains and meets the horizon. They stayed on the summit four hours, taking bearings and barometric readings and enjoying the view. It was not often one had the chance to survey such a panorama. On their return to camp they gave Whitney, who had been sick that morning, such a glowing description that he decided to attempt the climb. The following day he and Brewer reached the summit. Comparing it with the best he had seen in Europe, he told Brewer that this view was "the grandest he ever beheld."

Early on the morning of July 2, Hoffmann and Brewer set off from camp to climb the highest mountain in the Yosemite region (13,114 feet), the source of both the Merced and Tuolumne rivers. They gave it the name of Lyell, this time in honor of the famed British geologist Sir Charles Lyell. They found the ascent difficult: "In places the snow is soft, and we sink two or three feet. . . . We toil on for hours; it seems at times as if our breath refuses to strengthen us, we puff and blow so in the thin air." After more than seven hours of hard climbing, they reached the base of a pinnacle that breaks through the snow and forms the summit, only to find it inaccessible from that approach. Sorely disappointed, they had to stop some hundred and fifty feet short of their goal. This was the first of what was to become typical in the survey's mountain-climbing record.

Unfamiliar with such rugged mountain terrain, they were not aware of the need for careful study and reconnaissance of possible approaches, and often selected what recommended itself as the most direct route only to discover after it was too late that it was also the most difficult and hazardous. When faced with obstacles

that seemed insurmountable, they were often too ready to turn back
and label the peak "inaccessible." Even on their successful climbs
they reported encountering obstructions and dangers that mountaineers who followed failed to find. These descriptions of hazards
met and death defied were typical of most accounts written by
men who made first climbs in the Rocky Mountains and other
unexplored ranges of the West. In retrospect, perhaps, the dangers
and difficulties seemed greater. More probably, in retelling the
experience they succumbed to a natural temptation to exaggerate
the perils and so make a good story and add luster to their feat.
Not so John Muir. When he read Clarence King's colorful account
of his harrowing experience in climbing Mount Tyndall, he remarked: "He must have given himself a lot of trouble. When I
climbed Tyndall, I ran up and back before breakfast." But Muir
was a born mountaineer.

These designations of inaccessibility became part of the State
Geological Survey's official reports, which were widely read and
accepted, and years passed before the pronouncements were challenged. Not until 1871 did a white man reach the summit of
Mount Lyell. That summer John B. Tileston, a tourist from Boston
who was staying at Hutchings' hotel, made the ascent without
trouble. He wrote to his wife that he went nearly to the snowline
on August 28, and the next morning "climbed the mountain and
reached the top of the highest pinnacle . . . before eight." He was
aware that it was considered inaccessible.

Upon his return he told Hutchings that he had just conquered
the impossible. The innkeeper congratulated him, but privately
held some reservations. Ten days later, after John Tileston was on
his way to Boston, Hutchings and two companions tried it themselves. Encountering no obstacles, they made their way to the
summit, and, "incredible as it seemed at the time . . . found Mr.
Tileston's card upon the top."

While in the Yosemite highlands as guardian of Pat Delaney's
flock, John Muir made a first ascent of Cathedral Peak. Leaving
camp at dawn, he reached the topmost spire at noon, having
"loitered," as he said, along the way to study trees, hunt flowers in
alpine meadows, observe "lakelets and avalanche tracks and huge
quarries of moraine rocks." In his diary there is no mention of any
difficulties encountered during the climb of this challenging
mountain, 10,940 feet in elevation. He did record his delight at

finding gardens of white heather blooming on rocky ledges; he also described the dense mats of whitebark pine on the summit, dwarfed by the long seasons of heavy snow. Many were bearing cones, and Clark's nutcrackers were busily harvesting the seeds. Flowering among the dwarfed pines were asters and yellow daisies.

Mount Ritter was another of the survey's unattainable peaks, for Clarence King had tried to reach the summit and failed. Not until mid-October 1872 was it conquered. John Muir was then in the Mount Lyell region with his friends William Keith, Benoni Irwin, and Thomas Ross, who were so excited by the possibilities for picture subjects, they declared they needed at least a week to make color sketches. While they worked, Muir would use the time for an excursion to the "untouched summit" of Ritter, at 13,157 feet the highest of the middle Sierra peaks. After one day of travel over a maze of rugged canyons and crests, he came next morning to the summit of the divide. Immediately in front loomed the mountain's "majestic mass," its glacier sweeping down nearly to his feet, then curving westward and pouring its "frozen flood into a dark blue lake, whose shores were bound with precipices of crystalline snow."

After gazing "spellbound" for some time, he began scrutinizing "every notch and gorge and weathered buttress" with a view to ascent. What he saw was not encouraging: the entire front beyond the glacier appeared to be one steep, smooth cliff narrowing at the summit and bristling with jagged pinnacles and spires set one above the other, while to either side towered massive crumbling walls that offered no hope to the climber.

It was too late in the season, he decided, to attempt it, for even if he was successful, there was always that chance of being storm-bound. Instead of turning back, however, he pushed on across the glacier, intent on keeping to the lower slopes to learn what he could about the mountain's geologic history, and holding himself in readiness to retrace his trail at the first sign of a storm cloud. But as had happened before, he found himself going on, and up. "We little know until tried how much of the uncontrollable there is in us, urging us across glaciers and torrents, and up dangerous heights, let judgment forbid as it may." In this state, he worked his way up to the base of a cliff on the eastern edge of the glacier, and there encountering an avalanche gully, thought he would follow that as far as he could—if only to obtain "some fine wild views" for his trouble. It was not long until he was in the midst of the crumbling buttresses, finding their shadowed ravines glazed in many places with ice he had to chip away with rocks, having no axe. He knew that his position was becoming increasingly hazardous, and that it was too late to turn back: having safely passed a number of perilous spots, he had no wish to try them in descent, when a single misstep would plunge him onto the glacier below.

Pressing on, he came to the foot of a sheer drop in the channel he was following. Although only about fifty feet high, the cracks and projections on its surface appeared too small and fragile to serve as foot- and finger-holds. He tried scaling the walls to either side, which were less steep but so smooth he slipped back at nearly every step. Nothing remained but to try the avalanche channel. Studying it closely and choosing his holds carefully, he started up. When about halfway to the top he was brought to a sudden dead halt, "with arms outspread, clinging close to the face of the rock, unable to move hand or foot either up or down. My doom appeared fixed. I *must* fall."

With awareness of his danger, he became "nerve-shaken," and his mind filled with a "stifling smoke." This condition lasted but a moment: his "other self" took command, his trembling muscles firmed, he saw every crack and projection as though through a microscope, and his legs and arms began moving with a "positiveness and precision" that seemed outside his control. Although the mountain face above was still more hacked and torn, he made his way effortlessly over "yawning chasms and gullies," "beetling crags," and shifting talus, his iron-shod boots ringing on the granite. Soon he was standing on the highest summit pinnacle, exulting in the all-encompassing view—"giant mountains, valleys innumerable, glaciers, meadows, rivers and lakes, with the wide blue sky bent tenderly over them all."

Although darkness caught him before he reached the mountain's base, he was guided by the trends of canyons and by the peaks silhouetted against the sky. At length he heard the sound of the waterfall across the little lake where his camp lay, then saw the stars reflected on its surface. Using these as bearings, he soon found the pine thicket where he had slept the night before. With night his exhilaration was replaced by exhaustion. After building what he termed a "sunrise" fire and refreshing himself with bread and a cup of hot tea, he crept into his bed of pine boughs. In the morning, after thawing for a time in the sunshine (there was a heavy hoarfrost, and he had but one blanket), he "sauntered" back to the painter's camp, reaching there just at dusk. They seemed "unreasonably glad" to see him. Although he had been gone only three days and the weather had held clear the whole time, they had entertained thoughts that he might never return.

Half Dome, the Whitney Survey declared, was "the only one of the prominent points about the Yosemite which has never been, and perhaps never will be, trodden by human foot." In 1869, James Mason Hutchings and two companions set out to disprove this. They approached it by way of an Indian escape trail north of Grizzly Peak, which turned out to be merely an access to the High Sierra in time of danger, and was in itself a test of their mountaineering skill. However, once standing on the eastern shoulder of the dome, they were faced with the discouraging sight of an exfoliating granite slope of some forty degrees, whose surface appeared to be as smooth as glass, and they recognized defeat.

Two years later, John Conway, Yosemite's master trail builder, had a plan to refute the inaccessibility claim. Having a flock of young sons who were as skilled as lizards in climbing smooth rock, he called them together one day, announced his intentions, and taking along rope, hammer, and spikes, proceeded to the east shoulder. As the boys ascended the slope, they were to drive the spikes into fissures and tie the rope securely around each pin. Once they had reached the top he would follow, and with them (presumably) claim the honor of a first ascent. Climbing barefoot, the boys were able to fasten the rope for about two hundred feet, but above that point found the rock without flaws or fissures: in order to set the spikes it would be necessary to drill. Nothing remained but for Conway to call his lizards down and take the trail homeward.

At three o'clock on the afternoon of October 12, 1875, George Anderson, the Scottish sailor and gold seeker who at this time was the valley's blacksmith, stood on the summit of Half Dome. Determined to succeed, he had made extensive preparations, having built a headquarters cabin and set up a forge to make eyebolts, at a spring about a mile from the ascent point. Using Conway's old rope for a start, Anderson literally drilled his way to the top, inserting the bolts five to six feet apart, fastening his own rope to each in succession, and resting his foot on the last spike while he drilled for the next. He began the climb in his boots, but soon discarded them. Stockings slipped even more, so he tried bare feet, which were only a slight improvement. Returning to his cabin, he bound his feet and calves in sacking smeared thickly with pine pitch. Had he wanted to remain in one spot, this was the solution. Since he did not, a new problem arose: to get unstuck. His efforts several times caused him to lose his balance and nearly fall. In the end he made the ascent barefooted. Four "English gentlemen" who were staying in the valley next made the climb, with Anderson as their guide. A day or two later the handsome and adventurous Sally Dutcher, an assistant to Carleton E. Watkins, the famed San Francisco photographer whose views of the valley were largely responsible for acquainting the world with Yosemite's unique beauty, scaled the dome with the help of Anderson and Galen Clark, becoming the first white woman to reach the thirteen-acre summit.

That November, John Muir also made his way up Half Dome, in defiance of Whitney's pronouncement, for the pleasure of the climb and whatever lessons he could learn. The first storm of the season had covered the summit and lower slope with snow. Anderson tried to dissuade him, fearing that even with the aid of his rope, conditions would be hazardous. Further, clouds were gathering, and more snow threatened. But such risks meant little to Muir, and he was soon on his way to the top. As he stood on the overhang that looks down on Mirror Lake, he watched a flock of small clouds drift in from the north and fill Tenaya Canyon. Then the sun broke free, lighting the cloud surface, and making it glow. "Gazing, admiring, I was startled to see for the first time the rare optical phenomenon of the 'Specter of the Brocken.'" Muir's shadow, enlarged to gigantic proportions, lay clearly outlined upon the brilliant pearly-gray cloud surface. Delighted, he walked back and forth, waving his arms, and assuming all sorts of postures so as to observe each slight movement "enormously exaggerated." As often as he was to look down from heights upon cloud seas, this was the only time he ever saw the famed specter.

From a distance the summit of Half Dome appears to be barren, but Muir found growing there four clumps of contorted, wind-swept pines, representing three species. He also saw cinquefoil, Sierra onion, alpine daisy, spirea, buckwheat, goldenrod, and penstemon; and noted that blue jays, Clark's nutcrackers, and

chipmunks were at home there. He was disappointed in views of
the valley, which were foreshortened: North Dome was dwarfed
nearly beyond recognition, the sculpture of the Royal Arches was
hardly noticeable, while the towering walls to either side appeared
almost squat. Even so, this climb became one of the most popular
with tourists, and Anderson, anticipating a fortune to be made from
tolls, planned to build a substantial wooden stairway to the top.
However, while getting timber for the project, he suddenly took
sick and died alone in his little cabin.

During the heavy winter of 1883–84, masses of ice and snow
sliding down the smooth curve of Half Dome carried away all of
Anderson's rope and some of the eyebolts. No one had the ambi-
tion or the skill to replace the ropeway, and tourists that season
had to forgo the thrill of peering over the verge. Then, one evening
the following summer, shortly after dusk, valley residents were
startled to see a blazing bonfire on the summit. Unsure whether
this was a signal of distress or victory, a rescue party that included
Hutchings set off with ropes and bolts. At Snow's inn beyond the
summit of Vernal Fall, they met the makers of the fire: Alden
Sampson of New York and A. Phimister Proctor, a painter and
sculptor from Colorado—two friends making a horseback trip
through the Far West, "hunting, fishing, reading, and sketching."
While encamped at Glacier Point they had met Galen Clark, who
in answering their questions about Half Dome had told the story
of Anderson's daring. "But now we are waiting for some member
of the English Alpine Club to come over and have the goodness to
replace the rope," he added. "At that last remark our ears went
forward," Proctor said to Hutchings. "The thought passed through
both our minds at the same instant: 'No foreigner will do that job
till we have had a try at it.' "

"We quietly reconnoitered the place, and made all necessary
preparations in secrecy, so that no one should have the satisfaction
of laughing . . . if we failed," Sampson put in. Taking along two
hundred feet of "rather thin and frayed" picket rope, "a handful of
lunch, and a lemon apiece, in the early morning we rode from our
camp . . . to the base of the dome." Proctor could throw a lariat
"like a native Californian, so that when a pin was not over thirty
feet off, he would be sure to 'rope it' the first cast." Once the loop
was taut, he or Sampson would then pull himself up, stand on the
pin, and fasten Anderson's rope, after the other had tied the lower

end with the lariat. Proctor, who was working barefoot, told about hanging on to the eyebolt by his big toe. The only way this could be done was "to double up like a jack-knife, put my toe on the fingers by which I was holding the pin, and when I was balanced all doubled up, pull my fingers out with all my weight still resting on them." He was then standing on a two-inch surface, "my big toe the only support between me and the valley below. There was never a handhold." Once balanced, he would aim his lariat at the next bolt. The higher they climbed the more difficult this became, for many of the bolts were bent: "Often my loop would roll over a ring twenty times before I caught it"; and several bolts pulled out once there was weight put on them. One time his knot slipped, and he slid some twenty feet before it caught again: "This gave me a bad scare."

At length they came to a stretch where every pin had been carried away. Proctor found that here he could not cling to the glassy surface as well as Sampson with his hobnailed boots, so it was up to Sampson to do it alone. "The sensation was glorious. I did not stake my life upon it, for I was sure I could make it. If I had slipped in the least I would have had a nasty fall of several hundred feet. To be sure, I was playing out a rope behind me attached to my waist, but supposing I had fallen, with all this slack below me, my weight would have snapped it, or the rope would have cut me in two." As they leaned against the mountain for balance and support, each said later he had the feeling that it was trying to push him off.

By noon they had reached a ledge—"the only ledge, all of six inches wide"—where they could rest and eat lunch. At this point there was a corner to be rounded on naked granite that was steep and slippery, polished by the storms and snow slides of countless winters. Sampson gambled on a six-inch-high spirea bush and a length of partly rotted bale rope—and won. By the end of this first day they had made only half the distance. Before sunset they slid down the cable, mounted their horses, and rode back to camp.

The next morning they were back with all the rope they had. In the afternoon they came to another long, smooth stretch, not as steep as before, but like glass, and with only a few eyebolts left. In one place Proctor stood for an hour and a quarter on a two-inch pin while he tried to get his loop to hold on a bolt a hundred feet above. During this time his leg muscles would cramp and quiver from strain, and he would have to let himself down and hang by his fingers from the ring, "dangling over that empty mile of space." Below, he could see Sampson clinging to the rock face and looking little larger than a chipmunk. At last the lariat caught firmly, and as it was drawn taut, they gave a shout of joy. The rest of the climb was accomplished with comparative ease, and not too long after they were on the summit. There they sat for some time, resting and enjoying the view of Sierra peaks rosy in the glow of a setting sun. Then they built that fire on the highest point, as a signal of victory.

15

---◆···◆---

THROUGH THE
CAMERA'S EYE

CARLETON E. WATKINS' mammoth-plate views of Yosemite
were the first photographs of Western landscape to be proclaimed
works of art. The versatile Oliver Wendell Holmes, poet, physician, Harvard professor, and novelist, who was also the foremost
mid-nineteenth-century critic of photography, wrote that "as specimens of art they are admirable, and some of the subjects are
among the most interesting to be found in the whole realm of
Nature." Further, Watkins' approach was original: instead of photographing El Capitan and the Three Brothers head-on as they
soared into the air, as would ordinarily be done, he had captured
them in reflection, projected onto quiet stretches of the Merced
River. Holmes found each view to be "clear, yet soft, vigorous in
the foreground, delicately distinct in the distance, in a perfection of
art." Fellow photographers recognized his superiority. The distinguished British landscape photographer Charles R. Savage wrote
that "among the most advanced in the photographic art, none
stands higher than Mr. C. E. Watkins, who has produced . . . results second to none in either the eastern or western hemispheres."
Carleton Watkins, more than any one person, through his camera's
eye caught the world's attention and drew it to Yosemite Valley.

In 1849, the twenty-year-old Watkins, son of an upstate New
York innkeeper, joined the gold rush to California, going by way

of the Isthmus of Panama. Traveling with him was a friend, Collis P. Huntington, destined to become a financier and promoter of the Central Pacific Railroad. Perhaps neither man intended to dig for gold. Certainly Huntington did not, for he took with him a stock of merchandise to be sold at maximum profit to miners; by 1850 he had, with a partner, established a hardware business in Sacramento, which brought him his first fortune. Carleton Watkins may have tried his luck in the placers, but by 1854 he was clerking in a San Francisco store, apparently only on a part-time basis, since an acquaintance, Robert Vance, a successful San Francisco daguerreotypist who had two branch studios, asked him to take charge of his San Jose gallery until he could replace an operator who had left suddenly. Watkins knew nothing about photography, so when Vance came to San Jose that first Saturday, still without a replacement, he gave him some basic instruction in the hope that it would carry him through Sunday, the most popular day for portrait sittings. Bluff his way as best he could, Vance advised; he would return the following week and make the necessary retakes. When Vance came back, he found that Watkins had mastered the technique, and that his hunt for an operator was over. Having discovered his life's work, Watkins managed the gallery for a time, meanwhile learning the new wet-plate process; Vance, foreseeing the demise of the daguerreotype, had invested in the advanced equipment.

By early 1858, Watkins was working in San Francisco as a daguerrean operator, on his own, making a living from portraits and cartes de visite. But it was landscape photography that fascinated him, and in 1861 he made his first trip to Yosemite, taking with him a special 18-by-22-inch camera built to his specifications. It consisted simply of a wooden box with an opening in front for the lens and one at the back for the ground-glass plate. With this camera he was to make the largest outdoor views yet taken by any American photographer.

He started off from Mariposa with a train of twelve mules to carry his camping outfit and photographic equipment. Going by way of Wawona, he stopped at the Big Tree Grove, where he took the first photographs of the Grizzly Giant. He posed Galen Clark at its base, solely to indicate relative size, for Watkins' landscapes became noted for their absence of human figures. One London critic wrote that in none of his Yosemite views "do we see the least signs of man; not a log hut nor an ax-felled tree to indicate his presence: all seems wild, primitive nature, which give the great charm to these excellent photographs." This presentation of landscape as it may have looked before the advent of man appealed strongly to British and European viewers, whose own untouched wilderness had vanished so long before.

Once Watkins began photographing in the valley, five mules were required just to transport his professional outfit, for he was also working with a stereoscopic camera, useful in making studies of smaller subjects. One mule was needed solely for carrying the dark tent used for coating and developing plates. Before each photograph was taken, all supplies were unpacked and the portable darkroom set up; then after the exposures were made—each taking from ten minutes to an hour—and the plates developed, everything was carefully repacked, and the caravan moved on to the next scenic point, where the process was repeated. To avoid the blur of waving leaves or branches, exposures were often made in early morning or late afternoon, when the air was normally still. Because of light conditions at those times, such exposures required about sixty minutes. One of Watkins' finest pictures in this first series was a view of Sentinel Rock taken before the sun had risen on that part of the valley; exposure time was one hour.

Charles Savage, the English photographer who so admired his work, was curious to learn how Watkins managed to produce such clear, large views in a climate so dry and hard to work in, and called on him in San Francisco. He found Watkins not at all reluctant to reveal his methods, and spent "many pleasant hours" with him. Savage was surprised to learn that after his negatives were developed, Watkins kept them in a water bath until he was ready to finish them. This allowed him time to take the best advantage of light conditions. "Just think of carrying such huge baths, glasses, etc., on mule back, and you can have some idea of the difficulties in the way of producing such magnificent results," Savage pointed out to readers of *The Philadelphia Photographer*, the leading American journal in that field.

Watkins spent his first season in Yosemite Valley mastering his equipment and experimenting with aesthetic approach. He undoubtedly returned the following year to continue his work, but was certainly there in 1863, for he met William H. Brewer of the Whitney Survey, who wondered at the trouble Watkins took to make pictures and marveled at the results: "A series of the finest photographs I have ever seen."

From the start Watkins had a rival in Charles L. Weed, whose Yosemite scenes he was determined to excel. Weed had also learned the glass-plate technique in Vance's studio, and had an advantage in having preceded Watkins to Yosemite by two years. As a member of James Mason Hutchings' party, Weed had taken his camera to the valley in 1859 and made the first photographs by a professional. His work was widely acclaimed until Watkins began showing his views, when it became evident to the cognoscenti that Weed's work was inferior in composition and approach. Watkins emerged from this competition as the master photographer of Yosemite, and his rise to fame was rapid. By 1864 collectors throughout the United States, Great Britain, and Europe had bought his Yosemite views. In this same year an album of these prints helped convince Congress of the need to preserve Yosemite Valley, and doubtless influenced President Lincoln to approve the bill. Soon after Frederick Law Olmsted became chairman of the first board of Yosemite commissioners, he selected Watkins to make photographs of the area's most striking scenery, to be used in studies for its preservation.

Until 1866 Watkins limited himself to scenes within the valley and from Inspiration Point. But that year he accompanied geologists Clarence King and James Gardiner into Yosemite high country; King came to consider him the finest photographer he ever worked with. During this association Watkins produced some of his most dramatic pictures, made from the vantage points of Sentinel Dome and Glacier Point. Imbued with the general concern for rock, he included arresting foregrounds of exfoliating granite in fine rounded slopes, merging with boulder fields that seemed in turn to join the cliffs; then followed the flow of undulant ridges to a meeting with the far-off Sierra peaks—"communicating the infinite gradations from pebble to mountain," as one critic saw it. There were also closeups of rock structure and pattern, foregrounds for such majestic forms as Half Dome, El Capitan, and the mountain to be named Watkins. Many of the views he printed with distant perspectives faintly defined, in the manner of Oriental landscape paintings.

Watkins found, as others did, that the region never palled on familiarity. Moods and points of view seemed limitless, and inspiration was always fresh. But there was something beyond these —the indefinable magic of the place that held him and brought him back year after year for months at a time; he left no part unexplored in his continual search for the photographic.

In 1867 he opened his Yosemite Art Gallery on San Francisco's Montgomery Street, and this same year sent his mammoth-plate and stereoscopic views of Yosemite to the Paris Exposition Universelle. He received the only medal awarded for landscape photographs. He gained still further recognition with the publication in 1868 of Josiah Whitney's popular guide, *The Yosemite Book*, which was illustrated with fifty of Watkins' photographs made at Whitney's request.

As the gallery prospered and business expanded, Watkins was able to hire an assistant to operate it while he spent more and more time in the field, broadening his sphere in landscape work. In 1868 there was an expedition with painter William Keith up the Pacific Coast into Oregon, where Watkins made the first photographs of Columbia River scenery. Two years later he accompanied Clarence King to Mounts Lassen and Shasta in the Cascade Range; and in 1873 he toured Utah with Keith. Through his friendship with Collis P. Huntington, by that time a railroad magnate, he had an annual pass, and a flatcar always available to transport his two-horse photographic van, thereby making still more territory available to his camera's eye.

But he was an artist and not a businessman. Although he made large amounts of money, he was often in straitened circumstances and forced to borrow or to accept money gifts from wealthy admirers, for he gave generously and spent with no thought for the future. It was perhaps in keeping that he was also careless about financial obligations. During the tour of Utah an irate creditor, taking advantage of his absence, called in a long-overdue loan and ordered the gallery seized and the contents auctioned off.

I. W. Taber, a portrait photographer in the same building, acquired the Watkins negatives—some one hundred and fourteen mammoth plates of Yosemite scenes and over a thousand stereoscopic views—which he did not hesitate to print under his own name. Angered, Watkins told a friend: "That thief of a crook got everything away from me." But he did not propose to sit and cry about it, he added.

Soon he was on his way to Yosemite to recoup his artistic and financial losses, a project that was to cover many years. Setting up his camera at favorite viewpoints, he obtained results of the same high artistic order, many so similar to his earlier work they can be distinguished only by careful comparison for natural changes—the growth of foreground shrubbery; the absence of some prominent tree, storm-felled; or the presence of man-made structures. This similarity was not, however, indicative of artistic stagnation, for on close analysis, subtle differences marking increased sensitivity and a firmer grasp of the art are discernible. In some scenes there was a total change in approach, when, perhaps, a concern for strong contrasts in light and shadow replaced an earlier interest in details of rock structure.

Between 1867 and 1873, Yosemite became the most important working ground in America for mammoth-plate landscape photographers. The competition was keen, but Watkins' rank as Yosemite's foremost interpreter was not seriously threatened until the latter year. The challenge, presented by Eadweard J. Muybridge, came while Watkins was in the midst of remaking his lost work, a time when it was difficult for him to meet it. But Watkins had had rivals before, and his position seemed secure. In his absorption with photographing his "new series" in his favorite Yosemite, he perhaps gave little thought to Muybridge.

In 1880, at the age of fifty-one, Watkins married, and later this same year opened his gallery at a new location on Montgomery Street, next to the Palace Hotel. Reflecting the elegance of the famed inn, the gallery was "handsomely carpeted and fitted up with solid walnut showcases, tables and easels" for the display of his new Yosemite photographs. The walls were hung with photographs of a wide range of subjects—mining scenes in the Sierra foothills; Oregon, Utah, and Montana landscapes; views of San Francisco; studies of trees (almost botanical in perfection); and a recently completed series of California missions—many of them framed in heavy black walnut with gilt bands edging the mat next to the print.

But the spectacular and sensitive views of Yosemite that had first brought him fame remained his most popular work and the basis of his business. He continued portraiture, which was always profitable, and accepted commissions from rich friends (for he circulated in the upper strata of California society) to photograph their homes, gardens, and ranches.

Before 1870 landscape photographers in the Far West (relatively few in number) took pictures of what attracted them as artists, with the hope that these scenes might also appeal to prospective viewers and buyers. But after the completion of the transcontinental railroad, when increasing numbers of tourists began exploring the West, the demand for pictures of the spectacular and unusual sights along their routes of travel turned outdoor photography from an art form into a lucrative business. The field was shortly invaded by mediocre photographers whose products satisfied most travelers.

For Watkins the end of the 1880s marked the start of a financial decline. Money continued to slip from his hands; but in order to make more, he refused to compromise his art for the sake of good commercial prospects. Fortunately Huntington was aware of his old friend's improvidence and made some provision by deeding him an eighty-acre ranch in historic Capay Valley, Yolo County, as part compensation for the photographic work Watkins had performed gratis over the years for the Central Pacific. At first the property was leased, which brought an income. But during the 1890s, when his eyesight began to fail and his work was necessarily limited, he had for economic reasons to live in his studio. Then the ranch became a home for Frankie, his wife, and their children, Collis and Julia.

Recognizing the historical importance of his collection, which included the work of other and earlier photographers of the West, Watkins negotiated with Stanford University for its safekeeping. A friend who was cataloging for him (Watkins was almost totally blind by that time) wrote that on Sunday April 15, 1906, he unearthed an oaken chest in a crowded closet in the studio, and on opening it found the contents to be rare daguerreotypes of early California people and scenes, representing most of the noted photographers. Aware of its great value, he determined to send it to Palo Alto as soon as possible. Since it was too heavy for him to handle alone, he dragged it to the rear door and told Watkins that the next Sunday he would bring a helper.

Three days later, April 18, came San Francisco's great earthquake, and in its wake the devastating fire which swept through that part of the city where the Watkins gallery stood. Nearly his entire life's work was destroyed, for nothing had yet reached the Stanford archives. Broken in spirit and ailing physically, he retired to his ranch. He lived ten years more, in a kind of mental eclipse, dying at the age of eighty-seven. Unable to find inspiration for living from the world of nature he could no longer see except in his mind's eye, he turned inward.

As the master of Western landscape he set a standard for photographers who followed, many of whose careers might have been different had he not blazed the way. His classic style and candid expression of his own profound experience in nature, particularly in Yosemite, remained a major influence.

16

THE RIVAL

THE PHOTOGRAPHER Eadweard J. Muybridge was profoundly
influenced by Carleton Watkins and deeply indebted to his pioneer-
ing mammoth-view landscape work. In 1861 Watkins went to
Yosemite and set up his camera at many of the same viewpoints his
rival Charles L. Weed had used, in a determined effort to surpass
him. Seven years later Muybridge followed to Yosemite, intent on
excelling Watkins and establishing himself as the region's foremost
photographer. He spent five months there exploring with two
cameras—a 5½-by-8½-inch glass-plate and a stereoscopic—frequently placing his camera just where Watkins had. To distinguish
his work Muybridge manipulated, often stylized, his points of view
in order to achieve a romantic approach, and did not hesitate to
improve upon nature by adding a drift of broken cloud across the
face of Yosemite Falls or banking sullen thunderheads beside North
Dome—either painting them on the original negative or printing
them from separate ones. He made his headquarters at Hutchings'
hotel, where he was amused by the antics of the four-year-old Floy
and listened with interest to her father talk of Indian customs and
repeat legends. Sharing Hutchings' interest in perpetuating the
Indian names for landmarks, Muybridge used them in his picture
titles, lending yet another romantic touch.

At the age of twenty Edward James Muggeridge, the son of a

small-coals and corn dealer in Kingston-on-Thames, England, decided to make his way as a publisher's representative in the United States. By 1855 when he established an antiquarian bookshop on San Francisco's Montgomery Street, he had made the first in a series of periodic name changes that marked stages in his career, and satisfied a flair for the exotic: he had become E. J. Muggridge. The lack of euphony perhaps prompted him the next year to call himself Muygridge (*Muy* pronounced *My*), and not long after, in seeking the unusual, to spell his first name Eadward.

Genial, well-liked, and energetic, he became prominent in local bookselling and publishing circles (he continued to represent a London publisher), was active in civic affairs, and was elected to the board of directors of the Mercantile Library, one of the city's most esteemed institutions. Because he was an excellent businessman, his store prospered and expanded, and in 1860 he imported two younger brothers, Thomas and George, to help him. Shortly he sold the business to Thomas, and, with another name change— to Muybridge—embarked on a new career: a buyer of rare books and fine art.

Aware of the value of self-promotion, he kept the public well informed about his activities. In mid-May of 1860, the San Francisco *Daily Evening Bulletin* published an announcement that after Mr. Muybridge's return from a sightseeing tour of Yosemite Valley, he would be leaving on June 5 for New York, London, Paris, Rome, Berlin, and Vienna, and would accept orders for "the purchase of Works of Literature or Art," on a commission basis.

But he was delayed in returning from Yosemite and missed his sailing. Determined to get on his way as soon as possible, on July 2 he left on the overland mail stage, which carried up to eight passengers. It was a trip destined to change his life.

In northeastern Texas there is a hilly country wooded with post oaks and known as the Cross-Timbers section. As the stage driver left Mountain Station on July 21, he cracked his whip, and the "six wild mustangs" started off on a run. At the summit of the ridge he began applying his brakes for the steep downhill grade ahead, only to find that they did not hold. Uncontrolled, the team tore down the slope at top speed, first to one side of the road, then to the other. They were by then in the midst of a heavy forest, and Muybridge, anticipating the inevitable accident, took out his knife, slit the rear canvas, and was just ready to jump out when the horses swerved into a tree. The stagecoach was literally smashed into pieces; one passenger was killed and the rest were injured, some seriously. Muybridge was thrown on his head.

When he regained consciousness he found himself in a bed at Fort Smith, Arkansas, a hundred and fifty miles away. Each eye formed a different impression, he had no sense of taste or smell, and he was deaf, symptoms that remained acute for several months. As soon as he could, he went on to St. Louis by stage and by rail to New York, where he stayed eight weeks for medical treatment. He then sailed for England, and in London became a patient of Sir William Gull, Queen Victoria's physician. In recommending a course of "natural" therapy, Sir William prescribed an active life in the out-of-doors.

Muybridge decided to become a landscape photographer. It was a field in which he may have already had some experience, for he counted among his friends a number of professionals from whom he could have learned the art. It is certain that he practiced it in England during those years while he was still under medical treatment, for he said so. In 1867 he returned to San Francisco as Eadweard Muybridge, on the brink of a new career as master photographer.

His old friends in the city found him much changed since the accident: he was not the same "in any respect." The genial personality was gone, and he tended to be moody, irascible, eccentric, careless in dress, and lacking some of his business acumen.

He had not, however, lost his talent for self-promotion. Upon his return to San Francisco from his five-month photographic jaunt in Yosemite in 1868, he issued a brochure in which he posed as the publisher of twenty Yosemite views made by Helios, the name under which he now chose to work. "For artistic effect, and careful manipulation, they are pronounced by all the best landscape painters and photographers in the city to be the most exquisite photographic views ever produced on this coast [a broad claim in view of Carleton Watkins' having recently received the Paris Exposition medal for Yosemite landscapes] and are marvelous examples of the perfection to which photography can attain in the delineation of sublime and beautiful scenery." The list of subscribers for this series, he added, included nearly all "our best known connoisseurs and patrons of art." Whatever other reason he may have had for taking a pseudonym, there was the obvious one that allowed him to praise his own work in the highest terms.

Soon after the brochure's appearance he held a preview for critics, painters, and photographers. The identity of the mysterious Helios became a favorite theme for speculation in art circles. Which local photographer was hiding under the "significant classicism" of that name? Critics were in agreement that these Yosemite views surpassed in "artistic excellence" all others that had been published in San Francisco, and commended the painterly approach: "In some of the series we have just such cloud effects as we see in . . . oil painting."

Muybridge then sent one hundred and twenty-five of these prints to *The Philadelphia Photographer* for review; and still posing as the publisher, gave a number of them to San Francisco's Mercantile Library for display. Further attention was drawn to Helios by the publication of John S. Hittell's guide, *Yosemite: Its Wonders and Its Beauties*, illustrated with twenty Muybridge photographs. In the book's endpapers Edw. J. Muybridge of the Cosmopolitan Gallery of Photographic Art, on Montgomery Street, offered for sale two hundred and fifty of the "most comprehensive and beautiful" views of Yosemite Valley "ever executed." These works by HELIOS, he reminded the reader, were "justly celebrated as being the most artistic and remarkable photographs ever produced on this coast." Determined to compete with Carleton Watkins in all fields, Muybridge added that Helios was prepared to accept commissions to photograph "Private Residences, Ranches, Mills, Views, Animals, Ships, etc., anywhere in the city, or any portion of the Pacific Coast."

Not until the spring of 1872 did Muybridge return to Yosemite, equipped this time with a mammoth-plate camera larger than Watkins' and two cameras of smaller size, as well as a stereo; a sky shade of his own invention to prevent overexposure, for wet-collodion plates were extremely sensitive to blue light; and, in his own words, "an outfit of lenses and apparatus superior to any other in the United States." Traveling with him was the eminent landscape painter Albert Bierstadt, who shared his views on the aesthetics of landscape depiction and acted as his mentor. That Muybridge produced his finest work this season was certainly due in part to the painter's influence, reflected in such photographs as

"The Domes, from Glacier Rock"; "Tisayack, from Mount Waiya"; and "Valley of the Yosemite from Glacier Point," all containing highly effective cloud masses and hazy backgrounds typical of Bierstadt's work. There were also richly romantic moonlit scenes and, interestingly, mirror views in the style of Watkins.

To obtain these striking pictures, the San Francisco press reported, he often waited several days in one spot for the proper light conditions, went places where his packers refused to follow, and carried the equipment himself rather than forgo a scene—all of which Carleton Watkins had also done. But the critics and public were ready for a change, and Watkins was being temporarily eclipsed. Response to Muybridge's romantic, painterly approach was overwhelming. "Artistic," the novelist Helen Hunt Jackson called his work, and likened it to the landscape painting of Millet and Tenniers. It was unfortunate, she felt, that the world knew Yosemite mainly through the "big but inartistic" views of Carleton Watkins.

"The Watkins photographs are too well known to require comment," one San Francisco critic wrote, "but I would like to mention that Mr. Muybridge, a photographer not so long before the public"—the identity of Helios was finally discovered—"will exhibit . . . a series of large Yo-Semite views, finer and more perfect than any . . . ever . . . taken." By 1873 art connoisseurs were urging painters of Yosemite landscape to use Muybridge as their model and approximate his work as nearly as possible. His photographs were no longer to be compared favorably with paintings, but paintings were to be judged by his work. That year his Yosemite views were submitted to the International Exposition at Vienna and were awarded the medal for progress in landscape photography. Failing to recognize the stylistic difference between his approach and that of Watkins, the judges hailed Muybridge's work as evidence of advancement to a higher level of photographic art. At home, there was this same failure to perceive the fundamental dissimilarity between these two foremost interpreters of Yosemite, or to recognize Muybridge's debt to Watkins.

Before leaving for Yosemite in 1872, Muybridge received a telegram from Leland Stanford that was destined to change his career. Stanford, a former governor of California and a promoter, along with Collis P. Huntington, Charles Crocker, and Mark Hopkins, of the Central Pacific Railroad, owned a racing stable. From his ob-

servations Stanford advanced a radical theory that a horse in full
gallop had all four feet off the ground simultaneously at some
point in its gait. He was so certain of this, he bet a friend $25,000
and called on a photographer of no less eminence than Eadweard
Muybridge to furnish proof.

Muybridge was intrigued by the challenge of instantaneous
photography and worked with Stanford from April into early May,
long enough to establish the truth of Stanford's observations. After
the Yosemite sojourn they resumed the experiments with capturing various forms of motion on film, whenever Muybridge could
spare the time, for the demands his profession placed on him were
heavy now that he had reached the peak of his career. Then, in
October 1874, everything came to a sudden halt.

Three years earlier, at the age of forty-one, he had married a
twenty-year-old divorcée, Flora Stone, an aspiring actress, "petite
but voluptuous . . . with a sweet face and large lustrous eyes," who
had been retouching photographs in his studio. In May of 1874 she
bore a son whom Muybridge named Florado Helios. Six months
later he discovered the child was not his, but that of Harry Larkyns, a young and dashing British adventurer who had been
Flora's lover and lived with her during her husband's long absences on photographic assignments.

Learning that Larkyns had been sent by a San Francisco financial journal to report on the quicksilver deposits in Napa and
Sonoma counties, Muybridge set off to find him. Tracing him to a
ranch near the Yellow Jacket Mine, not far from Calistoga, he
entered the house and shot Larkyns to death. Then allowing himself to be disarmed and apologizing to several women present for
making a disturbance, he sat down in the parlor and began reading a newspaper. He was shortly placed under a citizens' arrest
and taken to the county jail for indictment and trial. That Muybridge had committed murder there was no doubt, but through
the endeavors of a brilliant young lawyer he was acquitted on
grounds of justifiable homicide. A man so wronged was entitled to
avenge that wrong, the defense argued, and the all-male jury con-
curred.

Soon after the trial Muybridge left for Central America to make
a photographic survey for the Pacific Mail Steamship Company,
a project that had been postponed by the Larkyns affair. The pictures taken on that assignment revealed him as a master photo-

journalist. He returned to San Francisco at the end of the following year. By then his wife had died, the scandal had quieted, and he took up his work with Stanford. He also assumed full responsibility for little Florado Helios.

In 1883 he was invited to continue his studies and experiments at the University of Pennsylvania. By that time he had made great advances, and was working with a battery of twenty-four cameras placed side by side, to capture the sequence of movement not only of horses, but of cattle, dogs, and men.

He never returned to Yosemite, nor did he go back to landscape photography. Acclaimed internationally for his research in photographing motion, he returned to England in 1892 to make his home, lecture, and prepare his studies for publication. Painters of animals were quick to recognize their debt to him, for prior to the publication of his illustrated books *The Horse in Motion* and *Animal Locomotion*, knowledge of this subject was slight. When horses and dogs—animals most often included in paintings—were shown running, they were almost always depicted with both forefeet extended to the front and both rear ones stretched behind, in the rocking-horse gallop. After seeing Muybridge's photographs in series, Jean Louis Meissonier, the noted French painter of animals, was said to have been unable to sleep that night, "so great was the shock to his sense of truth."

Muybridge's romantic views of Yosemite landscape brought him his first fame, established his artistry with a camera, and called Leland Stanford's attention to him. Had the pattern been ordered differently, the photographer might never have found his true life's work, and have achieved through his scientific research so important a place in the history of motion pictures.

17

THE LANDSCAPIST
AND THE
HASHEESH EATER

ALBERT BIERSTADT, the German-born New Bedford artist, had received his first major critical acclaim just prior to setting off for Yosemite Valley in the spring of 1863. He was by then the acknowledged "prince" of the painters of Western mountain scenery, noted for his mastery over broken light. It was predicted that he would soon "lead the brotherhood of American Landscape Painters."

He was two when his parents settled in the Massachusetts whaling port in 1832, and little is known about his early life or his art training until he was twenty. Then there appeared in the local newspaper an announcement that A. Bierstadt was prepared to give instruction in "the new and beautiful art" of monochromatic painting at his studio, where examples of his own work might be seen. That was in May 1850. The following year he had an exhibit of his paintings in New Bedford (which brought him a local patron), entered a crayon drawing in the New England Art Union show at Boston, and had an oil hung at the Massachusetts Academy of Fine Arts. In spite of this moderate success, he knew that he needed training, and in 1853, with the help of yet another patron, he went to Düsseldorf, an important German art center that drew students from all over the world. There he studied four years, at least part of the time with his mother's cousin, Johann

Peter Hasenclever, one of the country's leading painters. Study included travel throughout Germany, Switzerland, and Italy in search of subjects; training in making field sketches in pencil and charcoal, and color studies in oil, which were later developed into full-scale paintings in the instructor's studio. Two years after his return home, he joined a government expedition under Colonel F. W. Lander that was headed for the Rocky Mountains. The paintings Bierstadt made following this journey established his reputation.

In the winter of 1862, as he studied a collection of Carleton Watkins' photographs of Yosemite on display at Goupil's gallery in New York City, his response to the massive and unusual rock forms and to the waterfalls of tremendous height was immediate and strong. He felt their challenge to his brush and determined to go there. By early April he was on his way, with three friends. The most eminent was the twenty-seven-year-old New York art critic and author Fitz Hugh Ludlow, whose book *The Hasheesh Eater*— "a work of unrivaled eloquence and genius"—based on his own experiences, had made him a celebrity. At this time he had a contract with the *Atlantic Monthly* to write a series of articles describing the trip to California, with arrangements to publish them later in book form. The train took the party to Atchison, where they boarded the overland stage. Under their feet and within easy reach were their "commissary stores," to augment the often scanty and unsavory fare served at meal stations, and to supply them in the event of a breakdown in the wilderness. They were also prepared for possible Indian attack—"Our guns hung in their cases by the straps of the wagon-top"—and they were dressed for any emergency: "We wore broad slouch hats of the softest felt, which made capital night-caps for an out-door bed; blue flannel shirts," serviceable in "all weathers and climates . . . stout pantaloons of gray Cheviot, tucked into knee-boots; revolvers and cartouche-boxes on belts of broad leather about our waists; and light, loose linen sacks over all."

They arrived in San Francisco on July 17 and were welcomed by Thomas Starr King, then pastor of the city's First Unitarian Church, who planned to accompany them to Yosemite. At his home, where they spent many evenings, they "gazed by the hour" at more Watkins photographs of Yosemite hanging on the drawing-room walls. King added his impressions of the valley—which made Ludlow feel they were about to enter the original Eden—and told them he had it on the authority of two reliable British army officers who had explored the Himalaya wilderness that no precipice in Asia could compare in height and grandeur with El Capitan, just as no waterfall in the Alps could equal Yosemite Falls.

Much of their time before departure was spent in buying supplies; canned fruit and sardines, crocks of apple butter, and jugs of maple syrup were highly recommended to supplement the staples. Other necessities were ammunition for their shotguns, Ballard rifles, and Colt revolvers; and saddle horses. That called for a tour of all the stables in a city noted for fine horses. They were determined to have the best, and finally settled for animals at $70 apiece in gold—horses that would have cost over $150 each in New York. Saddles were next: "If there be a more perfect saddle than the Californian, I would ride bare-back a good way to get it," Ludlow announced. "It is not for a day, but for all time"; designed to conform to the rider's body and to ease the horse's burden. "There is no such thing as getting tired in it or of it."

By August first they were in Stockton, having gone by steamer. At the very last Starr King had been unable to come, but two San Francisco painters, Virgil Williams, whom Bierstadt had known while studying in Rome, and Enoch Wood Perry, an old comrade from Düsseldorf days, as well as Dr. John Hewston, "a highly scientific metallurgist and physicist," had joined them. Before embarking, they hired a former army teamster as factotum—"a meager, wiry fellow with sandy hair" by the name of Vance, a nephew, he said, of North Carolina's Confederate governor, Zebulon Vance. At Stockton they bought a secondhand Jersey wagon to carry their baggage to Mariposa, where they shifted to pack mules and took on the services of a fifteen-year-old youth to help with the train.

The painters spent a full day in the Mariposa Grove (with Galen Clark as their guide) making color studies and sketches of the giant sequoia, while the others pursued their special fields—botany and entomology among them—or wandered about gathering statistics on the Big Trees. The artists encountered problems when it came to depicting size, for in scaling them to fit a limited space, it was impossible to make the sequoia appear any larger than ordinary conifers. Bierstadt used Carleton Watkins' solution, placing Galen Clark at the base of the Grizzly Giant, the largest in circumference. He flanked it with a few pines of normal girth and height, and to emphasize comparative magnitude, stood a man and mule beside a tall, stout pine in the left foreground. Whether Bierstadt used Watkins' photograph of the Grizzly Giant as a model (it is almost an exact copy) or whether he received the advice in person has not been determined. But the two men must surely have met during their stay in the Yosemite area that summer. The photographer's influence is apparent in a number of other Bierstadt scenes, suggesting that Watkins pointed out special points of view. In approach, however, the two men differed radically, for the painter was a complete romanticist, dependent upon the broken light of brewing storms; the suffusing glow of dawn or sunset; cloud masses, shadow contrasts, and enveloping mists for theatrical effect. To Watkins, nature needed no embellishment: there was sufficient dramatic impact in the massive rock forms and towering falls alone. He shared John Muir's concept of truth and beauty in nature, and held that the most direct depiction allowed the essence of landscape to reveal itself.

As others had, the Bierstadt party found Galen Clark one of the best informed of men. He was handsome and wore "a noble, full beard" and shoulder-length hair; but, remarkable in this land of hats, he went hatless, for, he explained, the fever he had with his illness of 1856 had left his head so sensitive he could not stand the feel of even a featherweight slouch. They slept in his tavern, and at breakfast were treated to "the nicest poached eggs and rashers of bacon, home-made bread and wild strawberry sweetmeats" that could be found in the state.

For their midday meal they stopped at a "lovely green meadow walled in on one side by near snow-peaks." In the brook that wound through, the party's gourmands caught frogs enough for an entree. During the afternoon's ride they were aware of many wild-flowers—showy magenta fireweed; clumps of scarlet penstemon; hillsides thick with lupine in several shades of purple and blue; and among thickets on dry banks, the now rare Washington lily, "with an odor of tuberoses."

Traveling through the dense forest, they had no hint of Yo-semite's proximity until a sharp turn in the trail brought them into a clearing on an eminence, and the whole valley lay before them. They called this high clifftop Inspiration Point. "That name had appeared pedantic, but we found it only the spontaneous expression of our own feelings on the spot," Ludlow explained. "We did not seem to be seeing from that crag of vision a new scene on the old familiar globe as a new heaven and a new earth into which the creative spirit had just been breathed." They began picking out those prominent features made familiar through Watkins' photographs—El Capitan, North Dome, Half Dome, Cathedral Rocks, and Bridalveil Fall—and the painters sketched until nearly sundown.

"Like a nightmare of endless roof-walking was the descent down the face of the precipice. A painful and most circuitous dug-way, where our animals had constantly to stop lest their impetus should tumble them headlong, all the way." It was twilight when they rode into the meadow beside the Merced where they set up Camp Rosalie, named for Ludlow's wife, the beautiful Rosalie Osborne, with whom Bierstadt was in love. "We soon got together dead wood and pitchy boughs enough to kindle a roaring fire—made a kitchen table by wedging logs between the trunks of a three-forked tree . . . selected a cedar-canopied flat sward near the fire for our bed-room," and spread blankets over deep piles of fragrant evergreens.

Each morning during their stay in this camp west of Bridalveil Fall, the party rose at dawn, bathed in the icy Merced, breakfasted on game, flapjacks, syrup, apple butter, and coffee, then started out on horseback—"the artists with their camp-stools and color-boxes; the sages with their goggles, nets, botany-boxes, and bug-holders; the gentlemen of elegant leisure with their naked eyes . . . a fish-rod or gun." Ludlow's particular interest was collecting butterflies. At first he chased them on horseback, because the idea was romantic—a knight at some medieval game—but finding that he too often missed his quarry and netted his horse's head, he took to foot. Most of the party returned to camp for the noon dinner, but the painters took theirs in the field, the camp-boy carrying it to them in pails. There was often cold roast grouse, pigeon, or quail, or fresh-panned trout, for their sportsmen kept the table well-supplied. Bierstadt, Perry, and Williams stayed out until the light was almost gone; then after they had gotten back to camp, a half-hour was spent in a critical viewing of the day's field studies. Supper followed—another large meal—then brush-cleaning, the smoking of pipes, talk, and finally bed.

The three or four tourist parties then in the valley included several handsome girls whose informal mountaineering dress indicated shapely figures. It was a treat to see women undisguised by huge bell-shaped skirts; to observe the flow and grace of body movement free of encumbrance. Bierstadt and his friends denounced the fashion. "The bachelor who cares to see unhooped womanhood once more before he dies should go to the Yo-Semite," Ludlow advised.

After ten days or so, camp was moved five miles east to a grove of fine oaks and cedars just opposite Yosemite Falls. By then supplies had begun to run low, so Vance was dispatched to Mariposa with a horse and led mule, a list of purchases, and eighty dollars in gold. At the end of seven days when he had still not returned, Ludlow volunteered to track him down. At Clark's he learned that Vance had been there about noon on his first day out, had turned his animals loose instead of picketing them, and when ready to start on, had found they had disappeared. He accordingly borrowed Clark's only horse to search for them and had not been seen since. On the outskirts of Mariposa, Ludlow discovered their horse quietly grazing beside the road, threw a lariat over his head, and led him on into town, where the rest of the tale was soon pieced together. The pack mule had found his way back to the home stable; Vance had lost the eighty dollars in gold at a single game of cards; had then gone on with Clark's horse to Coulterville, where he sold it at auction, including saddle and bridle, for forty dollars; had promptly lost that money at cards; and had finally vanished, penniless and afoot, for parts unknown. Content with having found the three missing animals (Clark got his horse again upon proof of ownership), Ludlow started back for Yosemite with a load of provisions. He arrived there just as his comrades had emptied the final sack of flour for a last round of flapjacks, unleavened and syrupless.

After another ten or twelve days the artists were ready to move on, and camp was set up this time at Mirror Lake. They agreed that it was one of the most scenic parts of the valley, and enthusiasm ran high: "Painters, sages, and gentlemen at large, all turned out by dawn; for the studies were grander, the grouse and quail plentier, and the butterflies more gorgeous." Their wanderings led them east through Tenaya Canyon, where in following the stream for five miles, they discovered "some of the finest minor waterfalls in our American scenery."

Their final camp was pitched on a flat near the summit of Vernal Fall. There was at that time no horse trail beyond the entrance to the Merced Canyon. At this point they sent their animals back to camp, and packing the baggage themselves, "struck nearly eastward by a path only less rugged than the trackless crags around us. In some places we were compelled to squeeze sideways through a narrow crevice in the rocks, at imminent danger to . . . blankets and camp-kettles"; in others, they were forced to scramble on all fours up slippery inclines. "But for our light marching order—our only dress being knee-boots, hunting-shirt, and trowsers—it would have been next to impossible to reach our goal at all." But rewards were great, for these falls were the most beautiful they had yet seen. By August the peak of snowmelt and runoff is over, and those waterfalls that drop into the main chasm have dwindled—Yosemite Falls have shrunk to slender ribbons—and many lesser ones have disappeared. But the volume of the Merced River, fed by eternal springs and glaciers, remains relatively constant, and its falls full. Not far from Vernal (a "senseless" name, they thought; far better to have kept the Indian, Pi-wei'-ack—"sparkling water"), there was an "immense, overhanging, smooth-faced 'chip' of rock about the size of an ordinary village church," known as Register Rock. There were already a number of names inscribed when they added their record: "Camped here August 21, 1863. A. Bierstadt, Virgil Williams, E. W. Perry, Fitz Hugh Ludlow."

Bierstadt came completely under Yosemite's spell—it was to be his favorite painting ground—and within the next eight years he completed at least fifteen oils of Yosemite scenes. By early 1864 he had finished the first, a view west through the valley at sunset, showing Cathedral Rocks and El Capitan suffused with golden light. This was followed by "Camping in Yosemite," a view of Yosemite Falls that included their second campsite; "Valley of the Yosemite"; "Mirror Lake"; and "Vernal Fall." That same year the artist fulfilled the early prophecy, and critics pronounced him the peer of Frederic E. Church, America's foremost landscapist—perhaps even his superior in mastery of cloud effects and of light and shadow. Church was among the first to recognize this, and asked Bierstadt for criticism of a painting of Niagara he was about to send to a Paris exhibition.

Bierstadt's next Yosemite work, the second-largest canvas he ever painted (15 feet long by 9½ feet high), included the entire valley eastward from the base of Yosemite Falls. "The Domes of Yosemite," as he titled it, was shown in New York and Boston, and proclaimed by one critic to be "the best landscape ever painted in this country."

The visit of so noted a painter as Bierstadt stimulated Bay Area artists to unprecedented productivity. The result was "a violent outbreak of Yosemite views, good, bad, and indifferent . . . There is danger of having a little too much of even such a good thing as Yosemite," a San Francisco art judge observed.

Not long after his return home from Yosemite, Fitz Hugh Ludlow added alcohol to his hashish addiction, and within a year was considered by his family to have "sunk too low to be worth any consideration any more." He tried several cures, all unsuccessful, and Rosalie separated from him. He then went off to St. Louis with "his new lady," and Rosalie sued for divorce. Throughout these troubles she had turned to Albert Bierstadt, her husband's best friend, for counsel and help. The painter had loved her over a number of years, and in 1866 asked her to marry him. He took her to Europe on a wedding tour that lasted two years, and built her a mansion at Irvington-on-Hudson that was being constructed during their absence. Meanwhile Ludlow also remarried, but by then his health was completely broken. In an attempt to regain it he went to the Swiss Alps, but three months after his arrival died suddenly, at age thirty-four.

In July 1871, Bierstadt brought Rosalie to San Francisco. He planned an extended stay in California to enable him to paint in other parts of the Sierra as well as Yosemite. By this time he had been awarded the Legion of Honor, had his "Storm in the Rocky Mountains" praised by the noted poet and critic Théophile Gautier, and was soon to receive the Russian Order of St. Stanislaus. Of his Yosemite paintings one art judge wrote that they had probably done "more than all written descriptions to give persons abroad an adequate idea of that wonderful gorge. . . . The striking merit of Bierstadt in his treatment of Yosemite, as of other western landscapes, lies in his power of grasping distances, handling wide spaces, truthfully massing huge objects, and realizing splendid atmospheric effects."

He went first this season to look for subjects in the Donner Summit and Lake Tahoe regions; then in September he returned with Rosalie to New York on business that detained him several months. But in February 1872 he was in Yosemite in search of winter scenes. He went in by way of a trail that branches at Hite's Cove and led to the Merced canyon, which he then followed into the valley. At least two canvases resulted from his stay there, both painted in the studio he had built on the top of San Francisco's Clay Street hill. In May he returned with photographer Eadweard Muybridge. On their way into the valley, they discovered a small Indian encampment in a grove of alders and cottonwoods not far from the Merced River. There Bierstadt set up his easel and made oil sketches of the people and of their conical bark huts, and Muybridge set up his stereo camera and photographed the artist in action. From his color studies and perhaps with the help of Muybridge's photographs, Bierstadt painted "Indians in Council, California." With poetic license he clothed the figures in robes rather than the white man's cast-off garments they were actually wearing.

During this stay of several months, painter and photographer discussed the aesthetics of landscape, about which both had definite and similar concepts and feelings. Bierstadt had some knowledge of photography, for he had taken a camera on that first trip to the Rocky Mountains and also had two brothers who were professional photographers. It is known that Bierstadt and Muybridge worked together this season in selecting points of view that would achieve the high dramatic—theatrical—effect both valued in their work. To reach these special points the photographer would go so far as to have himself lowered on ropes down a cliff face to some narrow ledge or precarious overhang, and there set up what he called his "Flying Studio." The heightened sense of space and the atmospheric effects observed in these photographs may also be credited to the painter, for they were a part of his technique.

Meanwhile Bierstadt was not neglecting his own work, for while Muybridge was busy with his cameras, he was producing color studies and sketches. Together they took the new trail to Glacier Point and agreed that from there was perhaps the finest high view of all, especially of Half Dome and the Sierran peaks beyond, merging with infinity. Bierstadt made drawings from the summit, and of the valley from along the trail, for it was the walled valley that fascinated him. He seemed never to tire of painting it from many viewpoints, under various light conditions, in different moods and seasons, and with diverse approaches.

In August the geologist Clarence King, then at work on a survey of western mountain regions, was ready to leave Yosemite for the east side of the Sierra. He invited Bierstadt to accompany him and make drawings for the survey's report. The painter was struck by the contrasting character of the range's east escarpment—rugged, barren, rising almost sheer from the plain—and completed many studies for his own use. He traveled with King for about two months, then made his way north to paint again in the Lake Tahoe and Donner Summit regions.

Spring found him back in Yosemite at a time when the waterfalls were in full voice and flow; when spires and domes were veiled in morning mists; when masses of cumulus banked the horizon and topped the peaks, so that the Sierra seemed to sweep the sky—romantic visions he transferred to canvas. His wife and a group of friends came with him, and they stayed at Hutchings' hotel. In showing the valley to his party the painter revisited favorite haunts and made still more studies, for its essence was elusive; no other mountains had ever presented so great a challenge. At the end of six weeks they rode north some forty miles, with a guide and pack train, to camp in Hetch Hetchy, the valley of the Tuolumne River. The artist explored the gorge and its approaches with his sketchbook and colors, and subsequently painted four known oils of this lesser Yosemite.

On October 11, 1873, after more than two years in the West, Bierstadt and Rosalie boarded the train for home. In his portfolio were studies enough of Yosemite, the Big Trees, and Hetch Hetchy to last his lifetime. Seven years later he returned to California for five weeks to make preliminary studies for a painting of Mount Shasta and for one of the coast at Monterey. Trip time to Yosemite had by then been cut in half with the opening of a stage road into the valley, and Bierstadt evidently made a brief visit there, for a stage driver on the Wawona–Yosemite run distinctly remembered having him as a passenger. It would have been Bierstadt's final stay in the valley, for he did not come back to California again.

18

JOSEPH LE CONTE'S RAMBLES

"IT WAS IN YOSEMITE VALLEY that I first met him," wrote John Muir of Joseph LeConte; "he was making his first excursion into the high Sierra, and it was delightful to see with what eager, joyful, youthful enthusiasm he reveled in the sublime beauty of the Great Valley, and tried to learn how it was made. His fame had already reached me . . . and, like everybody else, I was at once drawn to him by the charm of his manner."

This was the summer of 1870, and Dr. LeConte, then forty-seven, was one of the most noted and respected scientists in the United States. His magnetic personality and the contagion of his intense and eager interest in his subjects was fast making him the most popular professor at the newly established University of California, where he taught geology, botany, and natural history. The affectionate relation between him and the students grew so rapidly that there soon was no lecture hall on campus big enough to hold his classes. Nine of his geology students had planned this first excursion to Yosemite and invited him to join them. Officially he was the party's surgeon, but in fact was simply one of them. He asked no favors; took his turn cheerfully as camp cook, dish-washer, or packer; joined in their games and gymnastics, for he was an outstanding athlete; and took part in their songs, stories, and jokes on the trail and around the evening campfire. Only when called upon to deliver a lecture in the field was he once again the professor.

Coming from a family of physicians and distinguished scientists, he began his career as a medical doctor in Macon, Georgia, following his graduation from New York's College of Physicians and Surgeons in 1845. The LeContes, of Huguenot origin, had settled in Georgia prior to the American Revolution, in which many of them took a prominent part. The young Dr. Joseph, soon finding that his real interest lay in scientific research and teaching, decided to give up his practice, move to Cambridge with his young wife and small daughter, and enter Harvard to study with Louis Agassiz, one of the great scientists and educators of his time. A strong bond of admiration and affection grew between the two men during a close working relationship of fifteen months, and the dynamic Swiss became a major influence in LeConte's development. After getting his degree he taught at a number of Southern colleges, subjects as far-ranging from his field as French and mechanics, before receiving a professorship in geology and chemistry at South Carolina College in Columbia. From 1860 through the spring of 1862 the school managed to stay open in spite of the Civil War, although by the latter year enrollment had dropped to fifty. But that June, when the Seven Days' Battle was fought for possession of Richmond, Virginia, and there came a call for all men over eighteen, every student volunteered, and the college closed.

"As a result of the war I lost everything I had in the world," LeConte was to write. Columbia was burned and sacked by Sherman's army. There was no money, and barter was the sole means of exchange. Obtaining permission from the federal commandant, the doctor hauled corn by flatboat from low-country plantations where some crops and stores had escaped destruction. The city government allowed him a hundred bushels, which he divided equally with his older brother, John; the rest he used in trade to support his own family. Dressed in a ruined hat and a ragged, castoff Yankee uniform, he worked as boatman until the college reopened as the University of South Carolina. He then resumed teaching, original research, and writing. But prospects were gloomy under Reconstruction rule and the LeConte brothers considered emigration to Mexico. Then word came from Louis Agassiz and other friends and colleagues in the North about the

proposed university in California, and both he and John, also a
distinguished scientist, applied for professorships. In 1868 they
received appointments—John to the chair of physics (later he became president of the university), and Joseph to the department of
natural history. The move to California came the following year.

That first trip to Yosemite Valley was "almost an era in my life,"
Joseph LeConte wrote. "I never enjoyed anything else so much . . .
the merry party of young men, the glorious scenery, and, above
all, the magnificent opportunity for studying mountain origin and
structure."

At ten o'clock on the morning of July 21, 1870, the start was
made. To a chorus of cheers from those left behind, the party set
off at a sweeping trot through the streets of Oakland. Each man
was dressed in flannel shirt, heavy trousers, sturdy boots, and
broad-brimmed hat; hunting knife and pistol were belted at the
waist. Most had rifles strapped behind the saddle.

Spirits were high, although the doctor, who had not been on
horseback in ten years, confessed to some misgivings when he
learned from their captain, Frank Soulé, that the first day's ride
would be thirty miles. It turned out to be nearer forty—ten hours
in the saddle—which took its toll from even the hardiest. As dusk
approached LeConte noticed that his companions' exuberance had
begun to wane. "After some abortive attempts at a song, some
miserable failures in the way of jokes, we pursued our weary way
in silence."

It took seven days to cross the parched, dusty plains of the San
Joaquin Valley—"hot, oh! how how!" the doctor noted. On the
morning of the twenty-eighth, as he sat in the shade of some sugar
pines at Galen Clark's, he wrote in his journal that the real enjoyment of their expedition had now begun: up to this point it had
been sheer endurance in anticipation of enjoyment. They encamped two days at Wawona (which they learned from Clark was
an Indian word meaning "big tree"), to recruit their jaded horses
in the fine meadows; to tour the Mariposa Grove; and to revel in
the welcome coolness of the deep forests and luxuriant grasslands.

Rested and refreshed, spirits were high again by the time they
were ready to leave Clark's on the morning of July 30, and they
joked and sang all the way to the alpine meadows where they had
their lunch. After eating, they pressed on with mounting excitement toward those points where they would get their first views of

Yosemite. Around six that evening they reached Sentinel Dome and climbed to the summit. "Such a sunset I never saw; such a sunset, combined with such a view, I never imagined," the doctor wrote.

In the morning they reached Glacier Point in time to watch the sun rise. Banks of horizon clouds caught and emphasized the colors of dawn alpenglow. Peaks and domes grew flushed and highlighted, but the valley far below still slept. Mirror Lake, gleaming black like obsidian, lay within the shadow cast by Half Dome. The silver Merced, a lifeless ribbon, wound through the stands of somber oaks and pines. Even the falls, massive columns of white, seemed motionless.

By ten o'clock the following day they were in the valley, coming in by way of the switchback trail from Inspiration Point. Camp was set up in a grove at the edge of Bridalveil Meadow, a quarter of a mile from the fall, which they visited late in the afternoon when light conditions are best. The doctor was "enchanted" by its grace and the beauty of its setting.

In the morning camp was moved to a pine forest edging a meadow along the bank of Tenaya Creek. After turning their horses loose to graze they walked a mile and a half to Mirror Lake for a swim. There Yosemite cliffs reached their climax of "imposing grandeur," LeConte saw. He had already observed the many evidences of glacial action in the valley—terminal moraines, striae and polish on cliff faces; and had noted two distinct kinds of granite structure, concentric and rude columnar, which singly or combined were responsible for the various forms. The Royal Arches, he pointed out, were a fine example of exfoliation of concentric structure, while columnar disintegration was seen best in Sentinel Rock and Cathedral Spires. Both were evident in Half Dome.

Several hours were passed in Tenaya Canyon, discussing its geology or observing it silently; watching the lake ripple in the wind, and the cloud shadows race. That night, exhilarated by their surroundings, they sang in chorus until nearly midnight.

Three days later the doctor stopped at Hutchings' sawmill to ask about the trail to Upper Yosemite Fall. The man who answered his questions and excited his interest proved to be John Muir, about whom he had heard much from Jeanne Carr. She had given him an introductory note to Muir, and had also written Muir of his coming. "We were glad to meet each other." Familiar with Muir's

theory of Yosemite's development and his studies in the high country, LeConte was anxious to discuss those findings and conclusions
fully and to examine with him the evidence. He invited him to join
the party on their crossing of the Sierra crest to the east side. Muir
was eager to go but would first have to obtain Hutchings' consent
to leave the mill.

The climb up the cliff east of Yosemite Falls proved strenuous
(it is still considered so). Like all who were new to the West, the
doctor was unprepared for the challenge. Later he became a renowned mountaineer, but now as he made his way over fields of
shifting talus and up perpendicular rock faces, having to inch his
way from crevice to crevice and to edge along minute joint cracks,
it seemed as though they were all defying death at every step. But
once he stood at the base of the great fall, following with his eye
the column of water that seemed to pour out of the clouds crown-
ing the summit, all else was forgotten. When one time the wind
swayed the fall far to the left, the party darted behind, and when
the water swung back again, peered through the mist veils at the
cliffs across the valley—dreamlike in character.

On their return they stopped at the mill and learned from John
Muir that Hutchings had agreed to his accompanying them over
the mountains to Mono Lake. As a result of the gold rush, California had a classless society. Mining had proved the great leveler.
Since the work involved was physical rather than mental, the old
superiority of people who worked with their heads over those who
worked with their hands did not exist. There was never a question
of dignity in the tasks men undertook. This situation struck every
new arrival to the state. Now as LeConte left Muir for a return to
camp, he reflected upon how strange it was to find a man of Muir's
superior intelligence tending a sawmill—"not for himself, but for
Mr. Hutchings."

The party rode down the valley in the cool of dusk. Light still
played on domes and spires; walls were silvery, shadows deep. As
they neared the encampment the doctor was surprised to catch a
distant partial view of Illilouette, one of the least known and visited of the major waterfalls, hidden in a gorge of the same name. It
now gleamed white from the midst of dark-gray granite. His companions seemed tired; there was not much talk, and no jokes or
songs. For himself, he felt fresh, and deeply under the valley's
spell.

The following afternoon, preparatory to leaving for the high country, where John Muir spent his first summer with Pat Delaney's flock, they removed to the old site in Bridalveil Meadow. Just as they were starting off, they heard a hollow rumbling to the left, then a thunderous crashing. Looking quickly in that direction they saw a vertical streak of white down the cliff of Glacier Point, a trail of dust, and large dust clouds rising from the base: a huge rock mass had fallen from the point. This was an example of the dismantling to which Yosemite walls are normally subjected, the doctor explained. Where joint cracks are numerous, a cliff becomes weakened internally over the years by the solvent action of acid-bearing waters—snowmelt, rain, springs—seeping into these fissures. Then the pull of gravity alone is enough to cause the loosened parts to break away and fall.

After supper they rode to the hotel (where the party received mail, and the doctor sometimes ate lunch) to take leave of Hutchings, Elvira, and Thérèse Yelverton, whom LeConte knew through Jeanne Carr. Thérèse, then in the midst of writing her Yosemite novel, was to cast him as Professor Brown, husband of the story's narrator.

Night had fallen by the time they started for camp. The black sky was studded with stars, the walls glowed in the moonlight—it was John Muir's great temple illuminated from above. Each landmark was as distinct as by day, clearly outlined and faceted. All in the party responded to the scene, but reacted differently: the young men, joyous, rode briskly, singing in chorus; the doctor fell far behind, his appreciation enhanced by the solitude and stillness.

Midafternoon the next day found him seated in Bridalveil Meadow alone, writing his impressions of Yosemite: "I sit in a kind of delicious dream, the scenery unconsciously mingling with my dream." Around five o'clock the entire party visited the fall. They saw the setting sun gild its summit, swam in the dark pool into which it drops, and ran behind the veil. After supper LeConte wandered off by himself to the riverbank to enjoy the valley by moonlight.

They were all up well before dawn to break camp for the start over the Sierra. The doctor could not resist the temptation to slip away from the bustle for a final farewell. As he walked through the dewy grass he saw the rising sun suffuse El Capitan with a "wonderful warm, transparent golden light (like Bierstadt's picture.) . . ." The entire south side of the valley lay in deep gloom; only the crest of Half Dome was touched with a rosy glow.

Up the steep zigzag of the Coulterville trail, object of terror to so many travelers, the cavalcade made its way. The doctor admitted to feeling a little uneasy on those stretches where the path clung to the outer edge of the almost perpendicular cliff. As had been agreed, John Muir overtook them at the junction with the old Indian trade route, then little-used, very rough, and nearly extinct.

Around two o'clock, after covering fourteen miles and much ground concerning the origin of Yosemite Valley, they stopped at Eagle Meadows just north of the Three Brothers. There on Muir's advice they pitched camp in a fine grove of fir. After dinner they lay on the forest floor, looking up through a lacework of treetops at the brilliant blue sky. LeConte noted that "Mr. Muir gazes and gazes, and cannot get his fill. . . . Plants and flowers and forests, and sky and clouds and mountains seem actually to haunt his imagination. He seems to revel in the freedom of this life. I think he would pine away in a city or in conventional life of any kind."

Muir in his turn observed that LeConte "studied the grand show, forgetting all else, riding with loose, dangling rein, allowing his horse to go where he liked. He had a fine poetic appreciation of nature, and never tired of gazing at the noble forests and gardens, lakes and meadows, mountains and streams displayed along the windings of the trail, calling attention to this and that with buoyant, sparkling delight like that of a child."

The talk turned again to the work of glaciers. LeConte agreed with Muir that a river of ice had moved down each side canyon, met, and formed the great Yosemite glacier that once filled the chasm. However, he attributed far more to stream erosion and preglacial action than Muir did. Later studies confirmed LeConte's ideas.

The two men then walked to the summit of Eagle Peak, the highest of the Brothers, to study the canyons opposite, and view the valley and the High Sierra. Half Dome, seen in profile, was the most striking feature from this point. Fascinated, they watched without word the changes wrought by the passing of daylight, the approach of dusk, the coming of night, and the rising of the moon, and were carried far beyond "human cares and human civilization," Muir remembered. The rest of the party joined them, and after it was fully dark, lighted a bonfire; answering fires soon appeared throughout the valley. Then the young men hallooed and shot off their rifles and pistols, and heard shouts and gunfire in response.

Travel the next day was mainly along a high ridge, with no trail and only an occasional blaze. Had it not been for John Muir's familiarity with the region they would have gone astray. The doctor saw in many places the evidence of those ice rivers. Much of the granite underfoot was so glassy from glacial abrasion that they had to dismount and lead their horses. Late in the afternoon they approached Tenaya Lake, set like a dark-blue gem in the midst of burnished granite. How fitting was the Miwok name, which meant shining rock. At its lower end they set up camp in a grove of lodgepole pine, where alpine chipmunks, birdlike in movement, foraged among the bushes for seeds.

After supper the doctor and Muir sauntered through the fragrant woods to the lake shore. There they sat on a large rock that stood islet-like a little way out in the shallow water. "The full moon and stars filled the lake with light, and brought out the rich sculpture of the walls of the basin and surrounding mountains with marvelous clearness and beauty amid the shadows; . . . a slight breeze ruffled the surface, giving rise to ever-changing pictures of brightness. At first we talked freely," Muir said, "admiring the silvery masses and ripples of light, and the mystic wavering dance of the stars. . . . But soon came perfect stillness, earth and sky were inseparably blended and spiritualized, and we could only gaze . . . in devout, wondering admiration."

"The grand harmony made answering music in our hearts," Le-Conte added. He was already completely captivated by the valley's charm; now he was caught by the magic of Yosemite highlands.

Before the sun had fully risen that next morning they were on their way up the canyon of Tenaya Creek, following it over the divide into the Tuolumne Valley. They were surrounded by the work of glaciers: ice lines at great height on the walls; a vast, snow-filled cirque on the north slope of Tenaya Peak, the fountain tributary to ancient Tenaya Glacier. Around noon they pulled up at the soda springs in Tuolumne Meadows. During glacial times two great rivers of ice had met there, and with the help of smaller tributary glaciers, filled the great Tuolumne Basin to a depth of 2,200 feet, creating the largest mer-de-glace, or ice sea, in the

Sierra—140 square miles. After the last glacier had melted, a shallow lake occupied the basin, and in the order of mountain landscape-making, this was eventually filled with silt and gravel by tributary streams and turned into a meadow. The doctor noted that it was now carpeted with flowers—buttercup, pink paintbrush, gentian, red heather, and whorled penstemon—doomed, however, for some 12,000 to 15,000 sheep were pastured in the area.

As they rode toward the summit, following a fork of the Tuolumne River, LeConte reflected that since leaving Yosemite Valley their way had been entirely through pristine wilderness. They had seen no other human beings beyond a shepherd or two.

From time to time Muir called his attention to rocks whose fine striae, examined through a lens, indicated positively the east-west direction of the glaciers. As they climbed, they noted the gradual dwarfing of trees and other vegetation. Near the crest was an alpine willow, a mere gray mat on the ground, no branch more than three inches high. Red heather and alpine daisy were in bloom there.

Descent to the east side lay through Bloody Canyon, the wildest of all Sierra passes, long a crossing for Indians and mountain animals. Sweeping down from the eastern crest of the range to the edge of the desert, it drops four thousand feet in three to four miles. Once within its snowy gateway, LeConte's party noticed that its black crags seemed to crowd close, almost threateningly, as though aware of their presence and not liking it. Carefully they led their horses over loose fragments of slate that were razor sharp and stood erect like knife blades, slashing the animals' legs and adding more blood to rocks already deeply dyed with it. But shortly the oppressive feeling of savage desolation lifted as they observed water ouzels darting into the cascades beside the trail, heard a robin sing, and saw below a chain of dazzling emerald-green lakes. They rested in a little meadow crowded with columbine and leopard lily that ringed one lake three or four times the size of Mirror.

LeConte was fascinated by the gorge's wild beauty. Geologically, it was the most interesting region he had seen. All about he found proofs that an ancient glacier at least a thousand feet deep had pushed through the canyon and on across the desert toward Mono Lake. Only occasionally were they able to see what lay beyond the towering walls enclosing Bloody Canyon. Then there were glimpses of Mono Lake merging with a shimmering sky; the uniform chain of extinct volcanic cones; the rugged east flank of the Sierra, peak piled upon peak, patched with glistening snow; the purplish sagebrush plains scored with traces of gray-green, marking the pathways of mountain-born streams.

On August 14, they explored the first of the volcanoes, riding down into its double crater. There they parted with John Muir, who was going on to climb the highest cone in the range. The doctor regretted that he could not go with him, but the university party's plans included geology studies in other parts of the Sierra. Now they were going to ride north, cross the range west at Monitor Pass, journey on to Tahoe, then make their way back to Oakland. LeConte was sorry to lose Muir's company, for he had grown fond of him and had formed a high opinion of his character and knowledge. He asked Muir to keep him advised of any important findings. Muir promised, and in December sent the doctor some huge lumps of ice from several living glaciers he had discovered.

The lumps of ice and the desire to continue his own glacial studies were not the only reasons for Dr. LeConte's prompt return to Yosemite at the start of vacation in the summer of 1872. The previous year he had been enchanted by the entire region and was drawn back by those myriad indefinable charms that had held so many others. He came prepared to spend the entire summer, making another horseback-camping trip, and to share the wonders with three friends and his nephew Julian LeConte, who had not seen them before.

John Muir accompanied the party into the highlands, led the doctor to those active glaciers he had found, and showed him the figures on movement computed with the aid of stakes. That September Joseph LeConte startled the world of science by his published announcement of Muir's discovery.

Muir habitually urged those with whom he felt a strong spiritual bond to forget time and responsibility, and go off with him into the heart of the mountains to learn their true meaning and experience a revelation. Now as they camped among the peaks, Muir spoke with regret that the doctor must so soon return to harness, and urged him to run away for a season or two in the "time-obliterating wildness." It seemed to Muir that as he pictured for him the "blessings" of such a truancy, the doctor was sympathetic to the suggestion. However appealing it may have been, LeConte was obliged to compromise.

Summer after summer he returned to the "grand valley" to pursue his studies, and like Muir, experience rejuvenescence. He attributed his continuing physical stamina and mental vigor to these excursions, which always included time in the high country, Tuolumne Meadows remaining a favorite camping spot. Important papers on ancient glaciers, on the structure and origin of mountains, on volcanic phenomena east of the Sierra, all of which were published, resulted from these expeditions.

The year 1875 found him in Yosemite again, with a party of four from the university, having once more ridden their horses from home. Many days were spent in the valley to relish its wonders, often in the company of John Muir and painter William Keith. Both parties went into high country, camped at Soda Springs, and traversed Bloody Canyon. Muir and Keith went on to Mount Whitney in search of picture subjects; Dr. LeConte was bound for Mono Lake to study the structure of its islands.

In June 1878 he again set off by horseback for Yosemite, escorting a kind of gypsy caravan in which rode his wife, teenage daughter, and eight-year-old son, a girlfriend of the daughter, and the family's Chinese cook. This elaborate outfit was in deference to Mrs. LeConte, who had no previous camping experience; at night she and the girls slept in the wagon. One of his students volunteered to drive; another rode his horse to keep LeConte company. Each of these expeditions was a happy combination of work and pleasure, for he pursued his mountain studies and his teaching to the end of his life. "I am firmly convinced," he once said, "that investigation ought not to be separated from teaching; . . . that not only is one a better teacher for being an investigator but . . . a better investigator for being a teacher. We never know a subject perfectly until we teach it."

He had such implicit faith in the restorative powers of Yosemite —its pure mountain air, its invigorating climate, its incomparable beauty—that he took there one summer his married daughter Emma, who lived in Georgia but had come West completely broken in health. They traveled in a hired coach-and-four (the first time the doctor had not ridden his horse), camping each night along the way. Emma had never seen Yosemite and was, according to her father, in an "ecstasy of delight" the entire six weeks. His faith was well-founded, for her cure was complete. He had a similar experience a few seasons later when in going by horse with a party of students he was overcome by heat and fatigue on the San Joaquin plains and feared he was losing his stamina. But once in Yosemite he could actually feel the return of his strength and endurance, and soon after climbed Dana and Lyell and trekked over the mountains for a first visit to Hetch Hetchy Valley, where he camped for a week, explored it from end to end, and "enjoyed life as much as the youngest of the party."

As often as he stayed in Yosemite, the spell was never weakened by familiarity. Many times he noted while encamped there that he seemed to appreciate it more with each visit. Once when he had been kept away nearly four years by studies in other places, he felt he could stand the separation no longer, and at the term's end, set off alone. Later his son joined him, and they spent three months camping in the valley and among the high peaks. At the end of their stay the doctor wondered to himself how much longer he would be able to come. That February (1893) he had been widely honored on his seventieth birthday. Although touched deeply by this evidence of appreciation and affection among his colleagues and students, it had the effect of impressing on him that he was now passed three-score and ten. Previously he had given little thought to his age; now he felt low-spirited, and rode out alone to take a tearful farewell of all the cliffs and waterfalls, as of "dearest friends." It was a premature parting, for the next summer he was back, and again in 1897.

In June of 1901, thirty-one years after his first trip, he had a strong desire to see Yosemite again and share it with his daughter Sallie, then on a visit from South Carolina. They would go by train, and join the Sierra Club encampment in the valley—he had helped John Muir organize it and was therefore a charter member. At the depot they met Frank Soulé, captain of that first student party, now also a professor at the university and on his way, with his wife, to the Sierra Club gathering. He thought the doctor as eager and enthusiastic as on that July morning in 1870.

After reaching the Sierra Club rendezvous at the foot of Glacier Point, the doctor spent the next two days driving with Sallie to distant parts of the valley to see Bridalveil and Yosemite falls, El Capitan, and the Three Brothers; walking with her to sites close by; and visiting with countless former students and with friends. It was a large gathering: among those there were John Muir; William Keith and his wife, Mary; the historian Theodore Hittell—friend of Grizzly Adams; the poet Edward Robeson Taylor; the well-known physician Benjamin P. Wall. LeConte was "the life of the party," one old student recalled; another wrote that he was "geniality personified."

On the evening of July 5 he admitted to feeling tired upon his return from Vernal Fall. A hearty dinner seemed to revive him, but not long afterward he mentioned to Sallie that he was having severe paroxysmal pains in his chest. Dr. Wall was asked to examine him and diagnosed the symptoms as angina pectoris, with which Dr. LeConte agreed. Medication brought relief, he slept soundly, and in the morning he seemed better. But a little after nine o'clock he grew suddenly worse. Sallie ran to the door of the Keiths' tent to tell them. William Keith called Dr. Wall, and they hurried back with Sallie. "Professor Joe's face was white and drawn but he urged us not to give up the trip to Illilouette on his account," Mary Keith remembered. "To satisfy him some of us started up to Nevada Fall."

Around ten o'clock Dr. LeConte turned over on his left side. Sallie cautioned him not to lie on that side. With a smile he replied, "It does not matter, daughter." Within five minutes he was dead. The news spread quickly throughout the valley. "A solemn sky seemed to lower upon the peaks and cliffs, and a heavy atmosphere of loss was all-pervading," Frank Soulé recalled.

The doctor's students and graduates prepared the casket and placed it in the coach that was to take him, Sallie, and Edward Robeson Taylor back to Berkeley. Then they covered it with boughs of pine, fir, and incense cedar, and decorated it with laurel wreaths and bunches of wildflowers. That evening the carriage made its slow way down the valley, lighted only by stars. Following was a large procession of students, friends, and acquaintances, bareheaded and afoot. At the bottom of the grade they stopped and watched in silence as the coach toiled on up the lonely mountain road and was finally lost in darkness.

Some weeks afterward, a granite boulder of handsome shape was taken from the foot of Glacier Point, near the spot where he had died, to mark his grave. Three years later (1904) the Sierra Club, in affectionate remembrance and to commemorate his work, completed the LeConte Memorial Lodge for its Yosemite Valley headquarters. Built of granite, on a rise just below Glacier Point, it contained a mountaineering and conservation library, reading room, and geological exhibits.

The doctor's close association with Yosemite and the High Sierra was continued by his only son, Joseph N. LeConte, who inherited his father's passion for camp and mountain life and shared his fascination with the valley. As a small boy he was introduced to Yosemite for an early exposure to its wonders, and for his father to impart his own great love of nature, as he said. Of his son, the doctor wrote: "He has since become the best camper and mountaineer I ever knew, tramping four or five hundred miles in the Sierra every summer, and probably knows them better than any other living man, unless possibly Mr. John Muir." Young Joseph, who continued the tradition of science and teaching, was a professor of electrical engineering at the University of California. He was also a photographer of distinction. Of his many pictures taken in Yosemite and the High Sierra, Ansel Adams, artist with a camera and today's foremost interpreter of Yosemite and the Sierra Nevada Range, has written that they are "the natural, inevitable selections of a man very much in tune with the world about him, very much aware of its beauty, and . . . reveal a sensitive reaction to the finest moments of the mountain scene."

19

STAGING DAYS

One of the best known of all Sierra whips was Alfred, a mulatto, who for many years had a daily run between Wawona and Yosemite Valley. He had the distinction of having driven more illustrious passengers than any other coachman in California: presidents and ex-presidents; royalty; diplomats; cabinet officers; senators, governors, and generals; journalists, painters, photographers, actresses, and noted belles. He remembered every one—Grant, Garfield, Hayes; the Princess Louise, the Lady Franklin, and the Duke of Sutherland; General Sherman and Carl Schurz; Albert Bierstadt and Thomas Moran; "Bull Run" Russell and Charles Nordhoff; Senator William Stewart; Flora Sharon, Jennie Flood, and Lillie Langtry. Proudly he wore the gauntlets given him by the French minister and carried the whip presented by the incomparable Jersey Lily—"the most agreeable and beautiful woman" he had ever driven into the valley.

Of medium height and build, Alfred dressed meticulously and wore "the whitest and handsomest gauntlets of any driver in the Sierra." He was a quiet man of reflective disposition, and often covered the entire distance from Wawona to Inspiration Point without saying a word. However, if he had a lively crowd aboard, he listened with obvious enjoyment to the jokes and stories, all the while keeping a vigilant eye on his team and the road. He always kept his schedule to the minute either way, knew every obstacle on the route, and never had an accident.

Only once did he permit a passenger to take the reins, and that was President Grant: "The General drove nearly all the way to Inspiration Point, and lighted at least four cigars," Alfred said. "He took in everything along the road, and made all the turns as perfectly as an old driver." There was a fine crowd aboard that day, he recalled. In addition to the general, Mrs. Grant, young Ulysses (called Buck), and their official party, there were the noted belles Jennie Flood and Flora Sharon, daughters of Comstock Lode silver kings.

A budding romance between Buck Grant and Jennie Flood caught the nation's fancy. It had begun just a short time before when the two met at a banquet given by the Floods in the general's honor, and blossomed in Yosemite. After the party's return to San Francisco, an announcement of the engagement was expected any day. When to everyone's surprise weeks passed without a word, family friends were called on to explain. Jennie's father, it seemed, had withheld his consent; he liked the young man personally but objected to his financial obscurity. To rectify the discrepancy in family fortunes James Flood introduced him to the possibilities of the stock market; furnished him with a stake; told him what to buy, when to sell, and at what time to reinvest. Within half a year, it was said, young Grant made a hundred thousand dollars in profit—and the engagement was then announced. But Buck had meanwhile gone home, and rumor had it that success had turned his head. As a man of independent means he found life in New York City so attractive he was in no hurry to return to Jennie. When at length he arrived in San Francisco, he was in no rush either to go on to suburban Menlo Park, where Jennie was summering. He lingered in the city so long that Jennie in a fit of anger sent him a curt note breaking the engagement. The newspapers made much of the jilting of the Comstock Lode heiress and were eager to label Grant a fortune hunter. Later he did marry; but Jennie, although she had no lack of eligible suitors and acceptable offers, remained single.

As more and more tourists made their way into Yosemite, the need for better transportation became apparent, and a company was formed to build a wagon road to the valley floor. On June 17, 1874, the first stages wound down the steep grades of a newly opened toll road—the Coulterville and Yosemite Turnpike. Competition was as keen among road builders as it had been with the promoters of the first horse trails, and soon a second company was organized to bring in another road from the west, from Big Oak Flat, just a few miles north of Coulterville. The Yosemite commissioners had granted exclusive rights to the Coulterville enterprise for a ten-year period, so when the Big Oak Flat combine applied to them for permission to construct a rival road that also would enter Yosemite Valley on its north side, it was refused. The investors immediately approached the state legislature with their plan, and that body, being constantly at odds with the commissioners, was only too willing to pass an act authorizing the second road, which was completed that July.

In the fall, the commissioners granted exclusive rights for ten years to a group of Mariposa businessmen to extend their stage road, which at that time terminated at Wawona, on into the valley. The following July (1875) a large celebration that included a barbecue, speeches, and fireworks marked its opening. Keeping pace with the roads was the construction of branch rail lines to convenient points throughout the San Joaquin Valley where travelers could transfer from train to stage, so that by start of the next decade the tourist had the choice of seven routes to Yosemite.

The road from Wawona was considered the most scenic approach, since it included the Mariposa Grove and the famed view from Inspiration Point. Its popularity transformed Galen Clark's peaceful haunt quite suddenly into a bustling stage center with stables large enough to hold a hundred horses; cavernous hay barns and granaries; blacksmith shops; carriage repair works; and crowds of milling passengers, porters, hostlers, and stableboys. Concord coaches; mud wagons; and four- to six-horse stages—boat-shaped vehicles with leather roofs and open sides—arrived and departed on schedule, or stood in waiting rows to be boarded. Private carriages, sulkies, surreys, buggies, and wagons deposited or picked up tourists at the station. Apart from all this dust, noise, and bustle were the stage drivers, autocrats of the high road, in the saloons wetting their throats for the dry run ahead; or if they were abstainers, as many of them were, seated in some quiet corner of the hotel parlor, watch in hand, anxiously awaiting departure time.

The man who "held the ribbons over a six-horse team on the

summits of the Sierra," wrote one regular traveler, "was more highly esteemed than the millionaire or the statesman who rode behind him. He was the best liked, and the most honored personage in the country through which he took his right of way." His clothes were made to order of the best material and tailoring. His boots and gauntlets were of the finest fit and pattern. His hat, usually cream-white in color, was half stiff, half slouch, and of superior felt. He cut a dashing figure and was greatly admired by all the women who lived along his route, most of whom he was privileged to call by their given names. No passenger offered coin as a tip, for only a fine hat, a pair of boots or gloves, or good cigars were acceptable. General Grant, at the end of his trip, gave Alfred a silver cigar case containing eight Havanas.

For many tourists the stage ride into Yosemite Valley was as harrowing as the horseback trip had been. Roads were "villainous," one British nobleman wrote—unpaved, narrow, winding, crisscrossed with gullies, interwoven with projecting tree roots of great size, and dotted with stumps and boulders. Turns were angular and often blind; the outside edge dropped into apparent infinity, and the pace was rapid. Most passengers acquired confidence by observing the coolness and dexterity with which the driver handled the six-horse team, and his ability to peer through impenetrable clouds of dust and define "trees and stumps and boulders . . . and horses' ears, when I could scarcely see my own hand before me."

"Uphill and down our Jehu pushed along, often furiously and always fast," circumventing every obstacle, as "now on the right pair of wheels, now on the left, he cut the 'outside edge' round a stump or rock," never going "one inch farther than necessary out of his way to save us from perdition." The consequent jolting, of "the most spine-breaking order," the baron continued, was nearly "unendurable." To his amazement the "ladies stood it gallantly."

Buffalo Jim was another well-liked and long-remembered Yosemite driver. Once he came close to spoiling his perfect record when after reaching the heights on his way from the valley to Wawona, he began having trouble with the "nigh wheel horse," a problem he could not discover. For a mile or more the animal became increasingly fretful; then he began to kick and buck. When he broke the dashboard in with his heels, all the horses started to run: "Jim put down the brake as hard as he could and yanked the team with all his might. His hat flew off and we went like the wind," reported a Yosemite commissioner who had been seated next to him. The commissioner was sure he could help but made no offer, knowing Jim would consider it a reflection. He did call to the inside passengers (in case there was any doubt) that the team was running away, and warned them under no circumstances to jump out.

After three or four miles had been covered at top speed, Jim handed him the lines: "Do the best you can, old man, for I am about gone up!" The commissioner noticed that the harness was loose and that two of the traces had broken. He could only hope the brake and reins would hold.

An almost level expanse of sand saved them, for the horses were forced to slow down and were finally brought to a halt within a few hundred yards of a relief station.

There was always a good chance for excitement of another kind, in the form of a stage robbery. The highwayman's calling had been a lucrative one since the first years of the gold rush. Then the concentration was on the robbing of bullion pack trains. But with the opening of roads and the coming of regularly scheduled stage-coaches carrying miners laden with gold dust and strongboxes packed with bullion bars and mine payrolls, it became an extremely popular occupation. Whether the highwayman worked alone or with confederates, success lay in surprise. After stages began running into Yosemite Valley, the tourists' cash, watches, and jewelry were other temptations in addition to the contents of the Wells Fargo express box; while the blind turns, thickets, and boulders along the mountain routes proved ideal for ambush.

At two o'clock on the afternoon of August 15, 1905, a San Francisco daily reported, "the Yosemite stage coach rolled with a great clatter of hoofs and creaking of wheels into the narrow gulch where the road from the valley drops down three miles below Ahwahnee, reeled smartly round the curve at the end of the gulch and was brought to a sudden, sliding halt by a trimly built young man who stepped out from behind a boulder with a black silk handkerchief tied round his face, just under his eyes, and a sawed-off shotgun aimed at the driver's heart.

"The six horses, maddened by the sudden check of the curb, reared and plunged in a heavy cloud of dust; the blue-shirted, sinewy driver, Walter Farnsworth, threw his weight against the brake, tugged desperately at the bundle of reins taut in his two strong fists, and swore softly between his teeth." The passengers "stared and gasped in panicky dismay."

"You got a gun?" the robber asked the driver.

"If I had I would have used it before this," Farnsworth said.

After the initial excitement had subsided, the highwayman ordered: "Get down out of that stage, every one of you men but the driver!" Suspecting a prank, two of them did not move.

"Get down! Get down, I tell you! Get down or I'll open up!" This time they were quick to obey, and the women jumped up on the seats.

"Sit down, you women!" he called out. They promptly sat. Lining up the men, one ahead of the other, their hands behind them, he proceeded to search their pockets, holding a small six-shooter to each victim's ribs, as he did so. The shotgun, in case of need, was slung over his right shoulder. "As every one of the passengers was a person of sufficient means to be traveling over a by no means inexpensive route," the San Francisco newspaper continued, "the gold which the highwayman was able to collect . . . amounted in all to several thousands of dollars." One of the heaviest losers was Anton Veith, Austrian consul at Milwaukee; another was the Wawona hotelman and stage-line owner, E. P. Washburn.

Stepping next onto the wagon wheel, his back to the men, he asked the women for their money. Anton Veith, seeing his chance, spoke softly to the victim behind him, suggesting that together they jump the highwayman while his attention was diverted; but he refused. The consul then approached two other men with the proposal, but they told him he had better keep quiet or he was likely to get a bullet in him. Veith was insistent: "If you help, I risk it; I take my chance." They shook their heads. The robber's attention was now on Veith, and pointing the six-shooter at him, he said in effect that if Veith turned around once more it might be the last time.

From the women the contributions were slim. Anna Agnes Wilkinson, a schoolteacher from Philadelphia traveling with her mother and sister, had quickly slipped their purses inside her blouse, and left out for the robber a coin purse with only a few dollars in it. Miss Annie Fullerton of Boston hid her sister's money and her own inside her camera. The highwayman was suspicious: "Say! I think you women have more money than this. I don't think you'd come into the park with so little."

"We heard beforehand there were fellows like you about; that's why we left it behind," he was told.

Then he ordered everyone to board and move on. But the Austrian consul had something to say: "You have my money; now I want a favor."

"What is it?"

"I want to take a snapshot of the scene." This gave Anna Wilkinson an idea, and she picked up her Kodak. "He seemed to be a rather nice young man," she told a reporter afterward. "Through the holes in his mask I could see his eyes. They were fine, great blue eyes, and he had such a lovely voice."

"You can let us have your picture. You can certainly do that much," Veith urged.

"I guess my makeup is all right," the road agent answered as he glanced down at his ragged linen duster and gave a tug to his battered slouch hat. "Nobody would recognize me. Go ahead."

"Stand still," Anna cautioned. "He stood still, posing like a good fellow, and snap, it was all over."

Although a reward was posted and a posse scoured the countryside, the highwayman, who was on horseback and had a sixteen-hour start, was never found.

But the most daring robbery of all on the Yosemite run took place on a hot July afternoon in the following year (1906). At exactly ten minutes to four, a young man with hat pulled low, face covered with a blue mask (one victim saw it as black; another as calico), stepped out from behind a thick stand of trees on the upper part of an S-curve, about a mile and a half north of the previous robbery site.

"A holdup!" shouted a tourist riding with the driver.

"And what is a 'holdup'?" asked a British traveler inside.

With his Winchester .44 leveled to cover the driver, the robber strode toward the stage. "Throw out that box!" he called as the sweating team was pulled to a plunging halt. A passenger complied. Hurriedly one woman slipped her rings into her mouth for safekeeping.

"Now get out and line up!" he ordered next. A witness described his voice as "musical and soft but determined." They all climbed out. The robber then called on a pretty young woman to pass the hat. She protested, but obeyed.

While standing with his hands held high, waiting to give up his valuables, one victim noted details of the highwayman's appearance: "On his left side hung an old canvas sack, and on his right an undershirt," forming a kind of skirt. "His shoes were wrapped in heavy cloth. The fourth and fifth fingers of his left hand were also wrapped. He had a blue handkerchief tied just above his nose, leaving nothing but his eyes showing."

"How many more stages?" he asked the driver, Will Palmer. "At least four more," was the reply. By the time the collection was made, the second stage was due to arrive. Keeping his victims within range of his rifle, he backed out of direct view.

The second driver, thinking there had been a breakdown, pulled his horses to a sudden stop. Within a minute he, too, was staring down the muzzle of the Winchester. His passengers were ordered out and lined up with the others, and a boy of about fifteen was told to pass the hat and search pockets and purses. But he was so unnerved by the request, so fumbling and slow, yet so thorough, an adult volunteered to substitute and managed to take only a small part of what each passenger had.

An amateur botanist with the party had at one point in the leisurely uphill climb stepped out of the stage to pick some wildflowers, expecting to overtake it during the next ascent. Now as he caught up and saw the others standing in line, he presumed they were being photographed. Anxious to join them, he hurried forward waving his flowers, and smiling. Then the soft-spoken man with the forty-four ordered him to put up his hands and get in line, which he did, still clutching his bouquet.

Within about fifteen minutes the third stage rolled up—they were traveling about a mile apart to avoid the other's dust—and the process was repeated. The fourth vehicle carried only women, who were allowed to keep their seats but instructed to drop all their money and jewelry into the sack. One woman who kept her valuables hidden in her stocking panicked and threw them secretly into the brush. Later she retrieved everything.

The fifth stage received the same treatment as the first. That being the last, everyone was told to board, and the drivers were ordered to move on. Then coolly shouldering the canvas bag of loot, which included a number of fine gold watches and a costly diamond ring, the highwayman melted into a wooded ravine where his horse was waiting. What he could not know was that the last driver, having seen the stage lineup as he rounded the bend and suspecting the reason, had quickly stuffed under the seat cushion a sack containing five hundred dollars in gold, a payroll for one of the foothill lumber mills.

Again a reward was offered and a sheriff's posse organized to search the mountains, but the soft-spoken lone bandit had once more vanished without a trace and was never caught.

With the steady increase in travel to Yosemite by both public and private conveyance, there was a great demand for tourist information—what to wear and what to take—and numbers of guidebooks were published. James Mason Hutchings' long experience in Yosemite made his advice the most authoritative: travel as light as possible; "eschew all Saratoga trunks," he urged. "Ladies would do well by providing themselves with woolen dresses of suitable length, color, and texture, made in the Bloomer style; durable linen riding habit; boots . . . made for wear more than ornament; and a warm shawl," all packed into as small a valise as possible; or, if an extended trip into the high country was planned, into a pair of saddlebags. It was a day when men tourists roughed it in three-piece business suits. Hutchings therefore advised "gentlemen" to see that they have one extra "suit of strong clothes (old ones would be best, as they will be good for nothing after your return)."

For those families or groups who preferred camp to hotel life—and there were a growing number of these—the primary requisite was "a light strong coach capacious enough to accommodate the entire party in case of bad weather" and to hold an incredible amount of gear. Heading the list of indispensables was a "flatish sheet-iron, bottomless cookstove," with two to four cooking holes on top and a generous length of stovepipe. Next in importance was the bake-oven, and nest of camp kettles; the frying pans, tea- and coffeepots; the bread, roasting, and dish pans; plates, cups, knives, forks, tea- and tablespoons—and of utmost importance, the large batter spoon for mixing bread and biscuit. "To these do not forget to add a whetstone, towels, soap, brooms . . . needles and thread, scissors, buttons, matches and candles; writing-paper, pens, ink, envelopes, postage stamps"; axe, hatchet, wedges, and rope in several sizes.

"Suitable tents should always be provided for the ladies, and one long tent for use as . . . a place of general rendezvous, and for social pleasures at all times." Horses must be of sufficient size and strength to manage such a load on steep grades.

Following his own advice in the fall of 1902, Hutchings packed his wagon with a camping outfit for a stay of several weeks in Yosemite. By then he had resumed a former occupation and was managing a hotel at the Calaveras Big Tree Grove, northwest of Yosemite, but his enthusiasm for the valley and its high country had never dimmed. Charles Loring Brace once wrote that he was "a 'Guide' in the highest sense"; and it was to act as guide that he went into Yosemite for the last time.

At seventy-three Hutchings had married again, a teacher and Yosemite enthusiast named Emily Edmunds. Emily had never seen the valley in fall, and it was to point out its special beauty at that time of year that he drove with her over the mountains.

Around four o'clock on the afternoon of October 20, as they were coming down the Big Oak Flat grade, Hutchings remarked that he had never before seen the dogwood, maple, poplar, and oak turned such brilliant reds and golds. They had already passed the worst curves and were nearing the bottom. Suddenly and for no apparent reason one of the horses shied and jumped over the wagon tongue, and both animals started to run (Emily thought later that the horse might have scented a bear).

Hutchings warned her that the team was out of control. Swerving madly from side to side, the wagon swung off the road not far from the base of El Capitan and struck a boulder. The impact jolted Emily to the ground. The team raced on, and "about twenty feet further down Mr. Hutchings was thrown headfirst upon a pile of rocks and expired within five minutes," reported a correspondent for the *San Francisco Chronicle*. Emily, who had been only slightly scratched and bruised, stayed by him until after dark in the hope that the runaway team would attract attention and a search party be dispatched. When no one came, she started for help. "Dazed, cold, almost in a dream, she walked into the office of the Sentinel Hotel two hours later and told her sorrowful story." The Sentinel was formerly Hutchings' inn.

His funeral service was held in the Big Tree Room, just as his daughter Floy's had been. "It would seem as if fate had ordained that his last hours be spent here, and his last night in the room he had helped finish in the early sixties," the *Chronicle* continued. "It was always his wish that it be so." It was also his wish that he might be buried in the valley. On Sunday morning, November second, he was laid in a grave next to Floy, in the little cemetery beneath the oaks.

It was not for the convenience of tourists, however, that one of the most spectacular roads in California was built through the Yosemite highlands. Known as the Great Sierra Wagon Road, it was constructed with Chinese labor by the Great Sierra Consolidated Silver Mining Company as a western approach to its Tioga Mine. Completed in 1883, it connected with the Big Oak Flat turnpike, then conformed generally to the old trade route used for centuries by Indians crossing the range, that same course followed in part by Joseph Reddeford Walker and his party of fur trappers in 1833, and later by John Muir and Dr. Joseph LeConte. However, instead of keeping to the Indian trail through Mono Pass and Bloody Canyon, the wagon road diverged at Dana Meadows to open a new passage through a gap also to be called Tioga, then branched north two miles to the town of Bennettville that had sprung up around the mine.

No money was spared to launch the mine. Up to 1883 its promoters had poured around $300,000 into the project, without return, for no ore had yet been milled; all funds were directed toward driving a mine tunnel. The additional expenditure of $64,000 for the road was more than the backers could meet: the following year the company failed and the enterprise was abandoned. For a time other mines in the area benefited from the wagon road, as did the more adventuresome traveler who came to Yosemite Valley in his own vehicle and was intrigued by what lay beyond the rim. But depressed gold and silver prices, rising production costs, and in some cases exhaustion of a lode finally forced all of the mines to close and their camps to be deserted. There are a few ghosts. Explorers in the vicinity of Gaylor Lakes, Tioga (once Bennettville), Lundy, Mount Dana, and Mono Pass are often startled to find the remains of a rock or log cabin in the wilderness, or some more pretentious decaying relic that was once the hotel and gambling saloon, the newspaper or assay office during the early days of prosperity.

The Great Sierra Wagon Road, untended, fell into disrepair and became a mere overgrown trace fast reclaimed by the wilderness.

After wheeled vehicles could no longer pass over it, it was still followed on foot and horseback, just as the old Indian trail had been, by those wanting to climb the peaks and explore Yosemite high country. John Muir recommended it for this purpose in his book on Yosemite. In 1915 the abandoned road, by then called simply the Tioga Road, was taken over by the federal government, and four years later was opened for public use.

No other trans-Sierra route equals its diversity of alpine scenery, for not only is it the highest road in California but it also has the rare advantage of winding among Yosemite peaks and domes, some of the most striking and unusual in the range. From the west the road climbs through forests; bridges streams (one of them, Yosemite Creek, the source of Yosemite Falls); and passes lakes, cascades, vast lush meadows, and flowering rock gardens. But a dramatic change comes with the crossing of Tioga Pass, where the highway reaches its maximum elevation of nearly ten thousand feet. Then the flowers, forests, and verdure of the west give way to barren, craggy cliffs and ravines of somber desolation typical of the range's steep eastern slope, which faces the arid Great Basin. Because of this variety in character no other Sierra roadway offers so many clear lessons in the creation of mountain landscape and the work of ancient glaciers. Here are the proofs of John Muir's discoveries.

One of the great appeals of this road lies in the number of alluring pathways that lead from it into a wonderland little seen by the general visitor to Yosemite Valley, who often does not venture far beyond its walls. Even among those who travel the Tioga Road many are unaware of what lies beyond the eye to either side. Yet this hidden world of lakes, streams, waterfalls, peaks, deep river canyons, and little valleys spread with meadows and shaded by groves of oak and pine comprises the larger portion of a national park that is nearly the size of Rhode Island.

In a region where almost no evidence remains of ancient occupation, some striking relics from prehistoric times have been discovered in one of those secret, pristine valleys. On a granite wall, protected from weathering by overhanging rock ledges, there are hundreds of pictographs in orange, red, white, and gray pigment —decorative art, symbolism, or record from some distant date and unknown hand.

20

THE
MOUNTAIN KING

*A*ROUND A HUNDRED YEARS ago a wanderer, a poetic dreamer whose name was John Lembert, set up his summer's camp at the soda springs in Tuolumne Meadows. He was a tall man of muscular build and striking appearance, with a Roman nose, keen blue eyes, and a full beard, a grizzled brown. Tales of California had lured him from his native rural New York a number of years after the gold rush, for in 1849 he was only a boy of eight. By the time he joined the hunt for gold the streams had been stripped of their flakes and pockets of nuggets, and men were at work in the heart of the Sierra, searching for what they called the Mother Lode, the supposed source of all the gold in the mountain streams. John Lembert followed the Merced River into the mountains and prospected among the peaks above Yosemite. He staked some claims, and later owned interests in one of the mining districts organized in that region before and during the launching of the Tioga Mine.

Tuolumne Meadows lies at an elevation of 8,600 feet above the sea. In spring and summer it is carpeted with a kind of slender-leafed grass that forms a close green sod. Flowers of many kinds bloom in season and attract a wealth of nectar feeders—honeybees, bumblebees, mining bees, and wasps; and a profusion of moths and butterflies. At the base of the silky grass is a world apart of mosses, rare fungi, and tiny flowering plants; of beetles, ants, leafhoppers, spiders, and harvestmen.

This abundance of life, appearing in successive stages, lasts until the night frosts of early fall sear the grass and flowers; then only a few hardy goldenrod and lavender asters continue to bloom, and the last of the butterflies feed on them. November's end usually brings the first heavy snow. Falling steadily in large flakes, hour after hour, sometimes for days, the bronzed meadows are soon turned to silent white. To John Muir they seemed to have burst into flower again—a mass of winter daisies. From December to May storm follows storm and the broad grasslands are buried ever deeper. Not until mid-June, and often later, are there signs of resurging life in those places where the softening snow has formed deep pockets, and spears of new grass are seen pushing through last year's rotted sod. Birds return from wintering below the snow-line; the air soon hums with insect sounds, and there are grass and flower fragrances in the wind. The cycle is complete.

John Lembert may have spent several summers encamped in Tuolumne Meadows before deciding to settle there, and applying in 1885 for a homestead on a quarter section. A lover of mountain solitude, a reader, a student of nature with a special interest in entomology and botany, he envisioned a nearly ideal life for part of the year in that vast flowery grassland with its wealth of insect life; he saw it as a kind of mountain kingdom of which he was ruler. He cut logs and built a small cabin with a granite foundation, fireplace, and chimney, near the soda springs whose waters he relished and protected with a log shelter against contamination by the flocks of sheep brought in each midsummer from the lowland ranches. Then he split rails, and packing them on his back, fenced the hundred and sixty acres. It was not a totally eremitic life, for an occasional hunter or prospector would stop overnight at the springs; and parties of university students—many of them Dr. LeConte's boys—spent their summer holidays climbing among the peaks; and the doctor himself, and his friends; and John Muir, and William Keith—all of whom camped at the springs, or used Tuolumne meadows as headquarters for the season. Many of these men shared their reading material with Lembert, for he hungered after books, and frequently sent him works of science or general literature upon their return home.

He had friends among the Indians who came to the big meadows late in the summer to trade. Ahwahneeches and other Sierra Miwoks, and perhaps Yokuts, too, brought acorns, pine nuts, bulbs, dried fruits and other plant foods to barter with the Eastern Monos for salt, rabbit-skin blankets, obsidian, and red pigment. Many of the Miwoks were Lembert's neighbors, for he had a winter cabin in the Indian village of *Po-ko-no'*, on the north side of the Merced River, just below El Portal. Others he knew from his residence in the valley, where he sometimes worked as a guide.

The trading parties encamped on the moraines in the middle of Tuolumne Meadows where the breeze blew strongest and dissipated the clouds of midges and mosquitoes. On a high moraine, just east of the soda springs, the arrow makers gathered to shape obsidian points. Lembert appreciated the meeting of tribes as a colorful spectacle and observed the activity with interest, for he had also undertaken a study of Indian customs and traditions.

Under the terms of the homestead law, title to land was given on condition of settlement, cultivation, and continuous occupancy as a home for five years, as well as payment of moderate fees. Since it was not possible to farm Tuolumne Meadows, Lembert decided to raise Angora goats, pasturing them on the rich alpine herbage until the coming of the first heavy snows; then he would drive them into the foothills to winter. While tending his flock in the highlands he began observing carefully the many kinds of flowers and the amazing variety of insects, especially moths and butterflies—from the large tiger swallowtail to the tiniest fairy moth; and he started writing down exact descriptions and making pencil sketches.

In the long summer evenings as he sat alone outside his cabin watching the sun set and the flush of alpenglow suffuse the craggy peaks and barren domes with shades of yellow, orange, red, and violet, he saw how many of the mountain profiles resembled human faces. In that dome just east of him (to be named Lembert), he found representation of three stages in his own development: the face of a youth and that of a mature man; and when viewed from the south side of the Tuolumne (which meanders through Tuolumne Meadows), the entire rock form was a man of his own middle years, with a long beard that flowed toward the soda springs. Many of the straight full trees and the contorted ones, the rock piles and boulders suggested to his imagination birds, deer, and bear; men afoot or on horseback; women in sweeping robes; hags, gnomes, and demons. He told himself long stories peopled with these characters and set in the domain he ruled. He wrote poems in blank verse descriptive of the power, fury, and awesome grandeur of the many mountain storms he had witnessed —the crash and rumble of thunder among the echoing crags; the blue flame of lightning striking the peaks; the roar of wind and tumult of rushing water. He occasionally told his tales or read his verses to those he felt would be appreciative.

One summer a party under Lieutenant M. M. Macomb, detached from the Wheeler Survey to map the Yosemite region, camped with Lembert's permission at Tuolumne Meadows. Hearing him mention one day some imaginary characters in his kingdom, several of the men concluded he was mad, and treated him as such. He was deeply hurt and incensed, for he was well aware of the differences between his fantasy world and reality. The botanists and entomologists with the party did not consider him crazy. They were impressed by his "faultless" English and "command of Latin," indicative of "a thorough classical education"; by the extent of his firsthand knowledge of plants and insects; and by his keen powers of observation. They urged him to collect professionally, for this area had been little explored scientifically. They instructed him in the preservation of insect specimens and in plant pressing, labeling, and packing, and left with him the names and addresses of museums and scientific societies to whom he could sell them. This introduced him to an absorbing life interest. He obtained some standard texts, and because of his knowledge of Latin progressed rapidly. Thereafter, as he herded his goats he collected seriously, and executed his drawings with so much skill he came to be known as the "hermit-artist."

The fine days of fall continued through November in 1889. Reluctant to leave his mountain retreat, John Lembert lingered. In early December he was caught by a blizzard, and snowbound. He tried to weather the storm in his cabin, but finding this impossible, for it was only crudely chinked with shakes, had to abandon his goats and with his donkey push through the snowdrifts to Yosemite Valley. Having lost both his investment and his living, he turned to whatever work offered—repairing Yosemite roads and trails, sometimes guiding—but continued with his collecting, in the valley as well as high country. John Muir came on him one summer's day at Black Spring, across the Merced from Bridalveil

Meadow, taking butterflies as they alighted to drink. "A rare man," Muir termed him, admiring his dedication to science.

Only once did his scientific investigations include Indians. He may have been asked to join a party of ethnologists in Yosemite, under the auspices of the Smithsonian Institution; or may have worked on his own at their request. Whatever the circumstances, he and several others, in their search for old baskets, shell beads and pendants, and for artifacts of rock and bone, disturbed some ancient burial sites and aroused the anger of the Miwoks. This resentment could not have been long-lasting, for he continued to occupy his winter cabin in the Indian village and to tramp the wilderness alone without fear of reprisal.

John Lembert was well-known and liked by the valley's permanent residents, was always welcome at their homes, and was a great favorite with their children because he never talked down to them when he told stories of his New York boyhood. He was sometimes asked to act as off-season caretaker for one of the hotels. During a winter spent at Snow's Casa Nevada, he made almost daily trips down the Vernal Fall trail to the valley to call on Nellie, a young woman who worked as an assistant in a photographic studio. In his diary he recorded the pleasure he derived from these visits. He courted her the entire season, but in vain, for Nellie had no desire to share the solitude of his mountain kingdom.

But in his fantasy world he married her. A new series of tales recounted the years spent sharing the throne in harmony. Then Nellie grew restless, irritable, and overbearing. The early days of bliss were over, and he, tired at length of being ordered about and led by the nose, revolted and turned her into a whitebark pine— for he possessed such powers. The tree, which resembled a hen in shape (for he had been a henpecked spouse) could be seen from his doorway, growing on a dome—a safe distance away. Toward evening when the sky forms a dark backdrop for Cathedral Peak, the mountain's outline suggested to Lembert a kneeling woman, pleading. She was woven into the saga as Nellie's best friend, who had tried to persuade him to spare his queen. For her pains he turned her to stone.

For all his flights into the realm of make-believe, John Lembert was recognized in the world of science as a well-rounded naturalist. But it was in the field of entomology, particularly that branch dealing with the order Lepidoptera—for butterflies were said to have been his "passion"—that he was widely respected for his discoveries of new and rare species. He was in regular correspondence with professors at universities east and west, with the heads of museums, and with entomologists in the federal Department of Agriculture—to all of whose collections he contributed. One previously unknown fawn-colored moth, taken by him at dusk in the meadows near Lyell Fork, was called *Hapialus lembertii*. There were other insects named for him, and several alpine plants.

Neither his pay for his specimens nor his earning as a laborer and guide were large, but his tastes being simple and his needs few, he was able to save some money. One winter day around 1894, he went into the valley's general store and paid for his purchases with paper currency taken from a "sizable" roll of bills. The clerk thought it might contain as much as $1,500 and asked him if he did not consider it "risky" to carry so much. Lembert was quoted as saying, "Oh, I am not worried about my neighbors—and I know you are all right."

April was too early for John Lembert to move up to Tuolumne Meadows, yet the door of his winter cabin in the Merced Canyon was padlocked on the outside. His Indian neighbors wondered, but did not investigate until almost two weeks had passed without seeing him.

On April 27, 1896, the *San Francisco Call* reported that John Baptiste Lembert, the entomologist, "a chum of John Muir when the latter was pursuing his studies of the glaciers in . . . Yosemite Valley some years ago . . . was found dead in his cabin last Sunday by Indians," one of whom took the news to Mariposa. The coroner determined that Lembert died after being shot in the head, above the right temple, and that he had been dead about two weeks. "It is hard to assign a motive for the deed, as Lembert was a poor man and was quiet and inoffensive, having no known enemies."

A few people, always ready to blame Indians for every crime, said they had killed him for having once dug up their burying grounds. But those who knew Lembert well and understood the Indians stoutly denied this. They assigned robbery as the motive, and held white men responsible, since a number knew about the roll of bills he carried. Nevertheless, for many months after Lembert's death, Indians refused to accept paper money in change or for sums owed them, fearing that possession of such currency might implicate them.

A sheriff's investigation turned up no suspects, and the case was never solved. Lembert's friends felt that the inquiry was far from thorough.

The Tuolumne Meadows kingdom passed to his brother, Jacob Lembert, who lived in Mariposa. Two years later he sold the property to James McCauley, builder of the Four-Mile Trail to Glacier Point and of the hotel there, and owner of the renowned hen. McCauley used the grass lands to pasture cattle. In 1912 the quarter section was bought by the Sierra Club for high-country headquarters. By then not a vestige remained of the log cabin in which John Lembert had meticulously preserved and described his plant and insect specimens; had written his long poems, created his fanciful tales, worked his magic powers, and dreamed of his lost love. Winter after winter of heavy snow had leveled the little house completely.

Some time after his death, members of the Sierra Club encamped at the soda springs discovered a packet of Lembert's papers hidden in a hollow stump. Included were many of his tales and verses, and the little diary in which he wrote about Nellie. These were taken to the club's archives in San Francisco for safe-keeping. Then in April 1906, ten years almost to the day after his murder, the San Francisco earthquake and fire destroyed the last of John Lembert's tangibles—relics of his two worlds.

21

---❖--

JOHN BURROUGHS AND JOHN MUIR

"An interesting man with the Western look about him" was John Burroughs' first impression of John Muir when they met in June 1893. Muir was in New York, soon to cross the Atlantic for a visit to his native Scotland, and called on the great nature essayist, disciple of Emerson and Thoreau, at "Slabsides," his rustic retreat along the Hudson River. Muir evidently saw much to admire in Burroughs, for upon a second meeting soon after, he suggested that they make the tour of Great Britain together. "Above all things" he would like to go with Muir, Burroughs said; but a few days later he sent a letter declining: he must be "free" when he went, "but circumstances would not allow it." The "circumstances," Muir knew, were Burroughs' wife, a notorious termagant. Three years later when Muir was at Harvard to receive an honorary master of arts degree, he traveled on to New York especially to see Burroughs. Then in June of 1899 they sailed with the Harriman Alaskan Expedition for a two-month scientific exploration.

It was during this period of daily association that the two men were drawn closely together through their shared interests in nature, and became fast friends. But a certain rivalry manifested by a bantering attitude toward the other also developed. Once when passing some magnificent views of mountains and glaciers, Burroughs, standing on the ship's bridge, called down to Muir, who had just appeared on deck: "You should have been out here fifteen minutes ago, instead of singing hymns in the cabin!"

"Aye," responded Muir, "and you, Johnnie, ought to have been up here three years ago, instead of slumbering down there on the Hudson!"

And again, one evening in the cabin when members and guests of the party were giving an entertainment, Muir did "a neat double-shuffle." Not to be outdone, Burroughs immediately followed with "an admirable clog-dance . . . an astonishing exhibition of agility in an old man with a white beard and hair," the ship's physician thought. It was not suspected that the youthful-appearing Muir was only one year his junior.

In the spring of 1909 John Burroughs came West to explore the Petrified Forest of Arizona with Muir, who had discovered it in his wanderings three years earlier and through articles had convinced President Theodore Roosevelt that it should be declared a national monument. From there he and Burroughs would travel on to the Grand Canyon, which Muir had likewise succeeded in having Roosevelt preserve. They would climax their tour with a trip to Yosemite Valley.

Burroughs, then seventy-two, had been reluctant to undertake the transcontinental train trip alone, but after his friend Clara Barrus and another admirer, a Mrs. Ashley, offered to go with him, he consented. Young Dr. Barrus, described as a handsome, vivacious little person with sparkling eyes and light-brown hair, was a practicing physician on the staff of a New York hospital and a naturalist. A close association of twenty years was begun in 1901 after she wrote a letter to Burroughs thanking him for his nature essays. Stuck by her sincerity, he replied at once. A regular correspondence followed; then an invitation to call at Slabsides. Shortly he was characterizing her in his journal as "the most companionable woman I have yet met in this world . . . a sort of feminine counterpart of myself."

Burroughs and his friends left the train at the little Arizona desert town of Adamana. It was night, and "out of the obscurity," Clara Barrus wrote, "a voice called, 'Hello, Johnnie, is that you?' And there under the Big Dipper, the two met for the first time since their Alaskan trip ten years before.

" 'Yes, Muir, I'm here, with two women in my wake. Are you surprised?'

" 'Surprised, mon, that there are only two. There were a dozen or two hovering round in Alaska, tucking him up with rugs, running to him with a flower or a bird-song. Oh, two is a very modest number, Johnnie—but we will worry through with them somehow.' And picking up part of our luggage, the lean, tall . . . Scot led the way to the inn. There . . . we got our first look at the big, simple, companionable John Muir. He had a lonely, far-away look in his blue eyes, except when he was hectoring some one, when he looked like a fun-loving boy. We found him the most entertaining and the most indefatigable of talkers." To this Burroughs would add: "You must not be in a hurry, or have any pressing duty when you start his stream of talk." Just now Burroughs was tired after his travels, and ventured at length to interrupt: "Muir, I'm sleepy —I'll have to go to bed."

"Sleepy, Johnnie! Why, lad, there'll be time to sleep when you get back to Slabsides, or at least in the grave!" Clara was soon to learn how indifferent Muir was to food, "how independent of sleep —when companionship was to be had" or some natural wonder absorbed him. Burroughs, in contrast, was "peculiarly dependent upon food and sleep—not only to do his best work, but to enjoy anything, or even maintain amicable relations with others."

Muir had an absolute genius for discourse, she realized: "Let him talk on and on unmolested, and his hearer is richly rewarded by talk discursive, grave and gay—adventure, anecdote, quotation, scientific data, glowing description, inimitable mimicry." Soon Burroughs was writing home: "The women have both fallen in love with John Muir, and no wonder."

As Clara Barrus became better acquainted with Muir she began comparing the two naturalists. They shared a keen sense of humor, a hatred of sham and display, a love of solitude and of their own kind; and each had much of the eternal boy in him. Otherwise they were as unlike in temperament and character as they were in face and figure. Muir's was the more complex and forceful personality, revealing in various moods the persevering student, the inspired seeker after knowledge, the practical man, the inventor, the adventurous explorer at home in any wilderness, and the mystic. Burroughs looked the contemplative investigator and the philosopher that he was, Emersonian in type. She thought of them as the "Wanderer" and the "Saunterer"—Muir needing a continent or a universe in which to roam; Burroughs finding inexhaustible interest in home acres. While Muir's thirst for new scenes was insatiable, a veritable homesickness afflicted Burroughs unless he discovered some touch of the familiar among alien surroundings. In Alaska it had been the Lapland longspur, for it recalled the bobolinks of his boyhood home. In Yosemite it was to be the robin that endeared the valley to him.

At the Grand Canyon, as they rode their mules down the Bright Angel Trail, Clara and Mrs. Ashley "caught snatches of geological talk from the 'two Johnnies' . . . in the rear. 'Muir, shall we find the Silurian and the Devonian down here?' " A tossing about of such terms as Jurassic, Triassic, and Permian drifted down to them, and she sensed the keen rivalry.

On their last day, as Clara stood at the rim contemplating the view, she realized how much the two naturalists had contributed to an appreciation of the canyon's wonders. Turning to Mrs. Ashley, she said: "To think of our having the Grand Canyon, and John Burroughs and John Muir thrown in!"

"I wish Muir *was* thrown in sometimes," retorted Burroughs, who had overheard, "—when he gets between me and the canyon."

Traveling on by train to California, the party was joined there by Francis Fisher Browne, distinguished editor of *The Dial* and friend of Burroughs, for the trip to Yosemite. During the stage ride into the valley, Muir was in a teasing and contentious mood, and those who did not know him well discovered his "perverse disinclination" to answer direct questions. He included not only his own party but a "sprightly" elderly woman who shared his seat. Let her ask him the name of some roadside flower, and he would give it in Latin; when she objected, he would overwhelm her with a list of its common names. When she protested that there were too many to remember, he would chide her for never being satisfied.

Muir had already discoursed on the part played by ice erosion in the origin and development of Yosemite Valley, but Burroughs was unconvinced. Privately he admitted to Clara Barrus, "Muir's glacier theory sticks in my crop." The controversy was still not settled, and Burroughs favored the Whitney subsidence explanation—perhaps only from a desire to disagree with Muir. Irked by what he considered obstinacy on Burroughs' part, Muir retaliated by cutting short his questions about Sierra geology with such a retort as "O Johnnie, get a primer of geology and study that!" Or if Burroughs advanced a theory, Muir would lapse into dialect and dismiss it with an impatient "Aw, Johnnie, ye may tak' all your geology and tie it in a bundle and cast it into the sea and it would na' mak' a ripple."

Following the roaring, foaming Merced River up through its narrow, boulder-filled gorge, they came at length to the valley. Burroughs responded immediately to "the spell of brooding calm and sheltering seclusion. . . . You pass suddenly from the tumultuous, the chaotic, into the ordered, the tranquil, the restful. . . . You can hardly be prepared for the hush that suddenly falls upon the river and for the gentle . . . sylvan character of much that surrounds you; the peace of the fields, the seclusion of the woods, the privacy of sunny glades, the enchantment of falls and lucid waters. . . .

"Yosemite won my heart at once. . . . Many things helped to do it, but I am sure a robin, the first I had seen since leaving home, did his part. . . . There he was, running over the grass or perching on the fence, or singing from a tree-top in the old familiar way. Where the robin is at home, there at home am I."

While strolling about the valley, through the stands of fragrant pines and oak trees in pink leaf bud; across wet meadows throbbing with frog choruses; along the turfy banks of the brimming, green river, Burroughs stopped often to gaze in "reverent amazement" at those awesome cliffs, their "faces scarred and niched, streaked with color, or glistening with moisture, and animated with waterfalls, rising upon either hand, thousands of feet, not architectural, or like something builded, but like the sides and four corners of the globe itself. What an impression of mass and of power and of grandeur in repose filters into you as you walk along! El Capitan stands there showing its simple sweeping lines through the trees as you approach, like one of the veritable pillars of the firmament. . . . It is so colossal that it seems near while it is yet far off. . . . It demands of you a new standard of size which you cannot at once produce." In the blending of the sublime and the familiar, the valley stood alone: "One could live with Yosemite, camp in it, tramp in it, winter and summer in it, and find nature in her tender and human, almost domestic moods, as well as in her grand and austere."

When he came to Yosemite Falls he gazed for some time in silent wonderment at that vision of a vast thunderous torrent dropping from the sky, then exclaimed under his breath: "Great God

Almighty!" Buffeted by wind and soaked by spray, he watched the mist rainbows "flit and hover," the laurel trees bend and sway, the water comets burst and spatter; and heard in the falls a chorus of voices. John Muir, satisfied with his response, ceased after that to challenge him at each new point of beauty with the question "And how does *that* compare with Esopus Valley, Johnnie?"

It did not, however, put an end to the daily tilts over the valley's formation. Whenever Muir called his attention to some evidence of glacier cutting and scouring, Burroughs would protest, "But, Muir, the millions of years before the Ice Age—what was going on here *then?*" to which Muir would respond with a shrug, "Oh, God knows—but, Johnnie—" and he would cite proofs: the marks of ice that swept over Glacier Point, the striae on the summit of Nevada Fall. One day at Mirror Lake, Muir described the great glacier that had once filled Tenaya Canyon, which as it pushed and ground its way through had trimmed back the walls and smoothed the face of Half Dome. "How is *that* for a piece of work, Johnnie?"

"Oh, Lord, that's too much, Muir!" Burroughs objected. He admitted that there were times when he "chafed a good deal" under Muir's "biting Scotch wit and love of contradiction," but he often found ways to repay him. Once, when Muir was showing the ruins of the sawmill he had built and run for Hutchings, Burroughs said accusingly: "You, such a student and lover of trees and forests, engaged in such vandalism as that!" Muir was hard pressed to explain that all the trees had been blown down in a gale, and that he was actually freeing the valley of "the unsightly ruin which the wind had wrought."

One bright morning the party set off early on foot for Vernal and Nevada falls. Up the steep trail they made their way, "touching melting snow banks in its upper courses, passing huge granite rocks also melting in the slow heat of geologic ages, pausing to take in the shaggy spruces and pines that sentineled the mountain side here and there." They lingered to watch ouzels dart in and out of the river cascades; saw a bluebird flash among the dark forest trees, and heard its song. "What beauty, what grandeur attended us that day!" Burroughs continued; "the wild tumult of waters, the snow-white falls, the motionless avalanches of granite rocks. . . . And that night, too, when we sat around a big camp-fire near our tents . . . and saw the full moon come up and look down upon us from behind Sentinel Rock, and heard the intermittent booming of Yosemite Falls sifting through the trees, and felt the tender brooding spirit of the great valley, itself touched to lyric intensity by the grandeurs on every hand, steal in upon us and possess our souls—."

Each new experience strengthened the spell, and Burroughs understood John Muir's response to these mountains: "They have called him as the desert used to call the old saints and hermits, and there has been a kind of religious enthusiasm in his response. His communion with mountains has stamped and molded his spirit; you can see the effects in his face and in the wistful, far-away look in his eyes; he hears their call incessantly."

As was usual, Muir urged Burroughs and his party to prolong their stay in Yosemite: he wanted to show them the giant sequoias and the incomparable view from Glacier Point. But like those others he had pressed over the years, they also were bound by schedules. Clara and Mrs. Ashley had planned a trip to Hawaii, and Burroughs was growing anxious to return home. To these reasons Muir replied: "Yes, I puttered around here for ten years, but you expect to see and do everything in four days! You come in here, then excuse yourself to God, who has kept these glories waiting for you, by saying, 'I've got to get back to Slabsides,' or, 'We want to go to Honolulu.' "

Muir believed that if he could get Burroughs into the highlands and let him read for himself the story of water action and ice action; see the glacier polish on the pavements beneath his feet and on the walls beside him; and follow the pathways of those ice rivers into Yosemite Valley, he might convince him of the truth. But this was the end of April, and those proofs were locked in by deep snow. He urged Burroughs to join him in July for a Sierra Club excursion into Yosemite high country.

Upon their return from Hawaii they spent a day with Muir at his ranch. "He showed us models of some of his early inventions," Clara Barrus recalled, "and literally barrels of notes of his wandering years and his Sierra studies and drawings—grist which Mr. Burroughs urged him to work up into loaves." Again Muir pressed them to go with him to the High Sierra, but for Burroughs the call of Slabsides was too strong. Once home, however, he wrote Muir: "Would I could have made it with you! I hope I may sometime—if not in the California Sierras, then in the Sierras of Paradise. . . . You contributed greatly to the success of our trip, and I know the

'fun' you had out of me was a very inadequate return. But we shall
. . . associate with you some of the great moments of our lives."
He had nearly finished a sketch he was calling "The Spell of the
Yosemite," he went on. "Don't wrinkle your nose now, I am only
trying to give my readers the impression those grand scenes made
upon me." He closed: "I salute you in love and comradeship."

John Burroughs never returned to Yosemite to follow those glacier pathways with Muir, but that one excursion to the valley, brief
though it was, left a lasting impression. "Those were days of pure
joy," he recalled in a letter to Francis Fisher Browne who had
shared them; "and I never expect to experience their like again."

22

---- ❖•❖ ----

SAVING THE YOSEMITE

IN OCTOBER 1874, John Muir reluctantly left Yosemite to pursue his mountain studies in other parts of the Sierra. The following June he was back, however, with William Keith and two other Bay Area friends. While Keith made color studies, Muir and the others, often joined by Dr. LeConte, rambled over the valley. Azaleas and shooting stars bloomed in the marshy meadows; mariposa tulips under the pines; spice-bush along the riverbanks. Muir visited the grave of his old friend, Yosemite pioneer James Lamon, who had died suddenly two weeks before. The east end of the valley seemed empty without him.

Muir had now begun an intensive study of forest trees. At the end of July, after he and his party came back from Mount Whitney, his friends went home, leaving Muir in the valley to plan an excursion through the sequoia belt south to the White River. He was gone for three months, with Browny the mule as his only companion. He found the Fresno and Kaweah groves already ravaged by lumbering, and the great Kings River stand threatened.

During this period of solitude he wrote some of his most profound concepts and observations, and foreshadowings of his coming crusade to preserve the wilderness. Will man cut down all the forests to build ships and houses? he mused in his journal. Will all alpine gardens become sheep and cattle pastures and be grazed and trampled to death? What will man's role be in the destiny of mountains? Will his destructions, like those of nature, work toward some finer beauty, some higher good? He doubted it, for the great obstacle was the doctrine which taught that the world was made especially for man's use. This was a dangerous fallacy, and one he was determined to challenge.

After his return, in the hope of prodding the state legislators to act, he wrote an appeal, "God's First Temples: How Shall We Preserve Our Forests?" that was published in a Sacramento newspaper. He expressed the opinion that sheep (hoofed locusts, he termed them) and sheepmen's uncontrolled burning to clear the undergrowth were worse enemies than sawmills. He pointed out that beyond aesthetic and spiritual reasons for preserving forests, there was that practical relation between stands of trees and climate, soil, erosion prevention, and water flow at river sources, factors few others considered at that time.

Jeanne Carr, in despair at trying to keep Muir out of the mountains and in the company of his peers, decided finally that marriage was the solution. She carefully reviewed her young women friends, selected a Miss Strentzel, then contrived to have them meet—contrived, for Muir, aware of the matchmaking schemes, avoided the introduction as long as possible. Five years after their first meeting Muir, then forty-one, married Louie Wanda Strentzel, the thirty-two-year-old daughter of a prosperous Polish medical doctor and horticulturist who operated a large fruit ranch in California's Alhambra Valley. That was 1880. A little more than twelve months later Muir, overcome by a longing for the wilderness, set off alone for Alaska to complete studies he had begun in 1879. He spent a year there, and his extensive collection of arctic flora, sent on to Asa Gray for identification, was for over forty years the only one from that region.

Following this expedition Muir settled into the routine of ranch life, clearing land for new orchards and vineyards and marketing the products. He proved an efficient and shrewd businessman and a superior agriculturalist, but at the expense of health, writing, and crusading on behalf of preservation. There was a single abortive attempt to find revitalization at Yosemite in the summer of 1884, with a wife who saw a bear behind every bush and was unable to keep up as he climbed to the heights in the hope of finding new strength. Their stay was brief, and Muir resignedly returned to harness.

"Have you abandoned literature altogether?" one of Muir's editors asked during these unproductive years. "Has the ink in your fountain entirely dried up?" At the urging of friends and publisher he agreed in 1887 to edit and contribute to an illustrated folio entitled *Picturesque California.* Although "all nerve-shaken and lean as a crow—loaded with care . . . and worry," he managed to write seven articles (the best and longest on Yosemite) by shutting himself up in a hotel room in San Francisco for two-week periods. There he pegged away "awkwardly . . . until the wee sma' hours," he said, "accomplishing little." Article writing was for him still as "rigid as granite and slow as glaciers." Between times he was hard at work "on vineyards and orchards while the publishers . . . are screaming for copy."

Two years later there came a turning point with his meeting of Robert Underwood Johnson, an editor of the *Century Magazine,* who had come to San Francisco. Muir had long been a contributor to the monthly when it was known as *Scribner's.* He called at the Palace Hotel, and the editor invited him to his room. Time passed, Muir did not arrive, and Johnson, sure he had lost his way, set off to find him. As he stepped out the door he heard him calling far down the corridor: "Johnson, Johnson! where are you? I can't get the hang of these artificial canyons." Then when they met, Muir said to him before offering any conventional greeting, "Up in the Sierra, all along the gorges, the glaciers have put up natural signposts, and you can't miss your way—but here, there's nothing to tell you where to go."

One result of this meeting with Johnson was to have far-reaching effects on Yosemite's future. Muir was always anxious to share the grandeur of that region with those he knew would appreciate it, and invited the editor to accompany him on a camping trip to the valley and the High Sierra. Overworked and far from well, Muir had been longing for an opportunity to escape to Yosemite. As soon as they reached the valley, Muir felt restored: it was "going home," he told a friend. Everything seemed more beautiful than he remembered it—the meadows more flowery, the favorite sugar pines nobler. It was as though he saw it with new eyes after five years' separation. He felt the power of its spell: "I fancy I could take up the study of these mountain glories with fresh enthusiasm, as if I were getting into a sort of second youth."

In the high country Johnson had difficulty keeping up as Muir "leaped from rock to rock . . . or skimmed the surface of the ground, a trick of easy locomotion learned from the Indians." Although he often had fun at the expense of "the Century's legs," when Johnson fell during their exploration of the Tuolumne River gorge, Muir gave him "a helping hand and cheering word"; he also found Johnson a comfortable resting place by the edge of Waterwheel Falls (one of the "most beautiful spots" Johnson had ever seen), and showered him with all those little attentions he usually reserved for children and animals.

As they rode their horses through the high meadows and forests, Muir pointed out the ravages of sheep and sheepherders' fires, and spoke with ardor about the need to protect the valley's environs. One night as they sat beside a campfire near the soda springs in Tuolumne Meadows, Johnson suggested that Muir open a campaign for the creation of Yosemite National Park by writing articles for his magazine. Illustrated with scenes of Yosemite, and supported by editorials and open letters from Johnson's pen, he knew wide interest and approval would be aroused, for there was a growing awareness of the need for preserving scenic and unusual natural sites—and there was precedent in the creation of Yellowstone National Park in 1872. Once this attention was gained, Johnson, who had a wide acquaintance among members of Congress, would then appear before the House Committee on Public Lands to urge establishment of the federal preserve along boundaries to be outlined by Muir.

Two articles, "The Treasures of Yosemite" and "Features of the Proposed National Park," appeared in *The Century* the following summer of 1890. Muir urged that the park include all of Yosemite's water sources, lying in a mass of scenic mountains that were readily accessible from the valley by way of trails and the Tioga Road. He also considered it necessary to stress that this region was "not valuable for any other use than the use of beauty. No other interests would suffer from this extension of boundary." That part of Tuolumne Meadows not homesteaded ought also to be included, since those fine grasslands made an unexcelled central camping ground for those going into the High Sierra.

The campaign aroused great enthusiasm, and "public-spirited

men all over the country rallied to the support of the National Park movement." A bill was introduced in Congress this same year, and though bitterly contested, was passed. On October 1, 1890, the park was created, its boundaries based on Muir's recommendations. A troop of cavalry was immediately dispatched to guard the area, and officers to administer it. Yosemite Valley, however, remained a state park within the federal holding, a situation that gave rise to a constant conflict over management, and duplication of expense and effort.

In the fall of 1894, Muir's first book, *The Mountains of California,* was published. Its wide acclaim encouraged him to write one devoted entirely to Yosemite. With that in mind he spent the summer of 1895 revisiting all of his favorite haunts, afoot and alone, carrying no blanket, and only some tea and crackers. In the high country he was overjoyed to find that since sheep had been banned from the new park, alpine meadows were once more deep in grass and abloom with gentians and daisies; and that rushes and sedges were again rank about Tenaya Lake. But he was heartsick over the state's administration of the valley—so dusty, frowsy, and forlorn it reminded him of some neglected backwoods pasture. Most of the meadows were fenced for hay fields or for the confinement of domestic animals. Each night some three hundred horses were let loose to graze and trample the remaining vegetation out of existence. The only flowers left were those on inaccessible ledges and recesses high on the walls. In the very middle of the "main hall" stood a pigpen. "Some of that stink I'm afraid has got into the pores of the rocks even."

In the six years since he was there, a clutter of new and unsightly structures had sprung up—warehouses, barns, livery stables and a blacksmith; ice house; vegetable stalls, a general store, a bakery, a butcher, and a laundry; a lumberyard, a cabinet shop (where he found Hutchings' crippled son working); saloons; express, telegraph, and post offices; a chapel; two art galleries, and two photographic studios. There were also countless private dwellings with attendant cow sheds and chicken coops. Most of the buildings were little better than shanties erected without plan or relation to one another in placement or style. Most had been built only to last the ten years granted lessees by the commissioners. Many of Muir's favorite sugar pines under which he had sat to write or read had been felled and turned into boards for these temporary constructions. Muir warned the innkeepers and other businessmen they were doing their best to keep away all lovers of wild beauty.

After what he described as a "tangly" search, he found his second cabin, the one opposite the Royal Arches, hidden like a bird's nest in a thicket of dogwood and azalea. The roof was mostly gone, and the floor overgrown with bushes and ferns. It had been used by campers who had left their litter—cans, papers, a whiskey bottle. Hutchings' charming old log house was in partial ruin and was being used to store farm implements and hay; his orchard was hip-high in weeds, and ground squirrels were feasting on the seeds of fallen apples. Lamon's fruit was also going to waste, the thrifty orchardist noted, and his famed berry patch was a mass of brambles. Like everything else, the little cemetery was sadly neglected; the graves of Floy Hutchings and the others were covered with briars.

The legislature, in its administration of the state grant, was totally indifferent to the fate of the incomparable valley, refusing to appropriate money for the most necessary work or to maintain a watch to prevent abuses. Since legislators and commissioners were almost constantly at variance, no defined policy could be agreed on. Yielding readily to pressures from private interests, both bodies granted special privileges, often in contempt of the other, as in the case of the rival stage roads to enter Yosemite Valley on its north side. There was also an instance of allowing a man to bridge the Merced River at the old ford and charge a fee for crossing. One outraged tourist stormed that at this rate every scenic point would soon have its toll taker. Californians in general, however, were apathetic toward this ruination of the valley. Too few were real lovers of nature, Muir regretted. The only solution was to alert the entire country to the abuses, and through the weight of public opinion force the state to recede the grant to the federal government. That, he knew, would provoke a battle: "A man may not appreciate his wife, but let her daddie try to take her back!" It was toward this recession that he now directed his efforts.

Muir was by this time recognized as a fearless and powerful leader in the growing conservation movement. His outspoken criticism of the legislature's indifference and the commissioners' mismanagement of Yosemite Valley prompted demands in Washington for an investigation. His friends—Robert Underwood Johnson in particular—foreseeing a long and hard fight, urged him to rally Pacific Coast supporters, lovers of Yosemite and the wilderness, and organize them into a united front.

With the help of a number of prominent Californians and Yosemite enthusiasts—among them Dr. Joseph LeConte—the Sierra Club was founded on June 4, 1892, with Muir serving as its first president, an office he held until his death twenty-two years later. Its declared purpose was dual: "to explore, enjoy, and render accessible the mountain regions of the Pacific Coast" and "publish authentic information concerning them"; and second, "to enlist the support and cooperation of the people and government in preserving the forests and other natural features of the Sierra Nevada Mountains." One of the club's first important victories was the defeat of a bill introduced into Congress that same year, calling for changes in the boundaries of Yosemite National Park and a consequent reduction in its size, for the benefit of stock- and lumbermen, and in recognition of some three hundred alleged mining claims.

When President Theodore Roosevelt first mentioned to Johnson of the *Century* that he was trying to plan a camping trip to Yosemite, the editor suggested that he go with Muir, who was a superb guide and knew more about that country than anyone else. Roosevelt, who was acquainted with Muir only through his writings and from reports of friends in common, approached him by letter: "I want to drop politics absolutely for four days and just be out in the open with you." Muir was reluctant at first to accept the invitation, since it meant postponing a trip to study the forest trees of Russia, Manchuria, and Japan. But after he thought about how much "forest good" he might do at home by informal talks with the President during the day's ride or around the campfire at night, he agreed to go.

After having dinner with William Keith, who had also been asked to join Roosevelt but declined because of his rigid schedule of daily painting, Muir boarded the presidential Pullman car at Oakland on May 15, 1903, for the night crossing of the San Joaquin Valley to Raymond. During the stage ride up through the foothills the next morning, Muir, seated between the President and California's governor, discoursed on the abuses in Yosemite Valley and urged recession of the grant. Before they reached the Mariposa Grove, he knew he had convinced both men. Once they had reached the valley they would see for themselves.

Late that afternoon, following a tour of the sequoia grove and a picture-taking session, Roosevelt dismissed with thanks the body of thirty cavalrymen who had escorted his party from Raymond. The inner circle who had accompanied him from Washington moved off, and the secret service, press corps, and photographers, taking this as a sign, followed to board stages for the hotel at Wawona, where the first in a round of formal receptions was to be held in the evening. Only those in Roosevelt's personal party knew that the guest of honor would not be there. Unobserved, he and Muir stayed behind to camp among the sequoias.

Responsibility for the President's comfort and privacy was in the hands of two rangers: Archie Leonard, a well-known guide and mountaineer, and Charles Leidig, a son of the Yosemite innkeepers. Leidig was an excellent outdoor cook, and having been born and grown up in the area, had an intimate knowledge of it. An army packer attended to the horses and camping outfit. For supper that evening Leidig prepared chicken and beefsteak, which Roosevelt ate with relish, and coffee, which he liked strong and black. His bed, to which he turned early after a long day, was merely a pile of blankets, some forty in number, stacked near the Grizzly Giant and arranged so that he could slip into any level for warmth or softness. There was no tent, only a tarpaulin stretched above him.

In the morning they had finished breakfast and were in the saddle by six-thirty. As they started out Roosevelt asked that they "keep away from civilization" and get into the wilderness as soon as possible. Knowing that he was anxious to avoid Wawona, where the official party had spent the night, Leidig led the way along an Indian trail that followed Alder Creek to Empire Meadows, south of the valley. Snow lay deep in many places, and they took turns riding ahead to break a path. By noon they were in the midst of a snow squall, and ate their lunch of cold chicken on an exposed ridge just east of the meadows. After covering many miles in the face of a bitter east wind, they welcomed the shelter of a little hollow behind Glacier Point which Leidig had selected for their camp.

That night Muir and Roosevelt talked late beside the campfire. Muir explained his glacier theory, and they discussed forest conservation, watersheds, and the need for setting aside scenic areas for parks throughout the entire country. Muir returned to the need for protecting Yosemite Valley through recession and enlarged on the damage already done. There were many times when the two men, both brilliant talkers accustomed to monopolizing a conversation, vied for that privilege. "Roosevelt talks his way through other people's talk like a snowplow going through a snowbank," his friend John Burroughs observed. Still, Muir insisted later that he managed to do most of the talking, and that he "stuffed" the President "pretty well."

Roosevelt awakened in the morning to find his blankets covered with four to five inches of snow that had fallen during the night. It was an experience he would not forget, sleeping "amongst the pines and silver firs in the Sierra solitude, in a snowstorm, too, and without a tent. I passed one of the pleasantest nights of my life. It was so reviving to be so close to nature in this magnificent forest."

After breakfast (over by six-fifteen) he and Muir rode on to Glacier Point to view that unexcelled panorama and keep an appointment with the official photographer. In spite of his determination to sever all connection with his party during these days, he had granted this one concession. He and Muir stayed for an hour, watching the rising sun (for it had cleared) gild the peaks and domes, which were mantled with new-fallen snow; then they posed for photographs. Two were taken of Roosevelt standing alone on the famed Overhanging Rock, with its straight drop of 3,200 feet to the valley floor, and two of him and Muir on the ledge.

On the trail that day John Muir talked further about conservation; and he identified trees and whatever small animals—squirrels, pine martens, and marmots—may have been out this early in the snowy highlands. Of the larger mammals they saw only deer, a band of seventeen. Roosevelt was especially interested in birds, could name many of them, and imitated their calls by whistling. He was pleased when sometimes they answered him.

The party took their nooning in the Little Yosemite along the upper reaches of the Merced River, where Muir directed attention to the many evidences of glacial action. Later in the day, as they neared the summit of Nevada Fall, Roosevelt was unpleasantly surprised to see quite a crowd awaiting him there. Unwilling yet to interrupt this wilderness experience by having to stop, shake hands, and chat, he requested the rangers to ask them to leave. Everyone in the valley knew that he was somewhere in the high country and would be coming down that day, although no one knew when or by which trail. People therefore stationed themselves at various points of entrance. Near the bridge at Happy Isles was another party, but he was able to greet them in passing. When those on horseback started to follow, he drew aside and asked them to ride ahead: "I do not like to lead a procession."

As they rode west through the valley Muir began calling Roosevelt's attention to the clutter of unsightly buildings and other encroachments of civilization. There was the Stoneman House, a hotel put up by the state to accommodate a hundred and fifty guests. Although generally considered "grand," it had been designed without regard to its natural surroundings and was so incompatible with them that it seemed to Muir to have a "silly look."

Close to four o'clock they drew up at Sentinel Bridge, where a throng had assembled. Roosevelt was ready by then to resume the role of president, and slipping down from his horse, greeted the people with his broad smile and customary friendliness. He talked for a few minutes with his personal party: "We were in a snowstorm last night, and it was just what I wanted!" A reporter for the *San Francisco Call* thought he seemed happy as a boy out of school. "When he reached the Mariposa Grove of Big Trees Friday evening the President was a tired, worried man. This evening he is bright, alert—the Roosevelt of old." He was wearing a khaki suit, an army hat (somewhat battered), and a handkerchief about his neck that was soiled and otherwise "much the worse for wear." In his buttonhole was a sprig of greenery supplied by John Muir. Although Muir had relinquished the tatters of former years in favor of a three-piece business suit and fedora, he had not abandoned his habit of wearing a spray of incense cedar or a cluster of carex; when he picked his own he also picked for the President.

Mounting again, Roosevelt led a procession this time across the bridge and on to Christian Jorgensen's studio-home, which had been prepared for his private use. With Muir and his official party he went inside (the only building he entered in the valley), looked at the painter's Yosemite scenes and Indian subjects, and talked about the wonders of the region. Although a buffet was awaiting him there, he took nothing but a glass of champagne; he was reserving his appetite for supper in the final encampment. He thanked the Jorgensens for their thoughtfulness and trouble, and explained his refusal of their hospitality: "Had I not wanted the complete rest I have had it would have been one of the great pleasures of my life to have spent some time in this building." He added: "This is the day of my life, and one that I will always remember with pleasure. Just think of where I was last night. Up there—" and with a sweep of his hand he indicated Glacier Point.

In about half an hour he left the Jorgensens'. Meanwhile, the entire population of the valley had gathered about his horse, which Charles Leidig was holding. Roosevelt once again shook hands and talked briefly and engagingly with children and adults. Then he, Muir, and the two rangers rode down the valley to Bridalveil Meadow. A throng followed, possibly a thousand people, in surreys and buggies, on horseback and foot, swarming over the grasslands and pressing close upon the campsite. Tired, and anxious to recapture a sense of tranquility and wildness during this last night, Roosevelt snapped: "These people annoy me. Can you get rid of them?" Leidig explained to the crowd that the President wanted to rest after a tiring day, and needed quiet. Would they leave? They all turned back.

Following dinner, he and Muir sat out in the meadows, talking until after dark. Then, returning to the campfire, Roosevelt entertained them with stories of his African adventures. In the morning, he and Muir boarded a special stage that took them over the mountains to Wawona, where they would have lunch, then press on to board the waiting train at Raymond.

A lifelong friendship was formed during those few days spent in Yosemite. It was an experience neither Roosevelt nor Muir would ever forget, and one they longed to repeat: "How I do wish I were again with you camping out under those great sequoias, or in the snow under the silver firs," Roosevelt wrote four years later; while Muir was to respond with, "O for a tranquil camp hour with you like those beneath the sequoias in memorable 1903!"

It seemed to John Muir that after he had convinced the President and California's Governor George Pardee of the need for receding the state grant and making it part of Yosemite National Park, the movement progressed with the speed of avalanches. It was not quite that swift, for it was bitterly opposed by one small but powerful group who believed in state's rights and saw the act of recession as "degrading to the State"; and by another vocal minority who held concessions they feared the federal administration would not approve.

When the battle was at its height in January 1905, Muir attended the state legislative sessions. He made speeches and "explained, exhorted, persuaded" lawmakers, journalists, and the public—anyone and everyone who would listen. He became an experienced lobbyist; his political education was complete, he told Robert Underwood Johnson.

That February (1905) the long struggle to save Yosemite Valley from its despoilers ended victoriously with the recession of the state grant to the national government. "Now, ho! for righteous management," Muir rejoiced. But acceptance of the grant met opposition in both houses of Congress and was delayed until the following year.

"Sound the timbrel and let every Yosemite tree and stream rejoice!" Muir wrote Johnson in that hour of final victory. "The fight you planned by that famous Tuolumne camp-fire seventeen years ago is at last fairly, gloriously won, every enemy down derry down."

23

TWO WORLDS

*I*N JULY of 1929, after an absence of seventy-seven years, Totuya, the granddaughter of Chief Tenaya, was persuaded to visit her native Yosemite Valley. She was by then the sole survivor of that original band of Ahwahneeches who had been driven out in 1851 by members of James Savage's Mariposa Battalion. Her exile was self-imposed, for the loss of her homeland was never forgiven and she had no wish to see white men living there. The only reason she agreed to return and spend several weeks was the abundant acorn crop that year. She joined a daughter's summer encampment at the mouth of Indian Canyon, in her girlhood the site of a large village, *Yo'-watch-ke*, and at the time of her visit the principal Indian settlement in the valley, populated mainly by Indians from east of the Sierra rather than Ahwahneeches.

Although slightly stooped, at eighty-nine Totuya was still strong and agile. She gathered several bushels of acorns in her burden basket, piled them beside her tent, cracked them with a hammer-stone, peeled the hard outer casing with her fingers, and pounded the plump kernels into meal. One day while she was at work, four women tourists stopped to watch. As a memento, each offered to buy from her five acorns at a penny each. Pushing the coin aside, she said: "No! not five dollars for one acorn, no! White men drive my people out—my Yosemite."

In 1851, Totuya had left Yosemite on foot; now she returned by automobile. As she toured the valley with her daughter and several white friends, she saw that there were stands of pine trees in the meadows where her people had played field games; azalea thickets, clumps of tall cow parsnip, and showy milkweed. She shook her head disapprovingly and observed in English: "Too dirty; too much bushy." The Ahwahneeches had kept the meadows open by firing the dry grass each fall. Only Leidig Meadow was yet free of encroaching forest and undergrowth, and she laughed in delight when she saw it. She greeted Yosemite Falls with a cry of joy: "Cho-lock! Cho-lock no gone!"

She noted the many man-made changes—the roads, the hotels, cabins, campgrounds, offices, stores, and other structures—and clasping her hands, remarked: "All fixed up! Ahwahne too dirty bushy!"

In the pioneer cemetery she stopped beside the grave of a cousin who had died a few years before. At first she was reflective and silent; then she began to moan and keen. Turning after a time to Rose Taylor, one of her white companions, she said brokenly: "All gone, long, long time 'go. I 'lone; no more Yosemite; long time 'go." Then she picked a handful of ferns and spread them over the grave.

In the park museum's Indian room she looked about in astonishment at the large collection of baskets of many kinds and uses; at the beadwork; the obsidian arrow- and spearheads; the sinew-backed bows; the flicker quill headbands; the feather dance skirts and plumes; the elderwood flutes and pipes. Her face lighted with joy. She knew at once which baskets were of Ahwahneeche make. Any basket that was carelessly woven she spoke of as "too dirty," and proceeded to point out the flaws in shape, evenness, or design, for she was a skilled basket maker. Examining some arrow points, she remembered the annual visits of Indians from east of the Sierra who came to trade obsidian for acorns. Recollections came flooding, and she spread her arms wide as if to encompass them all, repeating her litany, "Long, long time 'go." Then pointing to a girl of ten or twelve, a visitor in the museum, she added: "I so big."

There were unwelcome changes everywhere except in the great cliffs and waterfalls. In passing she stretched her hands in silent greeting to El Capitan. Her own village had faced Sentinel Rock, or *Loya*, once an Ahwahneeche lookout and signal point, and she gazed at it quietly for many minutes. Then giving expression to the crowding memories, she addressed it softly: "Loya, Loya— long time 'go."

Upon seeing Eagle Peak, the highest of the Three Brothers, she was reminded of those times spent in digging yampah root along the trail to its meadow, one of the best of the wild plant foods, relished for its sweetness and mealy texture.

When they came to Bridalveil Fall, the Pohono of her day, she spoke of it with awe. In time beyond memory several Indian people had drowned in its headwaters, and ever since, the stream and fall were inhabited by troubled spirits. She had no wish to go near it and warned away those who were with her. To the young man who was driving she spoke ominously: "Look out, boy! Pohono kill boy much!"

Totuya was the last to have heard those stories as they were told by the old people on winter nights around the fire in the earth-covered ceremonial house, and to repeat them in their purity. Mrs. Taylor would never forget "the Indian lore and history that fell from her lips" that day.

Rose Schuster Taylor, naturalist, conservationist, amateur ethnologist, writer, and lecturer was one of those caught in Yosemite's spell. As with Jeanne Carr and John Muir, there were close ties with the University of Wisconsin. Rose Taylor was an 1885 graduate, and her husband was a professor of Greek at the school. Following his death she moved to Berkeley, and after her first visit to Yosemite knew that she must return. Each year after that she lived in the valley for months at a time, devoting her energy, enthusiasm, and skills to scientific investigation, and interpretive work—a program just then being started in the national parks. She helped found the Yosemite Museum, acted as its librarian and docent, and did research and teaching in the Yosemite School of Field Natural History. Her studies included local Indians, and she became deeply interested in Totuya. She visited her every day for a week at the Indian village. As they sat on the ground cracking and shelling acorns Totuya, responding to Mrs. Taylor's sincerity and charm, talked readily in a mixture of English, Spanish, Indian, and explicit gesture about her personal life —her husbands, her children, her work as a shaman.

While still in her teens she married a fellow refugee, an Ahwahneeche by whom she had one daughter and four sons. After his early death she settled at Hite's Cove, about ten miles west and south of Yosemite Valley, on the South Fork Merced, where other of her people lived, and where her grandfather, Tenaya, was buried.

She watched the white prospectors at work along the river, learned how to pan gravel, and picked up a few flakes of gold from time to time, which she exchanged at the trading post for over-priced goods. She was aware of being cheated: "They robbed us of our findings," she recalled.

Often there was not enough to eat, for mining activities had made game scarce and destroyed many plant foods. When Le-brado Yerdies, a Mexican miner working at Hite's Cove, asked her to marry him, she consented. She accepted his religion—with res-ervations: "I . . . just little Catholic," she explained—while retain-ing her own beliefs; and took the baptismal name of Maria, by which she was known in the white community where she lived. To herself and her own people she was still Totuya, translated as Foaming Water.

Yerdies homesteaded acreage near Bear Creek on the oak-covered hills northeast of Mariposa, cleared land to build a log cabin, and ran some cattle. Totuya, a resident of two worlds, became a medicine woman or shaman, well known and highly re-spected. She spent most of her time out-of-doors, weather permit-ting, just as she would have done in Yosemite Valley, gathering and preparing acorns, baking the bread in a pit oven, and boiling the mush and soup over an open fire; digging roots and bulbs, harvesting herbs and other plants for food and curing, and collect-ing materials for basket-making.

Now she was a widow again; she had lost one of her four daugh-ters by Yerdies, and all of her Ahwahneeche sons, she told Rose Taylor. Each of the boys had died tragically as a result of con-flicts in culture. In recognition of Miwok mourning customs she wore her thick gray hair cut short.

Totuya spoke willingly about the Ahwahneeches' expulsion from their homeland. Vivid and accurate were those recollections of the climb out of the valley through deep snow, with her grand-father, Tenaya, as guide; and of their meeting with James Savage, "man with red shirt." All Yosemite Indians hated him, she said, although there were some foothill tribes who liked him.

She remembered that those battalion members who were escorting Tenaya's little band back to headquarters asked many questions her people could not answer. The white men grew angry, and when they came to a lake along the trail, and the Indians were marched up to it, Totuya thought for sure they were all going to be drowned in punishment. She would never forget how one trooper picked up a small Indian boy, and holding him by the heels over the water, threatened to drop him unless his parents gave satisfactory replies.

With mounting excitement she recalled the killing of Tenaya's son. Recollection of that loss was still keen, and poignantly she cried out: "O-o-o, too, too bad! Tenaya boy good!" She described the capture of her people at Tenaya Lake, which she knew as Pyweack, and told of the final ignominy when her grandfather, the chief, was marched at pistol point from his home valley. She talked about his death at the hands of the Monos, and told of the big "cry" in which she had taken part at Hite's Cove. She would not, however, tell just where Tenaya was buried.

Often when she relived a scene, a faraway look came into her eyes and her fingers stopped their work. When she spoke of wrong, suffering, and death at white men's hands, her voice became "harsh and powerful" and she glared at unseen enemies. Again, when talking of happier times, and there were many of those, or relating some amusing incident, her eyes sparkled, her tone grew animated, and she laughed heartily.

The day Rose Taylor came to say good-bye, she found Totuya standing beside her tent. Placing one hand on Rose's shoulder, she said, "Thank, thank; you white daughter." After a minute she turned suddenly toward Half Dome, threw back her head, extended her arms toward the mountain, and gave the "high-pitched, piercing call" that Tenaya had used to summon his people. Her voice was strong, clear, musical, and sustained; it echoed among the peaks and spires. She was the last of those to have heard the chief give that call, the last of those who had obeyed it.

The next year (1930), at her invitation, Mrs. Taylor visited the Bear Creek cabin in the summer, and again in the fall. On that last trip she brought Totuya a woolen blanket for the cold winter nights ahead, and Totuya presented her with a fine basket of her own making. Before Rose left for home she asked to hear Tenaya's call again. They walked together to a grassy knoll; Totuya lifted her head, and spreading her arms, gave a cry that "vibrated in the surrounding hills." After the echoes died, she repeated it.

Early the following spring (1931) Rose Taylor received word that Totuya was sick, and set off at once from Berkeley for Bear Creek. She found her wrapped in the woolen blanket, lying on top of her bed. Surprised and pleased by the visit, she stroked her friend's arm and said, "White daughter come far, far see me." Few words were spoken during that cloudy afternoon, for Totuya was very weak, but their silence was relaxed and comfortable. They were not alone, for daughters and grandchildren shared the cabin.

Rose spent the night there. "The Indian welcome, 'This house is yours,' invites refreshing rest," she wrote. In the morning the air was rain-fragrant and the sun bright. Totuya seemed stronger, but when they bid good-bye, she took Rose's hand in both of hers: "Gracias, gracias, you come far, far. . . . I sick. I go," and she pointed up, then toward the ground. Five weeks later she was dead. The funeral would be held at ten o'clock on the morning of April twenty-second.

As Mrs. Taylor walked up the trail to the cabin that morning, she could hear the keening and loud moans from within. Entering, she saw Totuya in a black silk dress, lying in state. A length of bright pink satin covered the lower part of her body. Placed diagonally across her breast was a belt, the design worked in beads by a daughter. Over her forehead lay a beaded headband, while around her wrists were narrower strips of beadwork. She had asked for a Miwok funeral, and her daughters had prepared the body themselves in the traditional way and had revived a dance ritual unused for many years. But like Totuya's life (typical of all her people), the ceremony reflected the culture of two worlds.

The elders decided that ten o'clock was too early for the funeral. One of them suggested two o'clock; another said three. But the majority favored four o'clock, since all who were coming from far away would have time to get there. Meanwhile, as relatives and friends arrived, they joined the ring of dancers and singers who circled the bier.

Around four, Totuya was placed in the coffin. Her daughters kissed her and said some final words; then a green veil was drawn over her face and the lid closed. Eight young men, grandsons and other relatives, picked up the coffin and started off on a trail that led through stands of oaks and thickets of blooming manzanita to the hilltop. Following them were some hundred and twenty-five mourners, Indian and white.

The burial site looked down upon meadows green and flowery, and viewed the distant Sierra. The grave was lined with white muslin, and overlaid with woodwardia ferns and wildflowers. Six Indian men stood beside it, chanting in their own tongue and swaying their bodies in rhythm, while at the foot an equal number of women accompanied them with arm movements. As the coffin was lowered, a part of the Catholic burial service was repeated. Then Totuya's most cherished possessions (the woolen blanket among them) were put in the grave, and her daughters began to wail with increasing fervor. Other Indian women soon joined them in a chorus of lamentation for the granddaughter of the last chief of the Ahwahneeches.

Following the white man's custom, the mound was covered with floral tributes. But at its head, apart from the rest, was a garland of blue and golden brodiaea—wildflowers picked from the banks and meadows where over the years Totuya had gathered medicinal herbs and harvested plant foods. It was just such a chaplet as she would have twined and worn as a girl, playing in the meadows of Yosemite Valley.

NOTES

1. DISCOVERY, PP. 3–9

George Nidever, a member of the Walker party, states in *The Life and Adventures of George Nidever* that their route west over the Sierra crest lay between the Merced and Tuolumne rivers. Zenas Leonard, the party's chronicler, gave the number of men as fifty-eight, in *Adventures of Zenas Leonard, Fur Trader*. Washington Irving, *The Adventures of Captain Bonneville, U.S.A.*, described Joseph Reddeford Walker and listed his various occupations. The oil portrait of Walker by Alfred Jacob Miller, who knew him, has been used as a source for Walker's appearance. Leonard records the lack of food and the cold. Bonneville's objectives stated in a letter of May 21, 1831, to General Macomb, applying for a leave; Appendix, Irving. Leonard was aware of Walker's enthusiasm for exploring new territory. The cross-country route and the difficulties encountered in pushing over the Sierra are also found in Irving, who drew on the journals, letters, and recollections of Walker party members. Since this was totally new country to all men in the party, they had no guide; and the territory had yet to be mapped, Leonard's account of just where they entered the Sierra and how they reached the divide is vague and lends itself to a number of interpretations. The ones followed here are the conclusions reached by Francis P. Farquhar, "Walker's Discovery of Yosemite"; and Dr. Vincent P. Gianella of Auburn, California. Both have explored all possible routes suggested by Leonard's account as well as supplementary evidence furnished by brief statements from other members of the party, and are in agreement. In letters of January 29, and March 3, 1979, to the writer, Dr. Gianella made his reasoning clear and stated he feels certain that it was up the East Branch of the West Walker River that Walker's party made their way. Joe Meek, quoted in Frances Fuller Victor, *The River of the West*, which is mainly Meek's story, recalled the ever-present hunger pangs. Leonard is the source for the rest of the journey. Lafayette Houghton Bunnell, *Discovery of the Yosemite and the Indian War of 1851 which led to that Event*, heard from Chief Tenaya of the Ahwahneeche Indians about the party of white men who crossed the mountains on the north side of Yosemite Valley. William Penn Abrams, "The Abrams Diary," recorded following the Indian trail that led past the future Yosemite Valley. Joe Walker was buried in the Alhambra Cemetery in Martinez, California. The date, November 13, 1833, appearing on his headstone as the time when he camped at Yosemite, is an error. By that date the party had already reached California's Great Central Valley and were following the San Joaquin River north, which Leonard makes clear. He also states that on November 12, 1833, while encamped along that river, they witnessed the great meteoric shower that was seen throughout the United States, and that their men and horses were "thrown into great consternation."

2. *THE SCENE AND THE SPELL, PP. 10–15*

C. Hart Merriam, "Indian Villages and Camp Sites in Yosemite Valley,"
gives the derivation of the Miwok word *yohamite* and the varying forms
of the word for grizzly bear in different territories. Fitz Hugh Ludlow
described the approach to the valley in "Seven Weeks in the Great Yo-
Semite." Frederick Law Olmsted's concept of the valley as a new kind of
park quoted in Tanya Edwards Beauchamp, "Renewed acclaim for the
father of American landscape architecture"; and Elizabeth Stevenson, *Park
Maker. A Life of Frederick Law Olmsted.* In *The Yosemite*, John Muir
asserted after years of observation that Nevada was the whitest of the
area's falls. In his journals, published as *John of the Mountains*, Muir noted
the difference in climate between the two sides of the valley. Merriam,
who was also a biologist, wrote about the meeting of plants and animals
from different zones, as did François E. Matthes, *Geologic History of the
Yosemite Valley.* Approximate date of the last grizzly bear to be killed in
Yosemite, found in Harry C. Parker, "Mammals of Yosemite National
Park." The grizzly became the victim of an uncompromising campaign of
extermination waged by hunters solely for the sport, and by settlers who
considered (often with good reason) the bear too dangerous a neighbor.
The last of his kind in California is said to have been killed in 1921. S. A.
Barrett and E. W. Gifford, *Miwok Material Culture*, identify the grass
hetchetci for which Hetch Hetchy Valley was named. In *The Yosemite*,
Muir applied the adjective "incomparable" to the valley. All descriptions
of Yosemite Valley and its high country based on firsthand observation at
various seasons over the years.

3. *DWELLERS IN AHWAHNE, PP. 16–32*

Dr. Albert B. Elsasser, research anthropologist, in a letter of January 30,
1979 to the writer, is the authority for the date of Yosemite's occupation by
Indians. He suggests that Indians from surrounding regions would have
been aware of the valley long before that time. A. L. Kroeber, *Handbook
of the Indians of California*, classified the Ahwahneeches and also discussed
the various influences recognized in Miwok culture because of their
geographical position, a subject likewise treated by Barrett and Gifford.
The count was started in 1877 by Stephen Powers, *Tribes of California*, a
former journalist and an amateur ethnologist. Merriam located and named
the permanent villages and summer camps and gave their size and prominence; he also located Chief Tenaya's ceremonial house and supplied the
reason for the valley being named Ahwahne. Barrett and Gifford; and Craig
D. Bates, "A History of the Indian People of Mariposa County," for methods
of building bark huts. Barrett and Gifford supply details of the construction
of the semi-subterrean dwelling, and of its living and cooking arrangements.
Kroeber discusses food supplies, while Barrett and Gifford list everything
that was eaten; describe the method of making acorn meal; the preparation
of various foods; the uses for manzanita cider. Kroeber, for first-fruit rites.
Barrett and Gifford, a source for deer-hunting ceremonies; for the ways
of taking deer, and the hunter's disguises. They are also sources for methods
of fishing; for grasshopper hunts; for the making of bows and arrows; and
for basketry techniques and designs. They likewise describe dress. Kroeber

brings up the interesting comparison between Sierra Miwok snowshoes and those of Mesa Verde. Personal adornment, ceremonial costume and paraphernalia, and face and body paint described by Barrett and Gifford. The curved pieces of obsidian attached to the fingers of the grizzly-bear impersonator were first found in ancient burials and were called "Stockton curves" by antiquarians; they remained a mystery until a description of the bear dance came to light. The bear dance is discussed by Kroeber, who also gives details of the Kuksu cult, its spirit and deity impersonations; he writes also of the fact that Miwok women were permitted to watch dances and allowed to participate in all but one. Barrett and Gifford explain step by step the building of the round ceremonial room, and point out those resemblances to the kiva of the Southwest; they describe the rites observed during the making of the foot-drum, and its special placement. They are a source for Miwok musical instruments. Pedro Font, a Franciscan missionary who accompanied Anza's California expedition, noted in his diary on April 2, 1776, that the split-stick rattle resembled the castanet in sound: "Font's Complete Diary of the Second Anza Expedition." Kroeber suggests the bull-roarer's possible use; as does William J. Wallace, "Music and Musical Instruments." The shamans' acquisition of power as well as their functions are treated by Kroeber. An account of sucking shamans in action given by James Mason Hutchings in "Scenes Among the Indians of California." The eighty-two herbs used by curing shamans are listed in Barrett and Gifford, who also tell of the shaman's personal use of datura. Ethnologist Frederick Webb Hodge, "Dreams and Visions," also consulted. Kroeber explains the existence of nonpolitical autonomous units rather than tribes, and makes the interesting observation that the Yokuts were unique in having true tribes. Chieftainship discussed by Kroeber; also the reasons for war, the preparations for warfare, and its methods. Kroeber speaks of the scalp dance and tells about the island of the dead and the tradition concerning an Indian Orpheus. Galen Clark lived in Yosemite for over fifty years, won the friendship and respect of the local Indians, and learned much of their lore. In his book *Indians of the Yosemite*, he tells of having learned from native informants about the island in the west to which departed spirits traveled; he adds that the Indians believed the island to have been their ancestral home. Descriptions of the mourning ceremony are found in many sources: eyewitness accounts by early white travelers in California; by miners, geologists, journalists, and later, in ethnological reports. Many have been consulted; those used are found in Kroeber and in Roland B. Dixon, "Death and Burial Among the Maidu." Field and sitting games played by Yosemite Indians are found in Barrett and Gifford. Kroeber describes the intense excitement among players and followers of Hand, called Hinawu by the Ahwahneeches, and its demand upon players for deep concentration and instantaneous decisions. *The Dawn of the World* contains many Ahwahneeche myths collected by C. Hart Merriam, who describes the setting for storytelling in the ceremonial lodge after the first rains of winter. Edward W. Gifford and Gwendoline Harris Block's book *Californian Indian Nights' Entertainment* is the source for Mouse the flute player.

4. "THE WHITE SACHEM," PP. 33–41

James Wilson Marshall recalled his excitement that January morning in 1848 for Charles B. Gillespie, "Marshall's Own Account of the Gold Discovery." Galen Clark describes the friendliness and hospitality of the native people toward the first gold seekers. In 1855, J. Ross Browne was appointed inspector of Indian affairs on the Pacific Coast, with orders to report fully on conditions. Following his instructions, he exposed fraud among Indian Service employees all over California, and inhuman treatment of Indians by those assigned to protect them. As a result, Browne was discharged. His book, *The Indians of California*, incorporating his report, is a scathing indictment of the reservation system and a revelation of appalling cruelty perpetrated by white men. Alonzo Delano writes in *Life on the Plains and Among the Diggings* about the "renegade whites" who stirred the Indians to acts of hostility in order to justify genocide. Another excellent source for that implacable hatred borne by Anglo-American gold seekers toward Indians and other minorities is Josiah Royce, *California . . . A Study of American Character*. Governor McDougal's attitude toward Indians quoted in Edward D. Castillo, "The Impact of Euro-American Exploration and Settlement." James Savage's story is told by his contemporaries: Heinrich Lienhard's two books, *A Pioneer at Sutter's Fort* and *From St. Louis to Sutter's Fort*; John A. Sutter, *New Helvetia Diary*; Joseph T. Downey, *The Cruise of the Portsmouth 1845–1847*; William J. Howard in Jill L. Crossley-Batt, *The Last of the California Rangers*; Benjamin Butler Harris, *The Gila Trail. The Texas Argonauts and the California Gold Rush*; Sam Ward, *Sam Ward in the Gold Rush*; Lafayette Bunnell, *Discovery of the Yosemite . . .* ; Cornelius Sullivan in George H. Tinkham, *California Men and Events, 1769–1890*; Robert Eccleston, *The Mariposa Indian War 1850–1851. Diaries of Robert Eccleston: The California Gold Rush, Yosemite, and the High Sierra*; William Penn Abrams' "Diary;" T. G. Palmer, letter of January 16, 1856, to his father, quoted in Bunnell; H. H. Bancroft, "Pioneer Register," quoting Savage's contemporaries. Heinrich Lienhard saw Savage's true character revealed by many of his acts and attitudes during the journey over the plains to California; while serving with Savage in the California Battalion, observed his looting activities; when working with him for John Sutter, became aware of his horse and cattle rustling, and had firsthand experience with Savage's petit larceny when the latter stole some of his valued personal possessions. Lienhard often heard his "foul" and abusive language, and realized the dangers of being Savage's enemy. Sutter's diary records Savage's various assigned tasks. Theodore H. Hittell, *History of California*, states that the success of the prospecting party of which Savage was a member was "phenomenal." Cornelius Sullivan watched Savage measure and pour gold dust into candle boxes. Bancroft states that Savage "exchanged hardware and whiskey by weight, ounce for ounce, with the Indians for gold-dust." Robert Eccleston reported the number of Savage's wives; Bancroft wrote that he "made it a point to marry a chief's daughter in every tribe." Bunnell tells the story of the raid on Savage's trading post in the Merced River canyon, west of Yosemite. Harris considered Savage an Apollo, polished in conversation; and had heard of his generosity. Although William Howard was one of those who saw Savage's real reasons for befriending certain Indians, and distrusted him, he had the impression that Savage was well-educated. Abrams, who looked over Savage's Merced River holdings for a possible mill site, found Savage "blasphemous"; he noted that he had five wives living with him, and took his authority for more than one from the Bible. Bunnell and Howard are sources for Savage's trip to San Francisco with José Juarez; for the stay in the city, the gambling losses, the quarrel with José; for the council at the Fresno River post. Both quote José's talk. Bunnell details the developments leading to the organization of the Mariposa Battalion. T. G. Palmer, who was a volunteer with the first punitive party organized by Sheriff Burney and led by Savage, gives a detailed account of that expedition in the letter to his father. Howard, who was also a member of that party, wrote about the confusion among green troops. Eccleston's diary records the expedition as he heard it from participants on their return to camp. Howard maintains that Savage helped Burney write his letter to the governor, and insisted upon exaggeration regarding the number and the extent of Indian "outrages," "depredations," and "massacres" suffered by the settlers in the area, and in giving the number of Indians under arms. Howard points out that Savage knew he could better influence the governor than the Pacific Division's commanding general, and makes it clear that Savage stressed and magnified the dangers of a general Indian rebellion. Letter of General Thomas B. Eastland to Governor John McDougal, regarding the peaceful nature of the California Indians, reprinted from the *Journals of the Legislature of California* for 1851, in Hutchings, *In the Heart of the Sierras*. Background: Annie R. Mitchell, "James Savage and the Tulareños."

5. THE TRAIL TO YOSEMITE, PP. 42–52

Lafayette Bunnell, who was there, is the authority for the recruiting of the Mission Indians; for the attempts to bring the Indians in to treat with the federal commissioners. A. L. Kroeber, "The Nature of Land-Holding Groups in Aboriginal California," discusses the Indians' sentimental attachment for their home territory, as does Robert F. Heizer, "Natural Forces and Native World View." Eccleston's diary gives an account of the march by way of Chowchilla Mountain in greater detail than Bunnell. Craig Bates gives the exact route. Bunnell is the source for the first interview with Chief Tenaya, and for the entry into Yosemite Valley. Eccleston, who stayed behind at headquarters camp, gives the number of men who left for the valley and tells about their preparation; he also kept a daily record of the weather. Indian sources were consulted for the Ahwahneeche opinion of James Savage, his appearance, and his acts. These were found in Bates; in Carl P. Russell's "Interview with Maria Lebrado at Bear Creek" and "A Last Link With the Past." Bunnell is the source for his own reaction to the valley's beauty, and the circumstances that led to his naming it Yosemite. Merriam, "Indian Village and Camp Sites . . . " states that in the early 1850s there was considerable dispute between Bunnell and Hutchings as to whether the proper form was Yosemite or Yohamite. Hutchings was right, Merriam says, for Yohamite was the name of the band living in a large and important village on the south bank of the Merced River. He adds that while these people called the grizzly bear *oohoomate'* or *ohamite'*, the Indian village next north of the valley called the grizzly *oosoomate'*, which he believes Bunnell must have heard, as this would account for his more euphonious form, Yosemite, later universally accepted. Eccleston recorded in his diary the story of the old Indian woman found in the talus cave, as he heard it from comrades who were there. Bunnell is an even more important source, since he discovered her. Totuya quoted on the return to the valley, in Russell, "A Last Link . . . " Letter of May 15, 1851, from John Boling to James Savage, gives a full report on the battalion's activities after entering the valley. It also contains his version of the killing of Tenaya's son. Bunnell, who had a more objective view of these events, is an important source. Totuya's recollections of the gunshots and smoke quoted in Russell, "Interview . . . " With the help of interpreters, Bunnell recorded Tenaya's speech; it is therefore not verbatim.

6. TENAYA'S STORY, PP. 53–60

Bunnell is once again the chief source. Hutchings, *In the Heart . . . ,* describes the downward rush of cold air at Bridalveil Fall after sunset, which stirs the trees and bushes, something that is still observed. Bunnell states that he obtained the names of the landmarks from Tenaya, since he was the authority: " . . . the words I noted down from the old chief's lips as they sounded to my ear at the time, getting the significance as best I could." The party's Pohono and Nutchu scouts, familiar with the Ahwahn-eeche dialect, helped Bunnell with the meanings, he says. Later he consulted Savage, "probably at that time the best interpreter in California of the different mountain dialects . . . as to the pronounciation of the names, and learned his interpretation of the meaning of them." Craig Bates, obtaining information from Indian sources, gives the significance of Tenaya's panto-mime. There have been some objections that Tenaya's story of the plague, the hegira, the stay with the Eastern Monos, his birth among them; and the return to Yosemite Valley is too detailed to have been obtained through interpreters. The embellishments are Bunnell's. Stripped of these the story is simple, is capable of being told in a few words, and contains nothing incredible. A number of ethnologists prefer to call Eastern Monos, Mono Lake Paiutes, a designation used by C. Hart Merriam. However, in the Smithsonian *Handbook of North American Indians,* vol. 8, "California," which was consulted for clarification, there is no agreement among authori-ties, many of whom still refer to these people as Eastern Monos. Others call them Owens Valley Paiutes, while some consider the Eastern Mono and the Owens Valley Paiute two distinct peoples. Since Eastern Mono is the designation most often used, and is therefore more readily identified by the lay reader, it is the name used here. Boling reported the charge over the snow in a letter to Colonel G. W. Barbour, quoted in Russell, "A Last Link . . . " This same article contains Totuya's recollection of the men in red flannels, and her statement that her grandfather, Tenaya, was marched at pistol point. Russell's "Interview . . . " is the source for Totuya's account of how she slipped away from the reservation. Miwok informant Leemee (Chris Brown) told about Tenaya's decision to return to Yosemite to take care of his son's body, quoted in Eugene L. Conrotto, *Miwok Means People.* Stephen F. Grover, a member of the prospecting party from Coarse Gold Gulch, gives a full account of their adventures in "A Reminiscence." Grover does not, however, mention the killing of the Indian boy. Totuya is once again the source for this information, in Russell, "Interview . . . " Bunnell writes about Lieutenant Moore's punitive expedition and Rose's safe return. Rose had escaped death by hiding behind a waterfall. Castillo discusses the failure to ratify the treaties. Bates, again drawing on Native American informants, records the hangings near the talus caves and the escape of some of the Ahwahneeches to the valley's rim. Merriam gives the meaning of Lahkoohah, the name applied to the caves. Bunnell is the source for the long-accepted version of Tenaya's death in Yosemite Valley. Totuya stated to Russell ("A Last Link . . . ") that no Indians were killed in Yosemite Valley except those killed by white men. In this article and in the "Interview . . . " she told the story of Tenaya's death as a result of the quarrel while engaged in Hand, in the Eastern Mono village across the Sierra. Jack Leidig, long a valley resident, in "Statements made to C. P. Russell regarding Tenaya's Death," disagrees with both Bunnell and Totuya. He contends that the chief died of natural causes near Savage's old trading post on the Fresno River. Since all of Totuya's other recollections of events were unfailingly accurate, there is every reason to accept her version.

7. *GRIZZLY ADAMS, PP. 61–77*

Bunnell tells about those prospectors who went into Yosemite Valley in 1853. Theodore Henry Hittell, *The Adventures of James Capen Adams, Mountaineer and Grizzly Bear Hunter of California*, is the chief source for this chapter, since Hittell was a friend of Adams and wrote down his story in a series of interviews taking place over many months. The editions of 1860 and 1911 have been used, the latter valuable for its informative introduction and postscript that tell how the book came to be written and what happened to Adams after he left San Francisco and joined P. T. Barnum in New York. The 1860 edition states that Adams settled in a little valley "on a northern branch of the Merced River, forty or fifty miles northwest of the famous Yo-Semite." In the 1911 edition the location of his winter quarters is still in a little valley on a northern branch of the Merced, but has become twenty or thirty miles northeast of Yosemite. Northeast is a misprint, since that would place Adams' headquarters in the vicinity of Tuolumne Meadows or Dog Lake, neither on the Merced River and both at an elevation between eight and nine thousand feet, where Adams would have been snowbound for approximately six months, a fact Hittell must have known. Twenty miles northwest of Yosemite Valley locates Adams reasonably on the North Fork Merced close to its sources in Pilot Ridge, not so high that he could not winter there comfortably and be enabled to carry on his hunting. John Muir, *My First Summer in the Sierra*, tells about stopping in a beautiful little valley, called Brown's Valley, on top of the divide between the North Fork Merced and Bull Creek. There David Brown, a miner and noted bear hunter, had his cabin, and there, just as in Adams' valley, the Miwoks had their bark huts. It is just possible that Adams' little valley was later occupied by David Brown. Howard's Ranch was owned by William J. Howard, who knew James Savage. Howard, a Virginia lawyer who came to California in 1849, set up a tent store to furnish miners in the Mariposa area. He later sold his store and bought 350 acres near the mining town Hornitos; this was to be known as Howard's Ranch. A. S. Evans, *À La California. Sketches of Life in the Golden State*, tells about Samson's escape during the museum's move. Notices written by Hittell for the San Francisco *Daily Evening Bulletin*, as well as advertisements appearing in that paper, record the moves, the changes in name, the addition of new attractions at the museum. Some appear in Hittell; most can be found in Tracy I. Storer and Lloyd P. Tevis, Jr., *California Grizzly*. William H. Wright, *The Grizzly Bear*, quotes Dean Caton on the sight of Adams walking along the San Francisco streets with his grizzlies. Storer and Tevis trace the history of Charles Nahl's drawing of the bear Samson. Hittell, in his book on Adams, as well as in a letter of December 15, 1907, to William H. Wright, published in Wright, gives his opinion regarding the excellence of the Nahl portraits. Although unsigned, the obituary on Ben Franklin in the *Bulletin*, January 19, 1858, is certainly Hittell's. Storer and Tevis detail the suit for back rent. Phineas Taylor Barnum, *Struggles and Triumphs: or, Forty Years' Recollection*, tells about his first meeting with Adams and their subsequent association. Lady Washington and General Fremont in costume described from an engraving of the two bears in Barnum. Wright recalls his boyish enthusiasm for Adams as the "prince of all hunters." Storer and Tevis have compiled the New York literary record. Hittell describes his method of getting Adams' story, both in the postscript of the 1911 edition and in the letter of December 15, 1907, to Wright. Barnum's account of Adams' death quoted by Hittell in the 1911 edition. In June 1870, Barnum visited the Yosemite.

8. THE NEW BONANZA, PP. 78–91

Information on James Mason Hutchings contained in manuscript and typescript form in biographical files, Yosemite Research Library. In 1853 his first publishing venture was an illustrated lettersheet, "The Miner's Ten Commandments," which sold 100,000 copies in one year. Hutchings tells the story of his first trip to Yosemite in his book *In the Heart* . . . James H. Lawrence, chronicler for the Sherlock's Diggings party, published an account of their adventures in the *Overland Monthly*, quoted by Hutchings, who is also the source for the number of tourists at the end of 1855. Bunnell; and John C. Ewers, *Artists of the Old West*, tell how Thomas Ayres' promising career was cut short on April 28, 1858, when the ship on which he was a passenger capsized in the Pacific and he was drowned. Bunnell names the first women who rode into Yosemite and chronicles the prevailing excitement over the possibilities of making fortunes catering to sightseers and through development of Frémont's gold mines; he tells, too, about the opening of the Mann brothers' horse trail. Galen Clark gives his own story in his manuscript "Reminiscences." He lived to be ninety-six and is buried in a plot along whose edges he planted seedling giant sequoia, in Yosemite's pioneer cemetery. Charles Loring Brace, philanthropist and author, was Clark's guest, as recounted in *The New West or, California in 1867–1868*. Hutchings named his publication *Hutchings' California Magazine*. Bunnell joined George Coulter and other investors in building what was known as the Coultersville Free Trail. In helping to survey and lay out the trail, Bunnell and his engineer partner named the three encampments Deer Flat, Hazel Green, and Crane Flat, the latter "suggested by the shrill and startling cry of some sand-hill cranes we surprised. . . . " In *Bits of Travel at Home*, Helen Hunt Jackson recorded the tourists' reactions to the saddle horses, and her own to the steep trail. J. H. Beadle, in *Western Wilds and the Men Who Redeem Them*, described his fears while descending the trail. He is also the source for Elizabeth Cady Stanton's decision to walk, and Anna Dickinson's request for a man's saddle. Biographical material on Dickinson in Giraud Chester, *Embattled Maiden. The Life of Anna Dickinson*. Beadle made the disparaging remarks about women riding astride. Hutchings (all reference to Hutchings, unless otherwise noted, will be to his book *In the Heart of the Sierras*) gives the history of Yosemite's pioneer hotels and stores and their problems. Stephen Cunningham described in an article appearing in the *Tuolumne Courier* of July 31, 1858; and by Benjamin

Butler Harris, *The Gila Trail*, who also gave Cunningham's background, told of his recent adoption by Indians, and related his and Bell's experiences as Cunningham's guest in the valley. James Lamson's diary, "Nine Years' Adventure in California," recounts finding Nina Frémont's petticoat, the making of a flag from it, and Hutchings' fastening it to the top of a pine tree. Hutchings gives an account of Horace Greeley's nonstop ride to Yosemite and his sufferings. Jesse Benton Frémont, *Mother Lode Narratives*, writes of Greeley's disappointment with the valley. Thomas Starr King tells his own story in the *Boston Evening Transcript*, January 26, 1861. Hutchings has been referred to again for the further history of early hotels and their keepers. J. C. Holbrook, *Recollections of a Nonagenarian, of Life in New England, the Middle West . . . together with Scenes in California*, was one of Mrs. Neal's first guests. The geologist Clarence King reported on Peter Longhurst's talent for flapjack frying, in *Mountaineering in the Sierra Nevada*; he also listened to his songs and stories. William H. Brewer, principal assistant with the Whitney Survey, commented in his journal (published as *Up and Down California in 1860-1864*) on Yosemite's reputation as one of the world's wonders. He spoke also about the arduous trip and the expense, which deterred many potential visitors. Hutchings is again the source for the annual number of tourists. J. S. Hutchinson told his father in a letter of June 7, 1857, about Cunningham's toll ferry. Bunnell records the failure of the Mann brothers' horse trail. Galen Clark, "Reminiscences," is the source for his and Milton Mann's discovery of the Mariposa Grove of giant sequoia. Caroline M. Churchill, *Over the Purple Hills, or Sketches of Travel in California*, was Mrs. Leidig's guest. A. P. Vivian, *Wanderings in the Western Land*, was the Leidigs' winter lodger. Hutchings describes the enterprising Snows, and Emily's special talents; the building of their hotel above Vernal Fall; the construction of a horse path to its door. He is likewise a source for the engineering of the Four-Mile Trail to Glacier Point; and for McCauley's Mountain House. Lady Constance F. Gordon-Cumming, who rode up the new trail to the Point in early May, wrote in her epistolary account, *Granite Crags of California*: "On our way down through the snow-cuttings, we had a rather awkward meeting with a long file of mules, heavily laden with furniture—or rather, portions of furniture—for the new house." The hen story was Derrick Dodd's, in *Summer Saunterings*, quoted by Hutchings. John Boddam-Whetham, *Western Wanderings. A Record of Travel in the Evening Land*, saw the Cosmopolitan as the valley's greatest wonder, and commented enthusiastically on the variety of drinks concocted at the bar.

9. EDITOR-INNKEEPER, PP. 92-101

Hutchings gave the reasons for his move to Yosemite Valley. The San Francisco *Daily Evening Bulletin*, February 3, 1860, carried the announcement of his marriage to Elvira Sproat. On October 5, 1941, their second child, by then Mrs. Cosie Hutchings Mills, stated in a letter to Elizabeth Godfrey of Yosemite that her grandmother Florantha Thompson Sproat was the daughter of the American painter Cephus Thompson, who made portraits of such notables as John Marshall and Stephen Decatur. *The New-York Historical Society's Dictionary of Artists in America*, consulted for information on Cephus Thompson and his children (Mrs. Sproat's brothers and sister) Cephus Giovanni, Jerome B., and Marietta, all celebrated painters. The Hutchings family biographical files for information about Florantha's impecunious husband and the family's peregrinations. In his book Hutchings gives the story of the midwinter journey to Yosemite, and his taking over the Upper Hotel. John Muir describes his friend James Lamon, quotes him, and tells about him settling in Yosemite Valley; in *The Yosemite*. Hutchings also writes of Lamon and states that his was the valley's first log cabin. The spirited New England woman who gave a detailed picture of accommodations and amusements at Hutchings' hotel is unidentified beyond the name Callie appearing at the end of her letter; in the writer's collection. Her entire account of the trip to Yosemite and back to San Francisco and of sightseeing in the valley is remarkable for keen observation and high good humor. There are no complaints about the hardships of the trip, no mention made of the steep descents. The guides' joke about locking hotel-room doors is found in Brace. Thérèse Yelverton described Elvira Hutchings in *Zanita, A Tale of the Yosemite*. Mrs. Sproat's importance to the household and hotel found in Cosie Hutchings Mills' letter of October 5, 1941. Linnie Marsh Wolfe, *Son of the Wilderness, The Life of John Muir*, for information on the births and dates of the Hutchings children. Hutchings tells about the move to the warm north side of the valley; the building of their cabin; the planting of orchard and garden. Charles Warren Stoddard, close friend of Robert Louis Stevenson, recalled with pleasure his winter passed in the Hutchings' cabin, and described Floy Hutchings: *In the Footprints of the Padres*; and "In Yosemite Shadows." Hutchings wrote of his personal library and the evening's entertainments. Mrs. Yelverton recorded her first meeting with Floy, and pictured her; she is also the source for the girl having learned much from John Muir. Floy's precocity was observed and noted by painter Charles D. Robinson, and quoted by Hutchings. The problems with the sawmill are recounted by Hutchings, who fails to credit Muir with their solution. Muir is the source for his reconstruction of the mill, for the cutting of lumber from fallen trees, and the building of cottages, in an unfinished memoir quoted in William Frederic Badè, *The Life and Letters of John Muir*, vol. I. The improvements at the hotel are from Hutchings; Wolfe gave Muir's part in them. Hutchings spoke with pride about the making of the wooden causeway and planting the avenue of elms. The evolution of the movement to create a Yosemite state park and its realization are traced in Carl P. Russell, *One Hundred Years in Yosemite*; and Alfred Runte, "Origins and Paradox of the American Experience." Runte discusses the growth of awareness for the need to preserve scenic areas, as does Hans Huth in "Yosemite: The Story of an Idea." Galen Clark told of Mrs. Frémont's part in the state park movement; his own efforts, his appointment as a board member and later as guardian. Hutchings, for the prolonged and unsuccessful legal battle with the State of California, and for the monetary settlement each petitioner received. Hutchings family papers tell about Elvira going off "with one Crocker," and the ensuing divorce. Hutchings is the source for his summer encampments in Yosemite; his writings; his appointment as guardian, and the return to the old cabin. Thérèse Yelverton, a keen observer, described Floy's disposition. John Muir wrote Harry Randall on December 20, 1901, about Floy having been expelled from school: he recalled her as a child, and spoke of her popularity as a "ladies' guide"; she "dressed in men's clothes [and] rode like a cowboy . . . " Charles Robinson characterized Floy's "warm and generous disposition." Augusta Hutchings' opinion of her as an original thinker, quoted by Floy's father. Family papers tell of Augusta's sudden death following a lung hemorrhage. Cosie Hutchings Mills recalled her grandmother in the letter of October 5, 1941.

0. ICE SCULPTURE, PP. 102–109

In "Mountain Sculpture: Origin of the Yosemite Valley," John Muir discussed the various theories of creation. Josiah Dwight Whitney, Yale graduate, geologist, head of the California State Geological Survey (known as the Whitney Survey), advanced the theory that the bottom of the valley dropped when support from underneath was withdrawn, in *The Yosemite Guide-Book.* His pronouncements concerning the formation of domes and of Half Dome being split "asunder," found in *Geology of California.* Professor Benjamin Silliman of Yale advanced the volcanic-convulsion/fissure hypothesis. Biographical material on Muir found in Badè, I. Muir's earliest observations of glacier erosion in the mountains above Yosemite Valley were recorded in his journal, *My First Summer in the Sierra.* His refutation of violent forces having been responsible for the Valley, contained in *The Mountains of California.* Badè discusses the acceptance of Muir's glacier theory by the noted scientists Louis Agassiz and Joseph LeConte. Muir in a letter of September 8, 1871, Badè, I, tells Jeanne Carr about having won John D. Runkle's support. The branding of Muir as an ignoramus and mere sheepherder in Whitney, *The Yosemite Guide-Book.* Muir's annoyance with Samuel Kneeland expressed in a letter to Mrs. Carr, October 8, 1872; Badè, I. In that same letter he tells about setting stakes on McClure glacier, an account he repeats in different form in *The Yosemite*; and in *The Mountains of California.* Muir's letter of December 11, 1871, Badè, I, to Mrs. Carr, is the source for the lumps of ice dispatched to Dr. LeConte. Clarence King's warning about Muir "the ambitious amateur," in his book *Systematic Geology.* François E. Matthes' two works, *Geologic History of the Yosemite Valley* and *The Incomparable Valley. A Geologic Interpretation of the Yosemite,* are sources for the remainder of this chapter.

11. JOHN MUIR: THE ALLURE OF YOSEMITE, PP. 110–126

Muir, in *A Thousand-Mile Walk to the Gulf,* tells about his plans to explore Cuba and drift down the Amazon, his illness, the failure to find a ship going to South America, and his trip to New York in order to carry out his decision to go instead to California. In *The Yosemite* he recounts the arrival in San Francisco, the meeting with the stranger on the street, and the walk with Chilwell to Yosemite Valley. In his autobiographical manuscript (unfinished) Muir also gives the story of the first Yosemite trip, at greater length and with many more personal details; quoted in Badè, I. Clara Barrus, "In the Yosemite With John Muir," for the anecdote, which she heard from Muir, concerning Chilwell's anxiety that they would be having to race over the Yosemite chasm. Muir, *My First Summer . . . ,* takes up where the unfinished memoir ends, and recounts the entire excursion to Yosemite highlands with Pat Delaney's flock in 1869. Muir, in a letter of November 15, 1869, writes Jeanne Carr that he is bewitched by Yosemite. All Muir letters, unless otherwise noted, appear in Badè, I. Muir recalled the walk into Yosemite with Harry Randall in a letter to Randall, December

20, 1901. Muir's relations with members of the Hutchings family are revealed in his letters to Mrs. Carr during this period, and in the letter cited, to Randall. Wolfe states that Elvira Hutchings was a diet faddist. Sarah Jane Lippincott writing about Muir, quoted by Badè, I. Personal description of Jeanne Carr and character study found in "Jeanne Carr, Naturalist, Writer, Educator, Was Spiritual Benefactress to John Muir." Muir's opinion of the ordinary tourist expressed in a letter of March 29, 1870, to Mrs. Carr. Muir locates his Sunnyside Bench as a ledge on the valley's north wall, just east of Yosemite Falls, and gives the significance of his observations from there in his journal, published as *John of the Mountains*. He recalled seeing the shadows cast by Venus, in the letter to Randall. His journal records his desire to become one with Yosemite. There he tells, too, about his reaction to the frenzy of Yosemite Falls at their peak of flow. He describes his baptism in the Upper Fall for Mrs. Carr, written on April 3, 1871, at the height of his excitement. In a letter of April 5, 1871, to his sister Sarah Muir Galloway, he admitted that adventure might well have been his last. His journal enlarges on the reasons for wanting to study the lower Merced River gorge. In the letter to Randall he speaks of them being probably the first white men ever to follow this route. Muir tells Mrs. Carr about his work at Delaney's ranch, expresses his annoyance with Hutchings, and makes clear his determination to return to Yosemite, homeless or not; letter of December 22, 1870. Badè, I, quotes parts of Mrs. Carr's letter to Muir (no date) visualizing him in his cabin. Muir described and made a drawing of his "hang-nest" for his sister Sarah, in the letter of April 5, headed: "In the Sawmill." As understanding as Jeanne Carr was of Muir's aims, she failed to comprehend the scope and depth of his mountain studies, as did most of those friends she sent to meet Muir, who thought he was wasting his talents in the wilderness. Nor did Mrs. Carr recognize his spiritual affinity with the mountains. Her first attempt to pry him away was a campaign to get him to join an American colonization scheme in the wilds of South America. "*But*, Mrs. Carr, why do you wish to cut me from California and graft me among the groves of Purus?" he protested. And again, "You confuse me. You have . . . encouraged me to read the mountains. Now you will not listen." On September 8, 1871, he writes her about quitting Hutchings' employ; as much as he dislikes the thought, he will have to work as a guide in the spring to earn pocket money. Muir's opinion of books found in his journal. Clara Barrus wrote about Muir's conversational powers. Muir outlined for Mrs. Carr his winter's work, in the letter of September 8. Badè, I, tells about the first series of articles in the *Daily Tribune*, and Mrs. Carr's placement of "Yosemite Valley in Flood." Muir writes about the formation of the ice cone and his exploration of it, in *Picturesque California*; "The Treasures of Yosemite"; *The Yosemite*; and in his journal. His account of the severe earthquake that took many lives in the town of Lone Pine, east of the Sierra, is found in "The Fountains and Streams of the Yosemite National Park"; *The Yosemite*; *Our National Parks*; and in a letter to Emily Pelton, April 2, 1872, in which he also tells her that he has written an article on his observations and experiences during the earthquake, for the *Daily Tribune*. It was published May 7, 1872. Muir's journal gives the exact location of his second cabin which, after he achieved fame, became a subject for much difference of opinion, and was fixed in various parts of the valley. He tells of awaiting Asa Gray's arrival at that cabin on the afternoon of July 18, 1872, in a letter to his sister Sarah. His rambles with Gray and his wife, recalled in a letter to Gray, October 1872. Muir gave his reasons for not wanting to teach, in a letter to Mrs. Carr, an undated fragment quoted by Badè. Mrs. Carr's letter to Muir, outlining her plan for his activities that coming fall and winter, quoted in part by Badè; no date. Badè also quotes excerpts from Jeanne Carr's letter introducing William Keith; also undated. Thérèse Yelverton described Muir's tattered appearance. Brother Cornelius, *Keith, Old Master of California*, is the source for the artists seeing in Muir a strong resemblance to Jesus; and for the close friendship that grew between Muir and Keith. *In the Mountains of California*, Muir told about Keith's wild enthusiasm for the Mount Lyell scene. Both Badè and Wolfe recount the hectic visit to Oakland and San Francisco. Back in Yosemite, Muir detailed for Jeanne Carr the process of purification in a long letter which she placed with the *Overland Monthly*; it was printed as "A Geologist's Winter Walk." Muir devoted a chapter to Galen Clark in *The Yosemite*. In another long letter to Mrs. Carr, September 1874, Muir explained the sudden departure from Oakland after the ten-month spiritual exile; described the long walk from Turlock to the ranch where Browny was pastured, the warm welcome given by Pat Delaney, the physical and spiritual renewal found in Yosemite, and the presentiment that he would be having to leave there.

12. *CAPTAIN YELVERTON'S CURSE, PP. 127-139*

Charles Warren Stoddard, an admirer and admitted "close friend" of Thérèse Yelverton, wrote at length about her life, based on material that she furnished him, on her published autobiographical writings, and on conversations with her, in his book, *In the Footprints.* . . . He spoke about her worldwide fame and position as a celebrity; about those plays and novels which used her story as their plot. During long walks together beside San Francisco Bay and over the hills of Sausalito where she rented a house for the winter, he came to understand her thoroughly. An account of her father's persecution of his family found in "The Great Yelverton Case," an article in *Harper's Weekly*. The editors, in introducing it, state: "Her story is one of the most romantic that has ever seen the light." While in Yosemite Valley, Thérèse talked to the journalist Mary Lawrence about having saved the life of Napoleon III, and of later becoming Eugénie's maid of honor. Lawrence wrote: "She told me much of Eugénie's charities and home-traits, and of her matchless beauty." Thérèse recounted for Mary Lawrence her experiences in the Crimean War, which the journalist also included in an article, "Summer With A Countess." Among those papers turned over to Stoddard by Thérèse were accounts printed and in manuscript of the entire relationship with Captain Yelverton. These have been used as sources, as has "The Great Yelverton Case," which includes testimony by (then) Major Yelverton in which he states that since Thérèse was beneath him socially he never had any intention of making her his wife; that the ceremony was but a farce; and that by the time they had reached Bordeaux he was tired of her and "had never wished to hear of her since." He insinuated that she was little above a cocotte; if by some she might be accepted as a "lady," then she was now "a woman of virtue lost." *Harper's* apologized to the reader for being unable to include "many parts of Major Yelverton's evidence which are painfully interesting, as showing the brutal purpose of the systematic seducer, and the abominable selfishness of the man.

But they are not fit for reproduction." Thérèse told Mary Lawrence about Yelverton's curse and about his being burned in effigy. Thérèse's voice was described by the *Dublin Morning News* quoted in *Harper's Weekly*; and by Lawrence. Both Stoddard and *Harper's* are sources for Thérèse's speech before the House of Lords, and the lords' decision. Editorial comment on "The Great Yelverton Marriage Case," in *The Nation*. Thérèse described in detail the interior of Hutchings' cabin in *Zanita* . . . , and gave there her impressions of Elvira. She spoke of her meeting with Galen Clark, in a letter (undated) to Stoddard. Mary Lawrence watched her playing with Floy and Cosie Hutchings. Thérèse's first impressions of John Muir are also contained in *Zanita*. . . . Muir told Mrs. Carr (July 29, 1870) about his introduction through Mrs. Robert Waterston. He added that he and Thérèse were already "pretty well acquainted"; and that he was glad to find that she was another of Jeanne Carr's friends. Thérèse's picture of Muir in *Zanita* is strikingly similar to that of Sarah Jane Lippincott, indicating the accuracy of Yelverton's portrayal of Muir. Lawrence noted that Thérèse was a good listener. The plan to ride together to Mono Lake is mentioned in Thérèse's October 1870 letter to Muir. Mary Lawrence saw Thérèse returning from the plant-collecting excursion. The Muir-Yelverton relationship is revealed in part through Thérèse's letters of October 1870 and January 22, 1872, to Muir; and in *Zanita*. . . . In this book Thérèse has Floy Hutchings (the Zanita of the title) fall to her death from the summit of Half Dome. There is conflict in the accounts of how Floy actually met her death. In both 1941 and 1949, her sister Cosie Hutchings Mills stated that while leading a party of friends up the Ledge Trail to Glacier Point (an especially dangerous route, now closed) she was crushed by the falling rock and died from internal injuries. Some years later Cosie is reported to have said that Floy contracted a "fatal illness" by swimming in Yosemite Creek. In the fall Yosemite Creek is but a trickle, and some years is completely dry. John Muir wrote Harry Randall in the cited letter that while Floy was guiding a group of women up the Four-Mile Trail to Glacier Point, she dismounted in front of Sentinel Rock and scrambled up to pick ferns "for one of the ladies. There is a small stream there and in climbing she slipped & got her feet wet . . . at a critical time, took sick & died. In so simple a way, notwithstanding her vigorous constitution & constant exercise, poor Floy lost her life." Cosie Hutchings' early accounts seem more reasonable, although Floy was more likely acting as a guide on the Four-Mile Trail, as Muir states. James Mason Hutchings tells about the naming of Mount Florence, a beautiful peak seen clearly from Glacier Point. Muir's letters of August 20 and November 4, 1870, tell Jeanne Carr about sending Yosemite flora by Mrs. Yelverton. On December 22, 1870, he wrote Mrs. Carr from Delaney's ranch that Thérèse had asked him to wait and guide her out of Yosemite. This trip of Muir's to trace glacier action in the lower Merced canyon was interpreted by Wolfe to be a means of escape from the unwelcome advances of Thérèse Yelverton. Without troubling to study the relations, further writers on Muir continue to repeat Wolfe's concept, with which the present writer does not agree. Mary Lawrence was with Thérèse when the letters arrived announcing the death of the old viscount and heard the baron invite Mrs. Yelverton to ride with them. She watched the party start off a few days later, and noted Thérèse's bloomer suit. Stoddard wrote that "she was probably the finest horsewoman in California at that time." Both Lawrence and Stoddard recount the adventure on the snowy heights. Lawrence gives more details, and describes Thérèse's terror at being lost and her fears that Yelverton's curse was coming true. She also identified Thérèse's rescuer as innkeeper George Leidig. Muir expressed puzzlement at not having been aware of Thérèse's anguish that night, and admitted feeling a "kind of guiltiness" at not having waited for her: the December 22 letter to Mrs. Carr. Stoddard tells about Thérèse's writing and publishing activities during her stay in San Francisco after the Yosemite experience. He also relates their amusement in reading together the sensational reports with their "frantically melodramatic woodcut illustrations." He mentions that she now took the title of Viscountess Avonmore. He was out of town the night she sailed, but a letter from Hong Kong gave him details of the circumstances under which she had set off and enlarged on her literary plans. She also wrote Muir from Hong Kong, on January 22, 1872. Stoddard tells the rest of her story. "At parting . . . we had promised to hunt each other up in the Old World by and by," he wrote. Although their paths crossed in England and he tried to find her, she was so secretive that not even her London publisher was able to direct him to her. They never met again, and Stoddard learned of her death by reading an obituary.

13. *TRANSCENDENTALISTS ON THE TRAIL*, PP. 140-147

John Muir spoke of the importance of his meeting with Emerson in an address made at Harvard on the occasion of receiving an honorary degree in 1896; quoted by Badè (I). Van Wyck Brooks, *The Life of Emerson*, listed some members of Emerson's party. Wilkinson James identified in F. O. Matthiessen, *The James Family*. James Bradley Thayer, in *A Western Journey With Mr. Emerson*, mentioned others in the group and told about the private Pullman car; about Emerson's ever-present purple satchel and its contents; about his study of German, and his work on "Parnassus." Thayer is relied upon for the stage and horseback trip to Yosemite; the stay in the valley; the sightseeing excursions; the observations made by Emerson and his companions; their reactions to the scenery; the meat of their discussions. The hen chose Thayer's bed as a possible nesting place. The reader of Thayer is impressed by the party's obvious delight in discovering links and reminders of home in the people met and the landscape viewed; and with the high intellectual level of general conversation that included frequent allusions to literature and art, and quotations from Goethe and other writers in tune with transcendental concepts. Muir narrated his experiences with Emerson not only in the Harvard address but also in "The Forests of Yosemite Park" and in his journal. Clara Barrus, "In the Yosemite . . . ," spoke of Muir's indifference to food. Muir likewise described for the Harvard audience the noon rest during which Emerson recollected his student days and called on his companions to tell stories or recite poetry. Thayer identifies the recitations as being from Sir Walter Scott. He is also the source for Emerson's meeting with Coleridge. Thayer quotes Emerson on the risks of sleeping out-of-doors. Of these opinions Muir was unaware and blamed his family and friends for refusing to allow him to camp. Galen Clark's attributes were enhanced in the Emersonians' eyes by the fact that he was from New Hampshire. Jeanne Carr told William Badè about Emerson groping his way by mistake to her back door; of his refusal to come in because his wife and daughter had gone ahead to the ferry for San Francisco, and he felt he must follow directly. Emerson's concept of Muir as a new kind of Thoreau, in John Burroughs, "The Spell of the Yosemite." Emerson, in a letter of February 5, 1872 (Badè, I), urged Muir to come to Concord. Muir's response was expressed in a note to Mrs. Carr: "I feel like objecting in popular slang that I 'can't see it'" (undated fragment).

14. CLIMBING THE HEIGHTS, PP. 148–157

William H. Brewer recorded the Whitney party's opinion of Yosemite Valley, described their climbs and the difficulties encountered, and gave their reactions to the summit views. Muir's remark about King's problems in climbing Mount Tyndall, quoted by Thurman Wilkins in his biography *Clarence King*. Hutchings reported on John Tileston's climb, and his own subsequent one. In *My First Summer* . . . Muir wrote about his ascent of Cathedral Peak, that "majestic temple of one stone." The challenge of Mount Ritter he detailed in *The Mountains of California*. Whitney's pronouncement regarding the inaccessibility of Half Dome, in his . . . *Guide-Book*. Hutchings gives an account of his first unsuccessful attempt to climb it. Muir, *The Yosemite*, is the source for Conway's "lizards" and Anderson's success. Sally Dutcher was a saleswoman in photographer Carleton E. Watkins' Yosemite Art Gallery in San Francisco. She also marketed his Yosemite views in the Valley, and sometimes accompanied him as an assistant on photographic excursions. She and Watkins were in Yosemite during the fall of 1875 when George Anderson reached the summit. Muir's experience with the Specter of the Brocken is told in *The Yosemite*, as are his discoveries of plants, birds, and chipmunks on the dome's apparently barren and inhospitable summit. Hutchings saw the signal fire on Half Dome, and obtained from Alden Sampson and Phimister Proctor the full account of their adventure. Later Proctor wrote "An Ascent of Half Dome in 1884."

15. THROUGH THE CAMERA'S EYE, PP. 158–165

Oliver Wendell Holmes, "Doings of the Sunbeam," contains his opinion of Carleton E. Watkins' work. In "A Photographic Tour of Near 9000 Miles," the English photographer Charles R. Savage includes his recognition of Watkins' artistry. Biographical data on Watkins furnished by Charles B. Turrill, a close friend and associate, in "An Early California Photographer: C. E. Watkins." The London critic is quoted by Weston J. Naef and James N. Wood, *Era of Exploration: The Rise of Landscape Photography in the American West, 1860–1885*. Turrill gives an account of Watkins' first excursion to Yosemite Valley, describes his outfit and the steps in the wet-plate process, as well as the care needed to obtain clear images. Savage tells about his visit with Watkins in "A Photographic Tour . . . " Nael and Wood treat with the rivalry between Watkins and Charles L. Weed. Hans Huth speaks of Frederick Law Olmsted's request for Watkins photographs. Clarence King's opinion of Watkins given by Nael and Wood, who grasp the essence of Watkins' concern with rock in his high-country scenes, which can also be discerned by the careful viewer. Turrill writes about the opening of the Yosemite Art Gallery. Naef and Wood; and Karen Current, *Photography and the Old West*, tell of Watkins sending his photographs to the Paris Exposition and of the photographs being included in Whitney's book on Yosemite. Turrill is the source of the annual pass and the railroad flatcar provided by Huntington, as well as for the trips into Oregon and Utah. Brother Cornelius identifies Keith as Watkins' companion on those excursions. Turrill stresses Watkins' lack of business sense, and recounts the foreclosure and the loss of his work. Watkins expressed his anger at Taber's actions, and his determination to carry on, in a letter of September 2, 1878, to Professor George Davidson, quoted in Naef and Wood. These authors carefully compare Watkins' "new series" of Yosemite with the earlier photographs. Whenever possible, these two series have been studied by the writer for similarities and differences. Turrill, for the elegance of the new gallery next to the Palace Hotel, and the range of subjects on exhibit. He also speaks of Watkins' close friendship with many prominent Californians; Naef and Wood state that he was invited to balls and other social functions by the owners of those houses and estates he photographed. These authors discuss Watkins' refusal to compromise his art and his consequent financial decline, as does Turrill, who is the authority for the Capay Valley ranch, the failure of Watkins' eyesight, and the economic necessity for living in his studio. Robert Taft, *Photography and the American Scene, A Social History, 1839–1889*, includes a letter from H. C. Peterson who was cataloging Watkins' collection, regarding the discovery of the chest packed with rare daguerreotypes, and the loss of most of Watkins' work in the fire following the San Francisco earthquake of 1906. Turrill is the source for Watkins' last days in San Francisco, since he took the blind and ailing photographer into his home and cared for him from April until October, when Watkins retired with his family to the ranch, which had up until then been leased. Watkins never recovered from the shock of losing his work for the second time. Taft states that he passed the final six years of his life in the State Hospital for the Insane at Napa, California. Watkins' daughter Julia has said that her father was not insane, but in his helpless state at an advanced age, was more than she or her mother could handle. At that time it was not unusual to place such cases in asylums.

16. THE RIVAL, PP. 166–172

Muybridge's debt to Watkins discussed by Naef and Wood. Mary V. Jessup Hood and Robert Bartlett Haas, "Eadweard Muybridge's Yosemite Valley Photographs, 1867–1872," establish his headquarters at Hutchings' hotel. Gordon Hendricks, *Eadweard Muybridge, The Father of the Motion Picture*, consulted for biographical detail, which includes the various name changes. Current; and Hood and Haas, write of his outgoing personality and his prominence in business and civic affairs. The May 1860 announcement in the *Bulletin* quoted by Hendricks, as is that paper's listing of Muybridge among the stage passengers. Muybridge's account of events leading up to the stagecoach wreck and the results of his head injury are also quoted by Hendricks; likewise the telegram of July 22, 1860, reporting the accident. Hendricks points out that the decision to become a photographer was a logical one, since Muybridge was already familiar with the art through his friend Silas Selleck, a photographer who had worked with Mathew Brady before establishing himself in San Francisco. "A family memoir," Hendricks states, indicates that Muybridge had already learned photographic processes from Selleck. Current quotes the *Sacramento Union*,

February 4, 1875, regarding the changes in Muybridge's personality and character after the accident. His name does not appear in the San Francisco directory until 1867, when he is listed at the same address as Silas Selleck's Cosmopolitan Gallery of Photographic Art. Muybridge's brochure announcing Helios' Yosemite photographs, quoted by Hendricks. Naef and Wood are of the opinion that Muybridge chose a pseudonym to clearly distinguish his work from that of Weed or Watkins, thereby preventing plagiarism. The opinions of various San Francisco art critics quoted from the *Evening Bulletin*, the *Morning Call*, and the *Alta California* in Hendricks. Hood and Haas are sources for Muybridge sending photographs to *The Philadelphia Photographer* for review, and for his presentation of others to the Mercantile Library, of which he was, before his accident, a board member. Muybridge's advertisement appears in John S. Hittell, *Yosemite: Its Wonders and Its Beauties*. Hood and Haas list the cameras and quote Muybridge's prospectus, which describes his additional photographic equipment. Naef and Wood; and Gordon Hendricks, *Albert Bierstadt, Painter of the American West*, are sources for the landscapist accompanying Muybridge. Naef and Wood discuss Bierstadt's influence on the photographer, which was pointed out by the *Alta California*, April 7, 1872, an article that told also about the trouble Muybridge often took to obtain his Yosemite views. Helen Hunt Jackson appraised Muybridge's work and regretted that Yosemite was known chiefly through Watkins' work, in *Bits of Travel* . . . Susan Coolidge's opinion of Muybridge's superiority over Watkins, in "A Few Hints on the California Journey." Naef and Wood call attention to the failure of the Vienna judges to perceive stylistic differences between Watkins and Muybridge in their approach to Yosemite, or recognize the latter's debt to Watkins. The experiments in animal locomotion treated at length in Hendricks, *Eadweard Muybridge* . . . ; also Naef and Wood; Current; Taft; and Hood and Haas. The tragedy of Muybridge's marriage and the killing of Harry Larkyns; the trial and acquittal; and the Central American photographic expedition, are in Hendricks, ibid. Naef and Wood assess Muybridge's achievements as a photojournalist. Taft treats with Muybridge's research at the University of Pennsylvania; his work in England; his lectures and publications, and quotes the painter Meisonnier.

17. THE LANDSCAPIST AND
THE HASHEESH EATER, PP. 173–183

Gordon Hendricks, *Albert Bierstadt* . . . ; and John C. Ewers, *Artists of the Old West* were consulted for biographical data on the painter; his early career, his European studies, and his recognition after painting Rocky Mountain scenes. Fitz Hugh Ludlow tells in "Seven Weeks in the Great Yo-Semite," about viewing the Watkins photographs on display in New York City. Hendricks quotes an unidentified opinion of Ludlow's *The Hasheesh Eater*; and notes that both he and Bierstadt were lionized. Ludlow describes their dress and equipment for the overland stage trip; their arrival in San Francisco; the evenings spent at Thomas Starr King's; the preparations for the trip to Yosemite; the trip itself, and the stay there. Ludlow, a keen observer, described in detail the scenery and flora. He is also the source for Vance's decampment. Hutchings described Register Rock and listed those members of Bierstadt's party who signed. Titles of Bierstadt's Yosemite paintings in checklist of known Bierstadt paintings in Hendricks, who is also the authority for the relationship with Frederic E. Church. Hendricks quotes the critic's favorable comment on "The Domes of Yosemite." B. P. Avery, "Art Beginnings on the Pacific Coast," II, talks of the effect of Bierstadt's visit on the local art colony. Through family letters Hendricks traces Ludlow's rapid decline as a victim of drugs and alcohol; his involvement with other women; Rosalie's divorce; and Ludlow's early death. A month after his wedding Bierstadt wrote a friend that his only regret was that he had not known Rosalie when she was twelve, enabling him to have married her then; quoted in Hendricks. The three-story mansion was built close to Washington Irving's Sunnyside. Avery comments on Bierstadt's success in capturing Yosemite on canvas, and in giving the world through the addition of color, an adequate idea of its wonders. The business that detained Bierstadt in New York was the planning of a buffalo hunt for the benefit of the Grand Duke Alexis of Russia. The painter called on General William T. Sherman and the secretary of war for help. Buffalo Bill Cody was hired for a thousand pounds of tobacco to see to it that the duke killed a buffalo. To add pageantry, Cody arranged with Chief Spotted Tail to bring a thousand Indians in war bonnets and buckskins to "Camp Alexis," set up on Willow Creek, south of the North Platte River. Wilkins tells about the association with Clarence King in his biography of King. Rosalie Bierstadt's sister, a member of the 1873 party going to Yosemite, kept a journal in which she mentions staying at Hutchings' hotel; she also recorded the camping trip to Hetch Hetchy. Bierstadt's paintings of Hetch Hetchy, the valley of the Tuolumne, in Hendricks' checklist. Alfred, a well-known stage driver on the Wawona–Yosemite run, remembered having Bierstadt as a passenger. Alfred quoted by Ben C. Truman, "Knights of the Lash: Old Time Stage Drivers of the West Coast," I.

18. *JOSEPH LE CONTE'S RAMBLES, PP. 184–197*

In "Reminiscences of Joseph LeConte," John Muir recalled his first meeting with Dr. LeConte. In his *Autobiography*, written at the urging of a daughter, Caroline, LeConte tells modestly about the popularity of his classes, and also mentions the affectionate relations with his students. His role in the university party is made clear through the journal he kept during that excursion, published soon after as *A Journal of Ramblings Through the High Sierra of California, 1870*. The autobiography is the source for his early life and education, and his career up to the Civil War. A spirited and often humorous account of his attempt to beat General William T. Sherman to Savannah, during the famed March to the Sea, and rescue his (the doctor's) daughter Sallie from the path of the invading army is found in LeConte's journal kept during those days, and published as *'Ware Sherman*. There the reader learns details of the events which prompted the remark in his autobiography that "as a result of the war I lost everything I had in the world." In an introductory reminiscence to *'Ware Sherman*, Caroline LeConte described her father's dress as he hauled corn by flatboat. She also told about those loyal friends and associates in the north who wrote her father about the new university in California, and sent letters of recommendation on his behalf and that of his brother John. Details of appointment of the brothers to professorships at the university, and John's appointment first as acting president, then as president of the university, supplied by J. R. K. Kantor, the university archivist, Bancroft Library, in a letter of October 5, 1978. Joseph LeConte emphasized the importance of his first trip to Yosemite, in the autobiography. *A Journal of Ramblings* . . . is the source for the horseback trip to Yosemite; the doctor's reactions to first views of the valley, and his continuing enthusiasm for each new scene and experience; for the party's stay in the valley, and the casting of the spell; for their travels with John Muir through the highlands and down Bloody Canyon to Mono Lake. Illilouette Fall was named by Josiah Whitney. According to Hutchings it is a faulty rendering of the local Indian name *Too-lool'-we-ack*. Muir wrote in "Reminiscences . . ." about LeConte's response to nature, and pictured the doctor as "sinewy, slender, erect." In this same article Muir recalled their experience in watching the coming of night from the summit of Eagle Peak. LeConte told about the bonfire, after the rest of the party joined them, the halloos, gunshots, and responses from the valley. Both men (Muir in "Reminiscences . . . ") wrote about the spiritual experience at Tenaya Lake. Description of ancient Tenaya Glacier in François E. Matthes, *Geologic History of the Yosemite Valley*. In a letter to Jeanne Carr, December 11, 1871, Muir speaks of sending glacier ice to LeConte. In *Autobiography*, the doctor admits succumbing to Yosemite's spell; and tells of his second excursion there. Badè, I, discusses LeConte's article in which he gave Muir full credit for discovering living glaciers in the Sierra. Muir in "Reminiscences . . . " recounts those efforts to persuade the doctor to run away. LeConte, Muir says, had told the "grand story" of his adventures in the Old Northwest when at twenty-one he and an Indian guide in a birchbark canoe had threaded all the waterways and gone to the sources of the Mississippi. This had prompted Muir to urge him to recapture the freedom of that adventure. LeConte in the *Autobiography* credits Yosemite for his continuing physical and mental vigor, and discusses the many scientific papers that resulted from these trips. One of the most important was the book *Elements of Geology*, published in 1878, which became a standard work, often revised. An account of the 1875 Yosemite trip is in the autobiography. It was LeConte's plan after finishing his examination of the Mono Lake islands to ride south through Owens Valley, to cross the Sierra by way of Kearsage Pass, and to join John Muir in the Kings River Canyon for a study of the sequoia of that area. However, the doctor was thrown by a runaway horse, and his entire body was so battered and bruised and one thumb was so painfully dislocated that he and his party did not go beyond the lake. The gypsy caravan trip of 1878 is also contained in the autobiography, as is the doctor's formula for the well-prepared teacher. This memoir is the source for all ensuing Yosemite trips; for LeConte's faith in its restorative powers; and for the realization that his appreciation of the valley increased upon each visit. Accounts of the final trip and Dr. LeConte's death are found in Frank Soulé, "Joseph LeConte in the Sierra"; and William Dallam Armes' Preface to LeConte's *Autobiography*. Brother Cornelius named many of those attending the Sierra Club gathering, spoke of Dr. Wall's diagnosis, and quoted Mary Keith's recollections. Armes reported Dr. LeConte's final minutes as told to him by Sallie LeConte. Soulé wrote about the decoration of the casket, and the night procession. Armes for the selection of the granite boulder as a grave marker. In the autobiography Dr. LeConte talked about his son as a mountaineer, and a talented photographer. Ansel Adams adds his opinion in "The Photography of Joseph N. LeConte."

19. STAGING DAYS, PP. 198–209

Ben C. Truman, "Knights of the Lash . . . ," described Alfred, whom he knew personally; quoted Alfred's recollections of famous people he had driven, of those gifts he most prized, and of the day he let General Grant take the reins. Truman gives a brief account of young Grant's jilting of Jennie Flood. Oscar Lewis and Carroll D. Hall, *Bonanza Inn*; and Oscar Lewis, *Silver Kings*, consulted for details of the romance, based on contemporary newspaper and magazine reports. Russell, *One Hundred Years . . .* ; John Outcalt, *History of Merced County, California*; and Hutchings, for a history of the stage roads. Hutchings describes the transformation of Wawona into a bustling stage center. Truman tells about the driver's social standing, and what he wore. Henry Hussey Vivian, First Baron Swansea, described the "villainous" roads leading to Yosemite, in his *Notes of a Tour in America from August 7 to November 17, 1877*. J. Ross Browne, *Washoe Revisited*; and J. D. Borthwick, *Three Years in California*, also wrote from experience about the Sierra roads and the drivers' skill. Truman was the Yosemite commissioner who rode with Buffalo Jim on the day his brakes failed. The stage holdup of August 15, 1905, was reported at length in the *San Francisco Examiner* the following day. The deposition of Anton Veith given on August 16, 1905, presents a clear and concise description of the robbery, even to the picture-taking. "The Yosemite Tourist" of July 13, 1906, carried an account of the photographing of the highwayman. This same issue reported the robbery of the five stages in July 1906. John C. Shay, *Twenty Years in the Backwoods of California*, recalled the numerous stage robberies that took place along this route to Yosemite, where he had a wayside blacksmith shop. James Mason Hutchings gave the advice to tourists and campers in his *Yosemite Guide Book* as well as *In the Heart of the Sierras*. Charles Loring Brace lauded Hutchings' talents as a guide. The *Sacramento Bee*, November 3, 1902, for an account of Hutchings' death, his funeral service, and burial. History of the Great Sierra Mining Road found in Russell. The diversity of alpine scenery along the Tioga Road, firsthand observation at various seasons. C. C. Presnall, "Indian Picture Writing in Yosemite"; Jim Snyder, "A Plea for Yosemite's Past."

20. THE MOUNTAIN KING, PP. 210–216

William E. Colby, who knew and admired Lembert, described his appearance in "Jean (John) Lembert—Personal Memories." Lembert is first listed in the *Mariposa County Great Register of Voters* in 1882, and his occupation given as a miner; it remains miner until 1890, when it is changed to rancher. A news item in the *Mariposa Gazette*, May 6, 1882, regarding a petition and remonstrance being circulated for signatures by Lembert among those opposing the extension of the Yosemite Grant boundaries, states that he owned interests in the Hoffmann Mining District. Firsthand observation of Tuolumne Meadows in spring; identification of indigenous insects made in Tracy I. Storer and Robert L. Usinger, *Sierra Nevada Natural History*. The Meadows in winter, described by John Muir in *The Mountains of California*. Joseph N. LeConte, son of Dr. Joseph LeConte, stated in "The Soda Springs Property of the Tuolumne Meadows," that the quarter section was homesteaded by Lembert on August 15, 1885. Colby described Lembert's rough cabin, and told about the shelter built to protect the springs. John Muir wrote in his journal that Lembert split the fence rails and packed them on his back. Colby remembered that many people shared their reading material with Lembert, and sent him books. Lembert told Colby about the Indian trading encampments on the meadow moraines; and about his friendly relations with these people, and his knowledge of their customs. Joseph N. LeConte and Colby locate the winter cabin in the Merced River Canyon; both write about Lembert's absorbing interest in the moths, butterflies, and flora of the alpine region. Colby won Lembert's confidence, and to him he talked freely about his dream world; told his stories, read his verse, and pointed out the figures he saw in the granite domes and gnarled trees. He also told Colby about those members of Macomb's party who thought him mad, and of the scientists among them who thought otherwise and encouraged him to collect. An article on Lembert in the *Entomological News*, September 1896, comments on his "faultless" language and command of Latin. Lawrence V. Degnan, who grew up in Yosemite Valley and also knew Lembert personally, stated in a letter of February 16, 1952, that Lembert had been well-educated. Hutchings is the source for Lembert being known as the hermit-artist. Both Colby and Joseph N. LeConte speak about the loss of his Angora goats. Degnan in the letter of February 16, mentions that Lembert worked as a guide and laborer. Colby is one source for Lembert's difficulty with the Indians over having disturbed some burial sites. The article in the *Entomological News* indicates that it was the Smithsonian Institution for whom he was collecting artifacts. Degnan, whose father was a pioneer Yosemite storekeeper, remembered in a letter of March 17, 1952, that Lembert was always a welcome visitor at his home in the valley. He spoke of his father's "great personal liking" for Lembert; and recalled that Lembert "used to entertain us youngsters with stories of his boyhood," and that he treated them as adults. Colby heard from Lembert the story of his unsuccessful courtship of Nellie who worked in George Fiske's photographic studio. After Lembert's death Colby saw his diary. Lembert's rank as a scientist is found in *Entomological News* article; and Degnan's letter of February 16, 1952. Description of the *Hepialus lembertii* in Harrison J. Dyar, "A New Hepialus from California." Degnan is the source for the "sizable" roll of paper currency carried by Lembert; the clerk's remark to Lembert, and his reply to the clerk, in letters of March 17, 1952, and March 6, 1961. The story of Lembert's murder was reported in the *Mariposa Gazette* of April 25, 1896, and the *San Francisco Call*, of April 27, 1896; and in a letter of Judge J. J. Trabuco of Mariposa, July 21, 1936, citing county records. Colby; and Joseph N. LeConte are also sources for Lembert's death. Lawrence Degnan in his March 6 letter states that those pioneer Yosemite families who "knew Lembert and the Indians as well as they knew their own families, stoutly absolve the Indians." In this same letter he expresses the generally held opinion that the authorities "made little or no investigation of the crime." LeConte gives the history of Lembert's Tuolumne Meadows homestead after his death, and its eventual purchase by the Sierra Club. Colby tells about the discovery of Lembert's papers and diary in a hollow stump, and their loss in the 1906 fire.

21. JOHN BURROUGHS AND JOHN MUIR, PP. 217–224

Unless otherwise noted the main source for this chapter is Clara Barrus, *The Life and Letters of John Burroughs*; likewise, all Muir letters appear in Badè, II. John Muir to his wife, June 13, 1893, speaks of Burroughs' refusal to accompany him to Great Britain and the reason. In a letter of July 3, 1896, Muir told his daughter Helen about calling on Burroughs; and to Walter Hines Page he wrote in May 1899 that he and Burroughs were going on the Alaskan expedition. Clara Barrus, "In the Yosemite With John Muir," comments on Muir's independence of sleep in contrast to Burroughs' need for it. She also quotes Muir's responses to the woman who shared his seat in the Yosemite stage, and his sharp retorts to Burroughs' questions. Burroughs describes his first reactions to the valley and the impressions gained during the stay there, in "The Spell of the Yosemite." In this article he also admits to accusing Muir of destroying trees when he worked as Hutchings' sawyer, and gives Muir's defense; he also notes here the many wonders seen on the walk to Vernal and Nevada falls, and that night in camp. He records his realization that he has succumbed to the valley's spell, and understands Muir's response.

22. SAVING THE YOSEMITE, PP. 225–236

June wildflowers, personal observation. John Muir told Jeanne Carr in a letter of June 3, 1875 about visiting Lamon's grave; and mentioned the success of Keith's sketches. Again, unless otherwise cited, all Muir letters appear in Badè, II. Brother Cornelius gives an account of this excursion as it influenced Keith, while Dr. LeConte records the pleasures of his camping trip at this time, in the *Autobiography*. Mrs. Carr learned of the Mount Whitney trip from Muir's letter of July 31, 1875; while his exploration of the sequoia groves is recounted in a letter to his sister Sarah of November 2, 1875. This trip with Browny the mule was also followed through Muir's journal, where he recorded his thoughts about the future of mountains and forests, and man's role in their destiny. In volume II, Badè quotes from Muir's article for the *Sacramento Record-Union*. He also tells of Mrs. Carr's problems in bringing about Muir's meeting with Louie Strentzel, and how after they had finally met and a romance seemed about to bud, Muir joined the U.S. Coast and Geodetic Survey's reconnaissance along the 39th parallel in order to study the mountains and trees of Nevada. Badè is also the source for Muir's unsuccessful attempt to find rest and revitalization with his wife in Yosemite. Wolfe, *Son* . . . , quotes the editor's inquiry about Muir's failure to produce any writings. Badè is the source for the offer to edit and contribute to *Picturesque California*. Muir described his nerve-shaken condition to his brother, David Muir, in August 1887. From a room in San Francisco's Grand Hotel, Muir wrote a series of letters to his wife, in July 1889, relating his struggles with article writing. Robert Underwood Johnson recounted with considerable amusement his meeting with Muir at the Palace Hotel when the mountaineer lost his way in the corridors; in "John Muir As I Knew Him." That feeling of "going home" was communicated to his old friend James Davie Butler, professor of Greek, whose presence in Yosemite Valley Muir had *felt* while in the heights in 1869; letter of September 1, 1889. This sensation of satisfaction at returning to Yosemite was also put into words in "The Wild Parks and Forest Reservations of the West." He spoke to Mrs. Muir in a letter of June 3, 1889, of his desire to take up his studies of Yosemite again. In his article Johnson gave an account of the exploration of the Tuolumne gorge on foot and Muir's fun at his inability to keep pace; the ride through Yosemite highlands, and his suggestion to Muir that he launch a campaign for the creation of Yosemite National Park. Badè writes about the publication of Muir's two articles, and the enthusiasm the campaign aroused. Muir's statement that commercial interests would not suffer, found in a letter of May 8, 1890, to Johnson, included in "The Creation of Yosemite National Park," a collection of Muir-Johnson letters on that subject. Russell, *One Hundred Years* . . . cites proof of the perpetual conflict between state and federal management. Badè tells about Muir returning to Yosemite as in the old days, alone, without a blanket, and with only tea and crackers to sustain him. To Johnson Muir expressed his delight at finding grass and flowers coming into their own again in the high country after sheep were banned; and of finding the valley frowsy and forlorn; in a letter of September 12, 1895. Hutchings listed the various business enterprises to be found in the valley; as did Muir in a letter to Johnson, March 4, 1890, in "The Creation . . . " Charles Nordhoff, grandfather of the co-author of *Mutiny on the Bounty*, lamented the shabby, "tasteless structures which form blots on the landscape"; and wished Frederick Law Olmsted might be hired to formulate a master plan for the valley, and direct the work: *California for Travellers and Settlers*. Muir records the "tangly search" for his second cabin; its condition as well as that of the Hutchings cabin and orchard; Lamon's fruit trees and berry patch, and the unkempt state of the old cemetery, in his journal. Muir remarked to Johnson about the regrettable lack of nature lovers among Californians, in the letter of March 4, in which he also spoke of a man's failure to appreciate his wife. Muir's outspoken criticism, Badè says, prompted an investigation of the mismanagement of Yosemite Valley. He is also the source for the founding of the Sierra Club, and its purposes. He likewise recounts the steps leading to the Roosevelt-Muir camping trip, as does William F. Kimes, "With Theodore Roosevelt and John Muir in Yosemite." Cornelius tells about the dinner at Keith's house, and gives the painter's excuse for not joining Roosevelt and Muir. "Charlie Leidig's Report of President Roosevelt's Visit in May, 1903," is almost a step-by-step account of the trip. A keen observer, Leidig missed little. Newspaper accounts also consulted for another point of view: "Roosevelt Pitches His Camp Near Bleak Sentinel Dome in Snow Storm," *San Francisco Chronicle*, May 17, 1903. Burroughs' remark about Roosevelt's ability to outtalk everyone, quoted in Barrus, *Life and Letters* . . . Muir wrote to C. Hart Merriam about stuffing Roosevelt; quoted in Kimes. *San Francisco Call*, May 18, 1903, "President Makes Camp at Bridal Veil Falls. Roosevelt Reaches Floor of Yosemite Refreshed and Delighted." Badè quotes from Roosevelt's 1907 letter to Muir wishing they were again camping together. Muir's recollection of the "tranquil camp" in a letter of April 21, 1908. Muir comments to Johnson on the speed of the recession movement, and relates his experiences as a lobbyist, February 24, 1905. His exultation in the final triumph, July 16, 1906.

23. *TWO WORLDS, PP. 237-243*

Carl P. Russell, "Last of Yosemite Indians Visits Valley After a 75-Year Absence," states that a grandson persuaded Totuya (or Maria Lebrado, as she was known in the white community) to visit her home valley. Rose Taylor, who was Totuya's friend, was aware of her feelings about the loss of her home, and knew that she went there only to gather acorns; Taylor wrote of this in *The Last Survivor*; and, "The Return of the Last Survivor." Unless otherwise noted, Taylor's writings on Totuya are found in these two sources, nearly identical. The village site is identified in Merriam, "Indian Village and Camp Sites . . . " Taylor, in the Preface to her book, tells the story of Totuya's response to the tourists; as does Russell, "Last of Yosemite Indians . . . " Mrs. Taylor, who accompanied Totuya on the ride about the valley, and on the visit to the cemetery and Indian Museum, is the authority for her reactions and comments, found in an additional source, "Maria Lebrado Is a Guest at Museum." Galen Clark, *Indians of the Yosemite*, writes about the troubled spirits inhabiting Bridalveil Creek and Fall, a tradition he had obtained from the Indians. Taylor quotes Totuya's warning about Pohono. Biographical material on Rose Schuster Taylor found in Carl P. Russell, "Mrs. H. J. Taylor, 1863-1951"; letter of February 24, 1948 to E. B. Fred, president of the University of Wisconsin, urging conferral of an honorary degree on Rose Taylor for outstanding accomplishment; and a letter from Herbert Eugene Bolton to Dr. Fred on this same subject; February 20, 1948. Also, "Bibliography of Published Writings of Rose Schuster Taylor." Taylor tells of the days spent with Totuya at her camp, shelling acorns, and retells her (Totuya's) story. Russell, "Interview with Maria Lebrado . . . ," is also a source for Totuya's two marriages, and for her settling at Hite's Cove. At that time she told Russell about being cheated by traders. She explained her Catholicism to Rose Taylor. In her Preface, Mrs. Taylor gives the meaning of Totuya. In the "Interview . . . ," Totuya talked to Russell about Lebrado Yerdies taking up a homestead and building several log cabins on the property. Taylor knew of Totuya's standing as a shaman. Newell D. Chamberlain, a neighbor, recalled Totuya living mainly out-of-doors, in *The Call of Gold*. Rose Taylor quotes Totuya's designation of Savage as "man with red shirt." In the interview with Russell, she spoke of all Yosemite Indians hating Savage; and also told about the threat to drown the little boy. Her poignant recollection of the death of Tenaya's son, quoted by Russell in "A Last Link With the Past." Totuya's version of her grandfather's death appears in Russell's interview, and in his two articles about her. In "Last of Yosemite Indians . . . ," Russell mentions Totuya's refusal to locate exactly where Tenaya was buried. Rose Taylor gives an account of her first visit to the Bear Creek cabin; of Totuya's illness, her death, the funeral rites, and the burial, in that part of her book she calls "Death of the Last Survivor."

BIBLIOGRAPHY

BOOKS

A London Parson. *To San Francisco and Back*. James Truscott & Son, London: 1860.

Badè, William Frederic. *The Life and Letters of John Muir*. 2 vols. Houghton Mifflin Co., Boston: 1924.

Bancroft, Hubert Howe. "California Pioneer Register and Index, 1542–1848," in *History of California*, vol. V. The History Co., San Francisco: 1884–1890.

Barnum, Phineas Taylor. *Struggles and Triumphs: or, Forty Years' Recollection*. American News Co., New York: 1871.

Barrett, S. A., and Gifford, E. W. *Miwok Material Culture. Bulletin of Milwaukee Public Museum*, March 1933.

Barrus, Clara. *The Life and Letters of John Burroughs*. 2 vols. Houghton Mifflin Co., Boston and New York: 1925.

Beadle, J. H. *Western Wilds and the Men Who Redeem Them*. A. L. Bancroft & Co., San Francisco: 1879.

Bingaman, John W. *The Ahwahneechees, A Story of the Yosemite Indians*. End-Kian Publishing Co., Lodi, Ca.: 1968.

Boddam-Whetham, John. *Western Wanderings. A Record of Travel in the Evening Land*. Richard Bently & Son, London: 1874.

Borthwick, J. D. *Three Years in California*. William Blackwood & Sons, Edinburgh and London: 1857.

Brace, Charles Loring. *The New West or, California in 1867–1868*. G. P. Putnam & Son, New York: 1869.

Brewer, William H. *Up and Down California in 1860–1864*. Francis P. Farquhar, editor. Yale University Press, New Haven: 1930.

Brooks, Van Wyck. *The Life of Emerson*. E. P. Dutton & Co., New York: 1932.

Browne, J. Ross. *The Indians of California*. Colt Press, San Francisco: 1944.

————. *A Peep at Washoe and Washoe Revisited*. Paisano Press, Balboa Island, Ca.: 1959.

Bunnell, Lafayette Houghton. *Discovery of the Yosemite and the Indian War of 1851 which led to that Event*. C. W. Gerlicher, Los Angeles: 1911.

Castillo, Edward D. "The Impact of Euro-American Exploration and Settlement," in *Handbook of North American Indians*, Vol. 8, "California." Robert F. Heizer, volume editor. Smithsonian Institution, Washington, D.C.: 1978.

Chamberlain, Newell D. *The Call of Gold, True Tales on the Gold Road to Yosemite.* Gazette Press, Mariposa, Ca.: 1936.

Chester, Giraud. *Embattled Maiden. The Life of Anna Dickinson.* G. P. Putnam's Sons, New York: 1951.

Churchill, Caroline M. *Over the Purple Hills, or Sketches of Travel in California.* Privately printed, Denver: 1876.

Clark, Galen. *Indians of the Yosemite Valley.* Reflex Publishing Co., Redondo, Ca.: 1907.

Conrotto, Eugene L. *Miwok Means People.* Valley Publishers, Fresno, Ca.: 1973.

Cook, Sherburne F. "Conflict Between the Californian Indian and White Civilization," in *The California Indians, A Source Book.* R. F. Heizer and M. A. Whipple, editors. University of California Press, Berkeley and Los Angeles: 1970.

———. "Historical Demography," in *Handbook of North American Indians*, Vol. 8, "California." Robert F. Heizer, volume editor. Smithsonian Institution, Washington, D.C.: 1978.

Cornelius, Brother. *Keith, Old Master of California.* G. P. Putnam's Sons, New York: 1942.

Crossley-Batt, Jill L. *The Last of the California Rangers.* Funk and Wagnalls Co., New York and London: 1928.

Current, Karen. *Photography and the Old West.* Harry N. Abrams, in association with the Amon Carter Museum of Western Art, New York: 1978.

Delano, Alonzo. *Life on the Plains and Among the Diggings.* Miller, Orton and Mulligan, Auburn and Buffalo: 1854.

Dixon, Roland B., "Death and Burial Among the Maidu," in *The California Indians, A Source Book.* R. F. Heizer and M. A. Whipple, editors. University of California Press, Berkeley and Los Angeles: 1970.

Downey, Joseph T. *The Cruise of the Portsmouth 1845–1847, A Sailor's View of the Naval Conquest of California*, Howard Lamar, editor. Yale University Press, New Haven and London: 1958.

Eccleston, Robert. *The Mariposa Indian War 1850–1851. Diaries of Robert Eccleston: The California Gold Rush, Yosemite, and the High Sierra.* C. Gregory Crampton, editor. University of Utah Press, Salt Lake City: 1957.

Elsasser, Albert B. "Development of Regional Prehistoric Cultures," in *Handbook of North American Indians*, Vol. 8, "California." Robert F. Heizer, volume editor. Smithsonian Institution, Washington, D.C.: 1978.

Emerson, Ralph Waldo. *The Heart of Emerson's Journals.* Bliss Perry, editor. Houghton Mifflin Co., Boston and New York: 1937.

Evans, Albert S. *À La California, or Sketches of Life in the Golden State.* George H. Bancroft, San Francisco: 1889.

Ewers, John C. *Artists of the Old West.* Doubleday and Co., Garden City, New York: 1965.

Farquhar, Francis P. *History of the Sierra Nevada.* University of California Press, Berkeley and Los Angeles; in collaboration with The Sierra Club: 1966.

————. *Yosemite, the Big Trees, and the High Sierra, A Selective Bibliography.* University of California Press, Berkeley and Los Angeles: 1948.

Font, Pedro. "Font's Complete Diary of the Second Anza Expedition." Herbert Eugene Bolton, translator; in *Anza's California Expeditions*, Vol. IV. University of California Press, Berkeley: 1930.

Frémont, Jessie Benton. *Mother Lode Narratives.* Shirley Sargent, editor. Lewis Osborne, Ashland, Oreg.: 1970.

Gifford, E. W. "California Indian Physical Types," in *The California Indians, A Source Book.* R. F. Heizer and M. A. Whipple, editors. University of California Press, Berkeley and Los Angeles: 1970.

————, and Block, Gwendoline Harris. *Californian Indian Nights' Entertainment.* The Arthur H. Clark Co., Glendale: 1930.

Gordon-Cumming, Constance F. *Granite Crags of California.* William Blackwood and Sons, Edinburgh and London: 1886.

Harris, Benjamin Butler. *The Gila Trail. The Texas Argonauts and the California Gold Rush.* Richard H. Dillon, editor. University of Oklahoma Press, Norman: 1960.

Heizer, Robert F. "Natural Forces and Native World View," in *Handbook of North American Indians*, Vol. 8. "California." Robert F. Heizer, volume editor. Smithsonian Institution, Washington, D.C.: 1978.

Hendricks, Gordon. *Albert Bierstadt, Painter of the American West.* Harry N. Abrams in association with the Amon Carter Museum of Western Art: 1973.

————. *Eadweard Muybridge, The Father of the Motion Picture.* Grossman, New York: 1975.

Hittell, John S. *Yosemite: Its Wonders and Its Beauties.* H. H. Bancroft and Co., San Francisco: 1868.

Hittell, Theodore Henry. *The Adventures of James Capen Adams, Mountaineer and Grizzly Bear Hunter of California.* Towne and Bacon, San Francisco: 1860.

————. *The Adventures of James Capen Adams, Mountaineer and Grizzly Bear Hunter of California.* Containing Introduction and Postscript by Hittell. Charles Scribner's Sons, New York: 1911.

———. *History of California*, Vol. III. N. J. Stone and Co., San Francisco: 1898.

Hodge, Frederick Webb. "Dreams and Visions." *Bulletin* 30, Part I, *Handbook of American Indians*. Smithsonian Institution, Washington, D.C.: 1912.

Holbrook, John C. *Recollections of a Nonagenarian, of Life in New England, the Middle West, and New York . . . together with Scenes in California*. Pilgrim Press, Boston: 1897.

Hutchings, James Mason. *In the Heart of the Sierras: The Yosemite Valley, Both Historical and Descriptive; and Scenes by the Way. Big Tree Groves*. Pacific Press House, Oakland: 1886.

Irving, Washington. *The Adventures of Captain Bonneville, U.S.A. in the Mountains and the Far West . . . from his Journal*. Edgeley W. Todd, editor. University of Oklahoma Press, Norman: 1961.

Jackson, Helen Hunt. *Bits of Travel at Home*. Roberts Brothers, Boston: 1894.

King, Clarence. *Mountaineering in the Sierra Nevada*. Charles Scribner's Sons, New York: 1923.

———. *Systematic Geology*. Vol. I *Report of the Geologic Exploration of the Fortieth Parallel*. Government Printing Office, Washington: 1878.

Kroeber, A. L. "Elements of Culture in Native California," in *The California Indians, A Source Book*. R. F. Heizer and M. A. Whipple, editors. University of California Press, Berkeley and Los Angeles; 1970.

———. *Handbook of the Indians of California*. California Book Co., Berkeley: 1953.

———. "The Nature of Land-Holding Groups in Aboriginal California," in *Aboriginal California, Three Studies in Culture History*. University of California Archeological Research Facility, Berkeley: 1963.

LeConte, Joseph. *The Autobiography of Joseph LeConte*. William Dallam Armes, editor. D. Appleton & Co., New York: 1903.

———. *A Journal of Ramblings Through the High Sierra of California, 1870 by the University Excursion Party*. The Sierra Club, San Francisco: 1930.

———. 'Ware Sherman. *A Journal of Three Months' Personal Experience in the Last Days of the Confederacy*. University of California Press, Berkeley: 1937.

Leonard, Zenas. *Adventures of Zenas Leonard, Fur Trader*. John C. Ewers, editor. University of Oklahoma Press, Norman: 1959.

Levy, Richard. "Eastern Miwok," in *Handbook of North American Indians*, Vol. 8, "California." Robert F. Heizer, volume editor. Smithsonian Institution, Washington, D.C.: 1978.

Lewis, Oscar, and Hall, Carroll D. *Bonanza Inn*. Alfred A. Knopf, New York: 1939.

Lewis, Oscar. *Silver Kings*. Alfred A. Knopf, New York: 1947.

Lienhard, Heinrich. *From St. Louis to Sutter's Fort*. Erwin and Elizabeth K. Gudde, translators and editors. University of Oklahoma Press, Norman: 1961.

———. *A Pioneer at Sutter's Fort, 1846–1850*. Marguerite Eyer Wilbur, translator and editor. The Califia Society, Los Angeles: 1941.

Matthes, François E. *Geologic History of the Yosemite Valley*. Professional Paper 160; United States Department of the Interior. Government Printing Office, Washington: 1930.

———. *The Incomparable Valley. A Geological Interpretation of the Yosemite*. Fritiof Fryxell, editor. University of California Press, Berkeley and Los Angeles: 1950.

Matthiessen, F. O. *The James Family*. Alfred A. Knopf, New York: 1947.

Merriam, C. Hart, editor and collector. *The Dawn of the World*. The Arthur H. Clark Co., Cleveland: 1910.

Morgan, Dale L., editor. *Overland in 1846. Diaries and Letters of the California-Oregon Trail*. 2 vols. The Talisman Press, Georgetown, Ca.: 1963.

Morgenson, Dana C. *Yosemite Wildflower Trails*. Yosemite Natural History Association: 1975.

Muir, John. *John of the Mountains, The Unpublished Journals of John Muir*. Linnie Marsh Wolfe, editor. Houghton Mifflin Co., Boston: 1938.

———. *The Mountains of California*. The Century Co., New York: 1894.

———. *My First Summer in the Sierra*. Houghton Mifflin Co., Boston: 1979.

———. *Our National Parks*. Houghton Mifflin Co., Boston: 1901.

———, editor and contributor. *Picturesque California, and the Region West of the Rocky Mountains from Alaska to Mexico*, 2 vols. J. Dewing, San Francisco, 1888.

———. *A Thousand-Mile Walk to the Gulf*. William Frederic Badè, editor. Houghton Mifflin Co., Boston: 1917.

———. *The Yosemite*. The Century Co., New York: 1912.

Naef, Weston J., and Wood, James N. *Era of Exploration: The Rise of Landscape Photography in the American West, 1860–1885*. Albright-Knox Art Gallery. The Metropolitan Museum of Art: 1975.

Nidever, George. *The Life and Adventures of George Nidever, 1802–1883*. William Henry Ellison, editor. University of California Press, Berkeley: 1937.

Nordhoff, Charles. *California for Travellers and Settlers*. Facsimile reprint, Ten Speed Press: 1973.

Outcalt, John. *History of Merced County.* Historic Record Co., Los Angeles: 1925.

Parker, Harry C. *Mammals of Yosemite National Park.* Yosemite Natural History Association: 1959.

Powers, Stephen. "The Indians of Yosemite Valley," in *The California Indians, A Source Book.* R. F. Heizer and M. A. Whipple, editors. University of California Press, Berkeley and Los Angeles: 1970.

Royce, Josiah. *California . . . A Study of American Character.* Houghton Mifflin Co., Boston: 1897.

Russell, Carl P. *One Hundred Years in Yosemite, The Story of a Great Park and Its Friends.* University of California Press, Berkeley and Los Angeles: 1947.

Sargent, Shirley. *Pioneers in Petticoats. Yosemite's Early Women, 1856–1900.* Trans-Anglo Books, Los Angeles: 1966.

Shay, John C. *Twenty Years in the Backwoods of California.* The Roxburgh Publishing Co., Boston: 1923.

Stevenson, Elizabeth. *Park Maker. A Life of Frederick Law Olmsted.* The Macmillan Co., New York: 1977.

Stoddard, Charles Warren. *In the Footprints of the Padres.* A. M. Robertson, San Francisco: 1902.

Storer, Tracy I., and Tevis, Lloyd P., Jr. *California Grizzly.* University of California Press, Berkeley and Los Angeles: 1955.

———, and Usinger, Robert T. *Sierra Nevada Natural History.* University of California Press, Berkeley, Los Angeles, and London: 1973.

Sullivan, Cornelius. Report about James Savage, in George H. Tinkham, *California Men and Events, 1769–1890.* Record Publishing Co., Stockton, Ca.: 1915.

Sutter, John A. *New Helvetia Diary: A Record of Events kept by John A. Sutter and his Clerks . . . from September 9, 1845 to May 25, 1848.* Grabhorn Press, San Francisco: 1939.

Taft, Robert. *Photography and the American Scene, A Social History, 1839–1889.* The Macmillan Co., New York: 1938.

Taylor, Rose Schuster. "Bibliography of Published Writings of Rose Schuster Taylor." Yosemite National Park Research Library.

———, (Mrs. H. J.). *The Last Survivor.* Jonck and Seeger, San Francisco: 1932.

Thayer, James Bradley. *A Western Journey With Mr. Emerson.* Facsimile reprint by Kennikat Press, Port Washington, N.Y.: 1970.

Tinkham, George H. *California Men and Events, 1769–1890.* Record Publishing Co., Stockton, Ca.: 1915.

Tressider, Mary Curry. *The Trees of Yosemite*. Stanford University Press, Stanford, Ca.: 1932.

Udvardy, Miklos D. F. *The Audubon Society Field Guide to North American Birds*, Western Region. Alfred A. Knopf, New York: 1977.

Victor, Frances Fuller. *The River of the West. Life and Adventures in the Rocky Mountains and Oregon*. Columbian Book Co., Hartford: 1870.

Vivian, A. P. *Wanderings in the Western Land*. S. Low, Marston, Searle, & Rivington, London: 1879. With illustrations from original sketches by A. Bierstadt.

Vivian, Henry Hussey (First Baron Swansea). *Notes of a Tour in America from August 7 to November 17, 1877*. E. Stanford, London: 1878.

Wallace, William J. "Music and Musical Instruments," in *Handbook of North American Indians*, Vol. 8, "California." Robert F. Heizer, volume editor. Smithsonian Institution, Washington, D.C.: 1978.

Ward, Sam. *Sam Ward in the Gold Rush*. Carvel Collins, editor. Stanford University Press, Stanford, Ca.: 1949.

Whitney, J. D. *Geology of California*. Vol. I *Report of Progress and Synopsis of the Field-Work from 1860–1864*. Caxton Press of Sherman & Co., Philadelphia: 1865.

———. *The Yosemite Book; A Description of the Yosemite Valley and . . . of the Big Trees of California*. Julius Bien, New York: 1868.

———. *The Yosemite Guide-Book*. University Press. Cambridge: 1869.

Wilkins, Thurman. *Clarence King*. The Macmillan Co., New York: 1958.

Wolfe, Linnie Marsh. *Son of the Wilderness, The Life of John Muir*. Alfred A. Knopf, New York: 1945.

Wood, Raymund F. *California's Agua Fria, The Early History of Mariposa County*. Academy Library Guild, Fresno, Ca.: 1954.

Wright, William H. *The Grizzly Bear; the Narrative of a Hunter, Naturalist, Historic, Scientific, and Adventurous*. Charles Scribner's Sons, New York: 1909.

Yelverton, Thérèse (Viscountess Avonmore). *Teresina in America*. Two vols. Richard Bently and Son, London: 1872.

———. *Zanita, A Tale of the Yosemite*. Hurd and Houghton, New York; Riverside Press, Cambridge: 1872.

Young, S. Hall. *Alaska Days With John Muir*. Fleming H. Revell Co., New York: 1915.

MONOGRAPH

Bates, Craig. "A History of the Indian People of Mariposa County." Yosemite National Park Research Library. Spring 1975.

PERIODICALS

Abrams, William Penn. Diary excerpts in Weldon F. Heald, "The Abrams Diary." *Sierra Club Bulletin*, May 1947.

Adams, Ansel. "The Photography of Joseph N. LeConte." *Sierra Club Bulletin*, October 1944.

Avery, B. P. "Art Beginnings on the Pacific Coast." II. *Overland Monthly*, August 1868.

Barrus, Clara. "In the Yosemite with John Muir." *The Craftsman*, December 1912.

Beauchamp, Tanya Edwards. "Renewed acclaim for the father of American landscape architecture." *Smithsonian*, December 1972.

Burroughs, John. "The Spell of the Yosemite." *The Century Illustrated Monthly Magazine*, November 1910.

Carr, Jeanne. "Jeanne Carr, Naturalist, Writer, Educator, Was Spiritual Benefactress to John Muir." Unsigned article; *Wisconsin Then and Now*, November 1979.

Colby, William E. "Jean (John) Baptiste Lembert—Personal Memories." *Yosemite Nature Notes*, September 1949.

Coolidge, Susan. "A Few Hints on the California Journey." *Scribner's Monthly*, May 1873.

Dyar, Harrison J. "A New Hapialus from California," *Entomological News*, January 1894.

Farquhar, Francis P. "Walker's Discovery of Yosemite." *Sierra Club Bulletin*, August 1942.

Gillespie, Charles B. "Marshall's Own Account of the Gold Discovery." *The Century Illustrated Monthly Magazine*, February 1891.

Holmes, Oliver Wendell. "Doings of the Sunbeam." *Atlantic Monthly*, December 1863.

Hood, Mary V. Jessup, and Haas, Robert Bartlett. "Eadweard Muybridge's *Yosemite Valley Photographs, 1867–1872*." *California Historical Society Quarterly*, March 1963.

Hutchings, James Mason. "Scenes Among the Indians of California." *Hutchings' California Magazine*, April 1859.

Huth, Hans. "Yosemite: The Story of an Idea." *Sierra Club Bulletin*, March 1948.

Jeffers, LeRoy. "John Muir: An Appreciation." *Appalachia*, June 1919.

Johnson, Robert Underwood. "John Muir As I Knew Him." *Sierra Club Bulletin*, January 1916.

Kimes, William F. "With Theodore Roosevelt and John Muir in Yosemite." *Westerners Brand Book Fourteen.*

Lawrence, Mary Viola. "Summer With a Countess." *Overland Monthly,* November 1871.

LeConte, J. N. "The Soda Springs Property of Tuolumne Meadows." *Sierra Club Bulletin,* January 1913.

Lembert, John B. Obituary, *Entomological News,* September 1896.

Ludlow, Fitz Hugh. "Seven Weeks in the Great Yo-Semite." *Atlantic Monthly,* June 1864.

Merriam, C. Hart. "Indian Villages and Camp Sites in Yosemite Valley." *Sierra Club Bulletin,* January 1917.

Mitchell, Annie R. "Major James D. Savage and the Tulareños." *California Historical Society Quarterly,* December 1948.

Muir, John. "The Creation of Yosemite National Park. Letters of John Muir to Robert Underwood Johnson." *Sierra Club Bulletin,* October 1894.

————. "The Forests of Yosemite National Park." *Atlantic Monthly,* April 1906.

————. "A Geologist's Winter Walk." *Overland Monthly,* April 1873.

————. "Mountain Sculpture: Origin of the Yosemite Valley." *Overland Monthly,* June 1874.

————. "Reminiscences of Joseph LeConte." *The University of California Magazine,* September 1901.

————. "The Treasures of Yosemite." *The Century Illustrated Monthly Magazine,* August 1890.

————. "The Wild Parks and Forest Reservations of the West." *Atlantic Monthly,* January 1898.

O'Meara, James. "A White Medicine Man." *Yosemite Nature Notes,* November 1951; December 1951.

Presnall, C. C. "Indian Picture Writing in Yosemite." *Yosemite Nature Notes,* October 1930.

Proctor, A. Phimister. "An Ascent of Half Dome in 1884." *Sierra Club Bulletin,* June 1946.

Runte, Alfred. "Origins and Paradox of the American Experience." *Journal of Forest History,* April 1977.

Russell, C. P. "A Last Link With The Past." *Yosemite Nature Notes,* June 1926.

————. "Last of Yosemite Indians Visits Valley After a 75-Year Absence." *Yosemite Nature Notes,* July 1929.

————. "Mrs. H. J. Taylor, 1863–1951." *Yosemite Nature Notes,* February 1951.

Savage, Charles R. "A Photographic Tour of Near 9000 Miles." *Philadelphia Photographer*, September–October 1867.

Snyder, Jim. "A Plea for Yosemite's Past." *Yosemite*, April 1973.

Soulé, Frank. "Joseph LeConte in the Sierra." *Sierra Club Bulletin*, January 1902.

Stoddard, Charles Warren. "In Yosemite Shadows." *Overland Monthly*, August 1869.

Taylor, Rose Schuster (Mrs. H. J.). "John Muir." *Yosemite Nature Notes.* April 1938.

———. "Maria Lebrado Is a Guest at Museum." *Yosemite Nature Notes*, September 1929.

———. "The Return of the Last Survivor." *University of California Chronicle*, January 1931.

———. "Some John Muir Reminiscences." *Yosemite Nature Notes*, September 30, 1927.

Torrey, Bradford. "On Foot in the Yosemite." *Atlantic Monthly*, August 1910.

Truman, Ben. C. "Knights of the Lash: Old Time Stage Drivers of the West Coast." I. *Overland Monthly*, March 1898.

Turrill, Charles B. "An Early California Photographer: C. E. Watkins." *News Notes of the California Libraries*, January 1918.

Yelverton, Thérèse (subject). "The Great Yelverton Case." *Harper's Weekly*, April 6, 1861.

———. "The Great Yelverton Marriage Case." *The Nation*, December 28, 1865.

NEWSPAPERS

Boling, John. Letter of May 15, 1851 to James Savage. *Daily Alta California*, June 19, 1851.

King, Thomas Starr. Letter to the *Boston Evening Transcript*, January 26, 1861.

Mariposa Gazette, April 25, 1896. "John Baptiste Lembert." Report on his murder.

———, May 6, 1882. Notice of "Petition and Remonstrance" being circulated for signatures by John B. Lembert.

Sacramento Bee, November 3, 1902. "Sad Death of J. M. Hutchings."

San Francisco Call, April 27, 1896. "Yosemite Murder." Report on the coroner's inquest held for John B. Lembert.

———, May 18, 1903. "President Makes Camp at Bridal Veil Falls." Report on Theodore Roosevelt's camping trip with John Muir.

San Francisco Chronicle, May 17, 1903. "Roosevelt Pitches His Camp Near Bleak Sentinel Dome in Snow Storm."

San Francisco Daily Evening Bulletin, January 19, 1858. "Death of a Distinguished Native Californian."

San Francisco Examiner, August 16, 1905. "The Yosemite Stage Is Robbed."

The Yosemite Tourist, July 13, 1906. "Five Yosemite Stages 'Held Up' by the Lone Highwayman of the Chowchilla."

————, (same date). "She Photographed the Highwayman."

MANUSCRIPTS AND DOCUMENTS

Bolton, Herbert Eugene. Letter of February 20, 1948, to E. B. Fred, regarding an honorary degree for Rose Schuster Taylor. Yosemite Research Library.

Callie. "The Switzerland of America." Epistolary diary of a trip from San Francisco to Yosemite Valley and back in 1864. The writer's collection.

Clark, Galen. "Reminiscences." Photocopy, Yosemite Research Library.

Corcoran, May Stanislaus. "Transcript of a Conversation Held in Mariposa with 'Maria' the Daughter of Yo-Semite's Chief Teneiya." Yosemite Research Library.

Degnan, Laurence V. Letter of February 16, 1952, to the United States Bureau of Entomology regarding John B. Lembert's work for them, and his position as an entomologist. Copy in Yosemite Research Library.

————. Letter of March 17, 1952, to Carl P. Russell, containing reminiscences of John B. Lembert. Original in Yosemite Collections.

————. Letter of March 6, 1961, to Douglass H. Hubbard, with further recollections of John B. Lembert. Original in Yosemite Collections.

Grover, Stephen F. "A Reminiscence." Original in Yosemite Collections.

Hutchings, Cosie, see Mills, Cosie Hutchings.

Hutchings, James Mason. Papers pertaining to James Mason Hutchings and other members of his family. Yosemite Research Library and Yosemite Collections.

Hutchinson, J. S. Letter of June 7, 1857, to his father. Original in Yosemite Collections.

Lamson, James. Diary. "Nine Years Adventure in California." Copy in Yosemite Research Library.

Leidig, Charles. "Charlie Leidig's Report of President Roosevelt's Visit in May, 1903." Original in Yosemite Collections.

Leidig, Jack. "Statement made by Jack Leidig to C. P. Russell . . . on May 27, 1949, regarding the death of Chief Tenaya." Original in Yosemite Collections.

Lembert, John Baptiste. Registration record taken from *Mariposa County Great Register of Voters, 1882–1894.* Yosemite Research Library.

Mills, Cosie Hutchings. "Chronicles of Cosie Hutchings Mills . . . " recorded by Elizabeth Godfrey, Museum Secretary. Original in Yosemite Collections.

————. Letter of October 5, 1941, to Elizabeth Godfrey. Original in Yosemite Collections.

————. "Miscellaneous Yosemite Notes." Originals in Yosemite Collections.

————. Recollections of John B. Lembert given in an interview with Carl P. Russell. Original in Yosemite Collections.

Muir, John. Letter of December 20, 1901, to Harry Randall. Original in Yosemite Collections.

Russell, Carl P. Interview with Maria Lebrado at Bear Creek (1928). Original in Yosemite Collections.

————. Letter of February 24, 1948, to E. B. Fred, regarding conferral of an honorary degree on Rose Schuster Taylor. Copy in Yosemite Research Library.

Trabucco, J. J. Letter of July 21, 1936, to Carl W. Sharsmitte [Sharsmith], regarding the murder of John B. Lembert. Copy in Yosemite Research Library.

United States Senate Document No. 57, Series 665. Report on investigation of fraudulent practices of James Savage, Indian trader.

Veith, A. G. "Deposition of A. G. Veith taken on the 16th of August 1905 at 2½ P.M. Mariposa Big Trees," regarding the stage robbery of the previous day. Copy in Yosemite Research Library.

Yelverton, Thérèse. Letter of October 1870 to John Muir. Original in Yosemite Collections.

————. Letter of January 22, 1872 to John Muir. Original in Yosemite Collections.

CORRESPONDENCE

Bates, Craig. Ethnologist; Assistant Curator of Collections, Yosemite National Park. Letter of July 13, 1979, regarding the final punitive expedition into Yosemite and the numbers of Indians who returned to live in the valley following expulsion.

Elsasser, Albert B. Associate Research Anthropologist, Lowie Museum of Anthropology, University of California. Letter of January 30, 1979, regarding Indian occupation of Yosemite Valley: "Fairly solid evidence from . . . the Yosemite region points to an ongoing occupation there about 1000 B.C."

————. Letter of April 23, 1979, regarding Indian superfamilies represented in California.

Gianella, Vincent P. Emeritus Professor of Geology, University of Nevada. Letters of January 29 and March 3, 1979 regarding Joseph Reddeford Walker's probable route into and over the Sierra Nevada Range in 1833.

Kantor, J. R. K. University Archivist, Bancroft Library. Letter of October 5, 1978, regarding the appointments of John and Joseph LeConte to the University of California faculty; the courses each taught; and John LeConte's tenure as university president.

INDEX

ABOUT THE AUTHOR

MARGARET SANBORN is a second-generation Californian with deep roots in the state's past: a great-grandfather who came to the gold fields at Placerville; a great-grandmother who taught Pomo Indians to read and write in the hope it would equip them to cope with the white man's world; a grandfather who kept school and served as a Wells Fargo agent in many wilderness settlements in Northern California. Mrs. Sanborn came under Yosemite's spell when at age eight she first hiked its trails with her father. Except for two years in Seattle, she has always lived in the Bay Area and now makes her home in Mill Valley, just north of San Francisco.